ENERGY AFTER RIO
PROSPECTS AND CHALLENGES

United Nations Development Programme
in collaboration with
International Energy Initiative
and
Energy 21
Stockholm Environment Institute

and in consultation with
Secretariat of the United Nations Commission on Sustainable Development

Authors

Amulya K.N. Reddy   Robert H. Williams   Thomas B. Johansson

Contributors

Samuel Baldwin	Mongi Hamdi	Michael Nicklas
Gustavo Best	Michael Jefferson	Michael Philips
David Bloom	Alexandre Kamarotos	Kirk Smith
Timothy Brennand	Johan Kuylenstierna	Wim C. Turkenburg
Elizabeth Cecelski	Gerald Leach	Ernst Worrell
Martha Dueñas Loza	Robert Lion	
Harold Feiveson	Susan McDade	

The views expressed in this volume are not
necessarily shared by the UNDP's Executive Board or other member governments of
the UNDP.

United Nations Publications
Sales No E.97 III.B.11
ISBN 92-1-12670-1

Cover photo credits: LA traffic: copyright
© 1996 PhotoDisc, Inc.; Australian solar
thermal technology: Imagenet stock
photography; rooftop solar water heater:
Jorgen Schytte, Solar Energy, Katmandu,
Nepal. Other photos courtesy of the
photographers: Andrea Brizzi, Cherie Hart,
Chuck Lankester, Costa Manzini, Ruth
Massey and Susan McDade.

Acknowledgments

This document was prepared by UNDP through the Energy and Atmosphere Programme (EAP) in the Sustainable Energy and Environment Division, Bureau for Policy and Programme Support (BPPS) in cooperation with International Energy Initiative (IEI), with support from Energy 21 (E21), the Stockholm Environment Institute (SEI), the World Energy Council (WEC), and in consultation with the Secretariat of the United Nations Commission for Sustainable Development (DPCSD). The EAP unit consists of Thomas B. Johansson, Suresh Hurry, Annie Roncerel, Susan McDade, Ad Dankers, Pepukaye Bardouille, Golda Kruss, Vivette Riley and Liliana Aberger.

Susan McDade and Annie Roncerel were the Project Coordinators for this effort and were assisted by Pepukaye Bardouille, Kimberley Heismann and Nada Kobeissi in the production of this work during their assignment in EAP. Special thanks to Ellen Morris who undertook the technical editing of this report. Amy Hosier's contribution to the final text editing was much appreciated. Maureen Lynch of the Division of Public Affairs (DPA), UNDP coordinated the printing process. The graphic design and cover was undertaken by Peter Joseph.

UNDP wishes to thank the Government of Austria for their contribution to this project which supported the initial submissions from the contributors. *Energy After Rio: Prospects and Challenges* benefited from the peer review process, especially the October 1996 review meeting held in New York, as well as the many timely comments and revisions suggested subsequently. UNDP wishes to thank all contributors and reviewers for their efforts, including:

Pepukaye Bardouille, Corinne Boone, Angela Cropper, Francois Coutu, Bernard Devin, Ad Dankers, Gordon Goodman, José Goldemberg, J. Gururaja, Ture Hammar, Kimberley Heismann, Richard Hosier, Suresh Hurry, Hisashi Ishitani, Harry Lehmann, Roberto Lenton, Andre Marcu, Ellen Morris, Nebojsa Nakicenovic, Frank Pinto, Paul Raskin, Annie Roncerel, E.V.R. Sastry, Stirling Scruggs, C.S.Sinha, Youba Sokona, Carlos Suarez, Joke Waller-Hunter, Anders Wijkman and Neville Williams. David Bloom acknowledges the collaboration of John Gallup (Harvard Institute for International Development) and David Beede (United States Department of Commerce) in the preparation of his contributions.

Notes on the Authors and Contributors

Authors:

Amulya K.N. Reddy is President of the International Energy Initiative and is a former Professor at the Indian Institute of Science, Bangalore, India.

Robert H. Williams is Senior Research Scientist at the Center for Energy and Environment Studies at Princeton University, USA.

Thomas B. Johansson is the Director of the Energy and Atmosphere Programme of the United Nations Development Programme and is a Professor of Energy Systems Analysis (on leave) at the University of Lund in Sweden.

Contributors (to different chapters/sections as indicated):

Samuel F. Baldwin is the Technical Director for International Programmes at the National Renewable Energy Laboratory (NREL), USA (section 3.4).

Gustavo Best is the Energy Coordinator at the Food and Agriculture Organization (FAO) in Rome, Italy (sections 2.1.4. and 2.2.4).

David Bloom is a Professor at the Harvard Institute for International Development in Cambridge, Massachusetts, USA (section 2.1.1).

Timothy Brennand is a Research Fellow in Environmental Sciences at the University of East Anglia, Norwich, Norfolk, U.K. (chapter 5).

Elizabeth Cecelski specializes in Energy, Environment and Development, and works in Germany (section 2.1.2).

Marta Dueñas Loza was Vice Chair-person of the United Nations Intergovernmental Committee on New and Revewable Sources of Energy (1990-92) and Member of the United Nations Solar Energy Group for Environment and Development (1990-92) (chapters 1 and 2, except section 2.1.2).

Harold A. Feiveson is Senior Research Policy Analyst, at the Center for Energy and Environment Studies at Princeton University, USA (section 2.4.2).

Mongi Hamdi is the First Economic Affairs Officer at the Department for Economic and Social Information and Policy Analysis at the United Nations in New York, USA (section 2.3.2).

Michael Jefferson is the Deputy Secretary-General at the World Energy Council in London, U.K. (chapters 2, 3, 4, and 5).

Alexandre Kamarotos is a Research Associate at Energy 21 in Paris, France (section 2.2.3).

Johan Kuylenstierna is Acting Director at the Stockholm Environment Institute at York, U.K. (section 2.2.2).

Gerald Leach is Senior Fellow at the Stockholm Environment Institute in London, U.K., and also Energy Advisor to the Industry and Environment Department at the World Bank (section 2.2).

Robert Lion is President of Energy 21 in Paris, France, and a member of the Earth Council (chapters 4 and 5).

Susan McDade is a Technical Specialist with the Energy and Atmosphere Programme, United Nations Development Programme in New York, USA (chapters 1 and 2).

Michael Nicklas is former President of the International Solar Energy Society and owner of Innovative Design Inc., in Raleigh, N.C., USA (section 3.3).

Michael Philips is the Washington Representative of Energy 21 in Washington, D.C., USA (chapter 5).

Kirk Smith is Professor of Environmental Health Sciences and also the Associate Director for International Programs at the Center for Occupational and Environmental Health at the University of California in Berkeley, USA (section 2.2.1).

Wim C. Turkenburg is a Professor and Chairman of the Department of Science, Technology and Society at Utrecht University in the Netherlands (section 3.1).

Ernst Worrell is a Co-Director of the Department of Science, Technology and Society at Utrecht University in the Netherlands (section 3.1).

Foreword

The 1997 Review of Rio is the first opportunity within the United Nations System to examine international progress made in sustainable development as a result of the first of the global conferences in the 1990's, which was the United Nations Conference on Environment and Development (UNCED). The Rio Conference drew international attention to linkages between environment and economic development, and underscored how the sustainable use of natural resources is an essential element of any international development strategy that addresses the needs of present and future generations.

One of the main goals of the United Nations Development Programme (UNDP) is to help the entire United Nations system become a unified and powerful force for sustainable human development. For UNDP, sustainable human development means concentrating efforts in four key areas: i) eradicating poverty; ii) increasing women's role in development; iii) providing people with income earning opportunities and livelihoods; and iv) protecting and regenerating the environment. Energy production and consumption are closely linked to these issues, and to reach the objectives established by the United Nations requires major changes in the approach to energy—focusing on energy as an essential instrument to meet basic human needs.

The importance of energy in development clearly emerged at the Rio Conference. However no integrated action programme in the field of energy was agreed upon at the Rio Conference in 1992. The essential linkages between energy and socio economic development were not approached in an integrated fashion. As a result, the recommendations concerning energy and development remain dispersed. Global consensus was reached only with regard to the important energy-related issues of climate change.

Shedding light and focusing international attention on the critical importance of energy to sustainable human development is UNDP's objective in preparing Energy After Rio: Prospects and Challenges. The current patterns of energy production and use, which shape the development process internationally, are unsustainable - and have become more so since Rio. In developing countries, energy financing as well as production and consumption patterns increasingly impede national development processes, and will continue to do so, unless new approaches are adopted.

Worldwide, an estimated 2 billion people continue to lack access to modern energy services. Though we know that energy is absolutely essential for development, little international attention has been devoted to this important relation. Agenda 21 called on nations to find more efficient systems for producing, distributing and consuming energy as well as for greater reliance on environmentally sound energy systems. Special emphasis was placed on renewable sources of energy. UNDP, through its Initiative on Sustainable Energy, is assisting programme countries to reflect these objectives—in national energy policies, investment plans, and sustainable development strategies. However, the achievement of Agenda 21 goals will require changes which go beyond aid policies and are reflected in international business, investment, trade, public and private sector policies and decisions.

What must be done? A more direct and dynamic debate on the essential linkages between energy and socio-economic development is needed, followed by translation into action in the short term, of the objectives of sustainable energy to achieve sustainable human development.

On behalf of UNDP, I hope that this report can serve to foster the international debate and consensus-building process concerning the importance of sustainable energy and refocus international commitment on this critical issue during the 1997 Review of Rio process. The authors of this volume describe the important links between energy and development, and suggest pathways that will allow energy to be deployed for the improvement of lives worldwide. This concern is at the heart of sustainable human development and, as we enter the next millennium, is one of the key global issues that will challenge all nations.

I congratulate the authors and contributors on their efforts, and am confident that Energy After Rio: Prospects and Challenges will be an important catalyst for decision-makers, policy-makers, academics, the international development community, non-governmental organizations and the media in highlighting the importance of energy for achieving sustainable human development.

James Gustave Speth

James Gustave Speth, Administrator
New York, January 1997

Table of Contents

Glossary of Abbreviations

Organisations and official bodies

ACEEE .... American Council for an Energy Efficient Economy
BPPS .... Bureau for Policy and Programme Support of UNDP, New York
DPCSD ..... Department for Policy Coordination and Sustainable Development, the Secretariat of the United Nations Commission on Sustainable Development, New York
EAP .... Energy and Atmosphere Programme of UNDP, New York
FAO .... Food and Agriculture Organisation of the United Nations
GEF .... Global Environment Facility
IEA .... International Energy Agency
IEI .... International Energy Initiative
ILO .... International Labour Organisation
IPCC .... Intergovernmental Panel on Climate Change
IREDA ..... Indian Renewable Energy Development Authority
NGO .... Non-Governmental Organisation
NPT .... Nuclear Non-Proliferation Treaty
OECD ...... Organization for Economic Cooperation and Development
SEI .... Stockholm Environment Institute
SIDS .... Global Conference on Small Island Developing States
UNCCD .... United Nations Convention to Combat Desertification
UNCED .... United Nations Conference on Environment and Development
UNDP .... United Nations Development Programme
UNFCCC . United Nations Framework Convention on Climate Change
UNIFEM .. United Nations Development Fund for Women
WEC .... World Energy Council
WHO .... World Health Organisation
WMO .... World Meteorological Organisation

Technical terms

BIG/CC .... biomass-integrated gasifier/combined cycle
CFL .... compact fluorescent lamp
CHP .... combined heat and power
CIG/CC .... coal-integrated gasifier/combined cycle
CNG .... compressed natural gas
CO .... carbon monoxide
CO_2 .... carbon dioxide
DCFC .... direct carbonate fuel cell
DME .... dimethyl ether
EJ .... exajoules (=10^{18} joules)
FCV .... fuel cell vehicle
GHG .... greenhouse gases
GJ .... gigajoules (=10^9 joules)
GtC .... gigatonne of carbon (=10^9 tonnes)
GW_e .... gigawatt of electricity (=10^9 watts)
HHV .... higher heating value
ICEV .... internal-combustion engine vehicle
kg .... kilogram
kW_e .... kilowatt of electricity
kWh .... kilowatt-hour
LHV .... lower heating value
LNG .... liquified natural gas
LPG .... liquified petroleum gas
Mha .... million hectares
Mtoe .... million tonnes of oil equivalent

MW_e .... megawatt of electricity
MW_p .... peak megawatts of electricity
NO_x .... nitrogen oxides
PAFC .... phosphoric acid fuel cell
PEMFC .... proton exchange membrane fuel cell
ppmv .... parts per million by volume
PV .... photovoltaic
SMD .... synthetic middle distillates
SOFC .... solid oxide fuel cell
SO_x .... sulfur oxides
SWH .... solar water heater
TWh .... terawatt-hour
W .... watt

Other terms:
BMVP ...... Building Measurement and Verification Protocol
DRE .... Decentralised Rural Electrification
ESCO .... Energy Service Company
FDI .... Foreign Direct Investment
GDP .... Gross Domestic Product
GNP .... Gross National Product
LSMS .... Living Standard Measurement Study
NFFO .... Non-Fossil Fuel Obligation (United Kingdom)
ODA .... Official Development Assistance
PURPA ..... Public Utilities Regulatory Policy Act (United States)
R&D .... Research and development
RECs .... Renewable Energy Credits
SBC .... System Benefits Charge

1 Introduction

Energy facilitates all human endeavour. Energy is used for heating and cooling, illumination, health, food, education, industrial production and transportation. Energy is essential to life. The development of human society and civilisation have been shaped by energy.

The original source of energy for all activities was human energy. The energy of human muscle provided the mechanical power necessary in the dawn of history. This era was followed by a time characterised by the control and use of fire from the combustion of wood, and with it, the ability to exploit chemical transformations brought about by heat energy to cook food, heat dwellings and extract metals such as bronze and iron. The energy of draught animals began to play a role in agriculture, transport and industry, supplementing human energy and energy stored in natural resources such as wood. Finally, in rapid succession, human societies acquired control over coal, steam, electricity, oil and natural gas. Thus, from one perspective, history is the story of the control over energy sources for the benefit of society.

Energy issues and policies have been concerned mainly with increasing the supply of energy. Countries around the world have considered the sufficient production and consumption of energy to be one of their main challenges. Modern economies are energy dependent. The provision of sufficient energy has been perceived as a central problem. Energy availability and consumption has been so important a consideration to economies world-wide that the magnitude of energy consumed per capita has become one of the key indicators of modernisation and progress in a given country. Recently, attention has begun to shift toward a more balanced perspective, including concerns related both to demand-side and energy consumption patterns. Either way, there is no escaping the fact that the use of energy is a necessary and vital component of development.

The benefits of modern energy supplies and services are unevenly distributed in the world and have yet to reach approximately one third of the Earth's population. People living in poverty have benefited very little from conventional energy policies and their implementation. More than 2 billion people continue to cook using traditional fuels, while 1.5-2 billion people lack electricity. At the same time, it has become widely recognised that development depends on access to appropriate energy services. Developing countries in particular often face constraints to growth and development that are directly related to the unsustainability of current patterns of energy production and use.

The appetite for energy has often exceeded the capacity of local sources of supply. During the 20th century, the energy supplies of many countries have been imported from distant suppliers. Efforts to establish influence and control over oil wells, gas fields or oil shipping routes have generated persistent tensions and political problems. This situation has often influenced national policies in foreign affairs, economics, science and technology. It has also been a factor in influencing the political map of the world. The security of energy supplies has been a geostrategic issue throughout this century. At the same time, the sheer intensity of energy production and use began to result in deleterious impacts on the environment.

By the late 1960s, the gravity of the environmental problems arising from toxic substances became clear. The problems of urban air pollution have been known for a long time. This was followed by the awareness of the environmental issue of acid rain. More recently, the accumulation of greenhouse gases in the atmosphere resulting from energy consumption has focused attention on the issue of climate change with the possibility of far-reaching consequences for all countries.

The oil shocks of 1973 and 1979 thrust the energy problem into the range of awareness of individuals throughout the world. The resulting price increases led to economic disruption at international, national and local levels. The vulnerability of all economies to energy price and supply fluctuations became evident to government policy makers and consumers alike. Some oil-importing developing countries faced serious balance-of-payments problems, and in some cases, became mired in debt. The indigenous development of fossil fuel resources and power generation was hindered by capital scarcity. Together with the lack of control over energy resources, this situation has highlighted the importance of national and local self-reliance and the need to diversify energy sources and production patterns as a means to distribute risk.

Energy is, and will remain, a crucial traded commodity in the international economy. Many countries, however, have unrealised energy potentials when renewable energy options are taken into account. Thus, quite apart from the critical issues related to the supply of fossil fuels, the political, social, and economic institutions dealing with energy are facing a series of new challenges in energy production, distribution and use. New issues associated with energy also are emerging. These include problems of economics such as access to capital, empowerment (self-reliance), equity and environment. Many of the human-based threats to the species and the biosphere are energy-related. Awareness of these issues has risen more recently, but they are still imperfectly understood.

This book is devoted to how energy is being dealt with amidst the most pressing issues of today's world. In the next chapter, attention will be focused on the main linkages between energy and global problems. It will be shown that global energy strategies are linked to major global problems, including: poverty, gender disparity (biases and discrimination against women), population growth, food, water and health, urban air pollution, climate change, acidification, land degradation, investment and foreign exchange requirements, energy imports and security, and nuclear proliferation. The implication of these linkages is that the issue of energy has to be tackled in such a way that other problems are not aggravated. Conventional energy strategies which are sectoral in nature tend not to address these other global problems in the responses, plans and solutions proposed. It will be argued that these linkages with energy can be utilised to help solve many wider problems. Within this perspective energy can be used as an instrument to promote sustainable development.

People want the services that energy provides; they do not demand oil or coal, or even gasoline or electricity. Therefore, it is essential to focus on the demand side of the energy system, the end uses of energy and energy services

Examples of energy services include: providing cooking, heating, cooling, lighting, and safe storage of food, clean water and sanitation, and other services required by society such as means of transportation, motive power for industry and agriculture, energy for commerce, communication and other economic activities. The demand side, end use-oriented, energy-services approach stresses the end users' preference for service, quality, affordability, reliability, safety, impact on the environment, and accessibility.

Energy issues need to be analysed from an end-use and service view-point, rather than from the traditional supply-side approach. The supply-biased approach tends to focus on forecasts of energy demand, based on projections of past and present economic trends, considering factors such as demography and economic growth. It takes limited account of the large opportunities for improvements in energy efficiency, shifts to modern energy carriers, and dissemination of renewable energy technologies.

Renewable sources of energy are now reaching commercial viability due to technology improvements and decreasing prices. Solar, wind, geothermal, and commercial biomass options offer feasible and attractive alternatives to conventional energy sources. The development of these resources has the potential to generate large scale economic activities in regions which currently face energy constraints. For the large numbers of people living in rural or remote areas, where grid extension of any sort will remain prohibitive based on infrastructure costs, decentralised renewable energy applications offer alternatives for the provision of affordable energy services while supporting local development and improved quality of life.

Finally, many modern technologies which are being developed through long term research and development (R&D) efforts offer the potential of deriving improved and cleaner energy services from conventional, carbon based fuels including coal, oil and gas. Barriers to the adoption of these technological options lie principally in the associated legislative, policy, trade, investment and international cooperation frameworks which currently influence energy sector development.

1.1 Energy in the United Nations Context

Over the 1990s the United Nations has convened a series of major conferences on global issues, starting with the 1992 Conference on Environment and Development (UNCED). The 1994 Cairo Conference on Population and Development, the 1994 Global Conference on Small Island Developing States (SIDS), the 1995 World Summit for Social Development in Copenhagen, the 1995 Beijing Fourth World Conference on Women and Development, and the 1996 Habitat II Conference in Istanbul have resulted in agreements on the social and environmental goals and objectives of the international community. The conferences have had in common a global vision of sustainable development that addresses the social, economic and environmental measures necessary to ensure sustainability of human activities and well being in relation to the natural resource base.

These conferences also have dealt with energy as it impacts sustainable development. In addition, two major global conventions negotiated in this decade concern energy. The United Nations Framework Convention on Climate Change (UNFCCC) and the Convention to Combat Desertification (CCD), respectively addressed energy issues as they relate to climate change and land degradation. These and the associated platforms of action from the United Nations conferences have been unanimous in articulating the need for changes in the current approaches to energy to include more attention to the sustainability of energy systems and the ability to provide energy services that can support the achievement of socio-economic and environmental goals and objectives. There has never been, however, an integrated and cohesive treatment of energy and sustainable development.

From Rio to Istanbul, consistent and clear calls for improved energy efficiency, commercialisation and dissemination of renewable energy, technology transfer, legislative and price reform to create what has become known as an "enabling environment", including capacity building, women's and community involvement in energy planning, and improved natural resource man-

agement, have emerged in the platforms of action from each of the major United Nations conferences in the five years since Rio. The basic elements of a global strategy for sustainable energy can be pieced together from these statements which have been negotiated and agreed within the intergovernmental process provided under the auspices of the United Nations. However, a focused approach to energy, with emphasis on the role of energy in overall socio-economic development and the adoption of sustainable energy practices, has not emerged.

Five years ago the United Nations Conference on Environment and Development (UNCED) held in Rio de Janeiro drew international attention to, and enhanced awareness of, the imperative of sustainable development. Over 150 governments committed themselves to sustainable development and the protection of the environment in Agenda 21 and the "Rio Declaration".

According to Maurice Strong, the Secretary-General of the Rio Conference, "Agenda 21 constitutes the basic framework and instrument which will guide the world community on an ongoing basis in its decisions on the goals, targets, priorities, allocation of responsibilities and resources in respect of the many environment and development issues which will determine the future of our planet."

The debate at Rio led to the conclusion that while energy problems could hamper attainment of key development objectives, if handled wisely, solutions to energy problems could contribute to meeting these objectives. At that time, international attention was very much focused on the issue of climate change. Agenda 21, in Chapter Nine makes the important statement on energy: "Much of the world's energy is currently produced and consumed in ways that could not be sustained if technology were to remain constant and if overall quantities were to increase substantially. The need to control atmospheric emissions and other gases and substances will increasingly need to be based on efficiency in energy production, transmission, distribution and consumption, and on growing reliance on environmentally sound energy systems, particularly new and renewable sources of energy" (UNCED, 1993).

Thus one essential conclusion of the discussion of energy at Rio was the unsustainability of energy production and con-

Energy and the Major United Nations Conferences

Agenda 21 programme areas, activities and objectives from the Rio Conference describe numerous links between sustainable development and energy issues. These are reflected in the chapters of Agenda 21 on Promoting Sustainable Human Settlement Development, Health, Integrating Environment and Development in Decision-making, Protection of the Atmosphere, Combating Deforestation, Combating Desertification and Drought, Sustainable Mountain Development, and Promoting Sustainable Agriculture and Rural Development. Chapter 9B dealing with Energy and Chapter 34 on Environmentally Sound Technology, Cooperation and Capacity Building are particularly relevant and contain many elements of a sustainable strategy. Energy efficiency, new and renewable energy, dissemination of modern, clean technologies for conventional fuels, supporting policy frameworks and capacity building are central among these.

The Programme of Action adopted at the United Nations Conference on Population and Development emphasises the need to integrate population concerns into all aspects of economic and social activity. Chapter 3 of the Program of Action addresses the interrelationships between population, sustained economic growth and comprehensive sustainable development, particularly for the implementation of effective population policies and meeting basic human needs. The Cairo Conference subsequently recognised poverty as a major obstacle to solving population problems.

The Global Conference on Sustainable Development in Small Island Developing States (SIDS) produced a Plan of Action which deals with energy resources in Chapter 7. It concludes that SIDS "are currently heavily dependent on imported petroleum products, largely for transport and electricity generation, energy often accounting for more than 12 percent of imports. They are heavily dependent on indigenous biomass fuels for cooking and crop drying". The absence of energy alternatives is a clear factor in unsustainable development patterns in SIDS. As a result it is concluded that "increased efficiency through appropriate technology and national energy policies and management measures will reap both financial and environmental benefits for small island developing states".

The Copenhagen Social Summit Programme of Action represents a global effort to address issues related to social development and the negative impacts of underdevelopment and poverty. Global consensus was reached on the need to create an enabling economic environment aimed at promoting more equitable access to sustainable development, and the goal of eradicating poverty. Chapter 2 recognises that improving the

sumption based on current technologies in the face of growing demand.

Agenda 21 programme areas, activities and objectives from the Rio Conference describe numerous links between sustainable development and energy issues. These are reflected in Chapter 6: Protecting and Promoting Human Health; Chapter 7: Promoting Sustainable Human Settlement Development; Chapter 8: Integrating Environment and Development in Decision-making; Chapter 9: Protection of the Atmosphere; Chapter 11: Combating Deforestation: Chapter 12: Combating Desertification and Drought; Chapter 13: Sustainable Mountain Development; and Chapter 14: Promoting Sustainable Agriculture and Rural Development. Chapter 34 on Environmentally Sound Technology, Cooperation and Capacity Building is particularly relevant to energy and modern clean energy technology (UNCED, 1993). Agenda 21 contains many of the elements of sustainable energy strategy. The various dimensions of this complex relationship will be examined further in Chapter 2 and through out this book.

Since UNCED, many other initiatives to promote sustainable energy, including increasing energy efficiency and promoting the use of renewable energy sources, have been undertaken. As a result there are now good examples, significant benchmarks, and success stories all around the world in these areas. But, these efforts are dispersed. Although providing a good starting point, they cannot meet the tremendous challenge that availability and accessibility of transportation, communication, power and energy services at the local and community level is a way of improving the access to productive resources and infrastructure necessary for poverty eradication, especially for isolated, remote, and marginalised communities.

The implementation and follow-up of recommendations from Cairo and Copenhagen related to health, education, safe food, potable water and sanitation, transportation, employment and poverty eradication , as well as the needs of special groups such as the ageing, handicapped, victims of natural disasters, children, refugees and the displaced, will all require a substantial increase in energy services.

The Beijing Conference Platform for Action, Objective K "Women and the Environment" refers to women's numerous roles in the management and use of natural resources, as providers of sustenance for their families and communities, as well as women's needs and requirements as users, consumers, managers and decision-makers. It stresses the need to integrate gender concerns and perspectives in all programmes for sustainable development.

The United Nations Conference on Human Settlements HABITAT II statement "Sustainable Human Settlements Development in an Urbanising World" explicitly deals with sustainable energy use. Chapter 4 states that the use of energy is essential in urban centres for transportation, industrial production, household and office activities. "Current dependence in most urban centres on non-renewable energy sources can lead to climate change, air pollution and consequent environmental and human health problems, and may represent a serious threat to sustainable development. Sustainable energy production and use can be enhanced by encouraging energy efficiency, by such means as pricing policies, fuelswitching, alternative energy, mass transit and public awareness. Human settlements and energy policies should be actively co-ordinated". The promotion of efficient and sustainable energy use and actions for Governments, the private sector, non-governmental organisations, community-based organisations and consumer groups to solve many of the crucial social and economic requirements of sustainable development are recommended.

The World Food Summit in its Rome Declaration on World Food Security noted that "unless governments and the international community address the multifaceted causes underlying food security, the number of hungry and malnourished people will remain very high in developing countries, particularly Africa south of the Sahara and sustainable food security will not be achieved". The importance of energy in agricultural production, food preparation and consumption is clear.

mankind will have to grasp in the field of energy during the next century.

In its resolution 47/190, the United Nations General Assembly decided "to convene not later than 1997 a special session for the purpose of and overall review and appraisal of Agenda 21". In the same spirit, resolution 50/113 invites relevant organisations of the United Nations system to contribute to the special session in co-ordination with the Commission on Sustainable Development. The fifth anniversary of the Rio Conference therefore offers a propitious moment to assess the critical issue of energy in relation to other major global problems.

1.2 Energy After Rio: Prospects and Challenges

The analysis presented in this book draws together a large number of dispersed elements that are relevant to sustainable development, where the issues of supply and demand of energy are significant. It builds on the work of the conferences, drawing new insights from research and development with respect to: *i)* the role of energy in sustainable development; *ii)* technological options to supply energy services; and *iii)* experiences in energy policies to achieve objectives in areas linked to energy, such as those contained in negotiated conference documents. Later chapters will present options for using energy more efficiently, and also will explore how both renewable and fossil sources of energy can be used in cleaner and more efficient ways, to help create a more sustainable future for the world.

Starting from a discussion of the social, environmental, economic and security issues of today's world, the linkages between these issues and energy are described. This book advances an integrated perspective on the linkages between these vital issues and energy. Not only is energy one of the determinants of these problems, but actions related to energy can contribute to their alleviation, if not solution. Implementing sustainable energy strategies is one of the most important levers humankind has for creating a sustainable world.

Energy therefore must be an instrument for the achievement of sustainable development. It is vital to reveal the linkages between energy and the major global issues (Chapter 2), to identify the technical opportunities for sustainable energy (Chapter 3), to bring the technical options together at a global scale, and to assess the manifold implications of sustainable futures associated with the implementation of these opportunities (Chapter 4). The policy issues for bringing about a sustainable future in the context of current trends and constraints (Chapter 5) are addressed suggesting a basis for future action.

2 Energy and Major Global Issues

2.1. Energy and Social Issues
2.1.1 Poverty

Poverty is indisputably among the world's largest, most urgent, and most fundamental issues. The concept of poverty refers to an individual's, or family's, inability to achieve minimal standards in fulfilling basic human needs such as food, clothing, shelter, health, education, and sanitation services. Its pervasiveness, as revealed by the extent to which elementary minimum needs are not satisfied, is undeniable.

Poverty is most naturally conceptualized and measured in terms of the proportion of people who do not achieve specified levels of health, education, and body weight. Operationally, however, poverty standards typically are expressed in a single dimension—either in terms of the monetary resources that would enable an individual to consume a fixed bundle of basic goods and services (i.e., absolute poverty)[1] or as some fraction of the bundle of goods and services that a reference group is able to, or actually does, consume (i.e., relative poverty).

The poverty measurement refers to the proportion of some population whose income or consumption expenditure falls below the specified level. The poverty income gap refers to the average size of the difference between income/expenditure and the standard, for those below the standard.

International comparisons of absolute poverty raise a number of important and difficult issues. These issues include the comparability of estimates based on income and consumption expenditure data, the comparability of the populations to which the estimates pertain (e.g., national or urban), the inclusion of imputed values of consumption from own-production, and the treatment of in-kind earnings and business profits and losses.[2] It has also become common to adjust national currencies for differences in their purchasing powers.

In perhaps the most ambitious and careful attempt yet undertaken to measure absolute consumption poverty, it has been estimated that, as of 1993, roughly 1.3 billion people in developing countries (30% of their total population), daily consume less than the equivalent of US$1 in goods and services.[3]

Statistics on the inability of people in developing countries to satisfy basic human needs corroborate the enormous scale of poverty and highlight its breadth and complexity. For example:
- an estimated 20% of people in developing countries do not have access to health services;
- 30% lack access to safe water; and
- 60% lack access to sanitation (HDR, 1996).

In comparison with industrialised countries:
- infant and child mortality rates in developing countries are more than five times higher;
- the proportion of children below age five who are underweight is eight times higher;
- the maternal mortality rate is 14 times higher; and
- the proportion of births not attended by trained health personnel is 37 times higher.

Although these and other standard indicators of poverty are fraught with a variety of conceptual and measurement problems, they collectively paint a compelling picture of severe human deprivation in all areas of basic human needs.

---

[1] Estimates of absolute poverty are quite sensitive to the methods used to make these adjustments. In addition, all such methods focus on the cost of a standardized bundle consumed by an average household, not on the typical bundle consumed by a low-income household. Insofar as market baskets consumed by low-income households tend to be filled with relatively high proportions of less costly non-tradeable goods and services, absolute poverty will be overstated under all methods of estimation.

[2] For a concise discussion of these and related issues, see (World Bank, 1996).

[3] This number has been adjusted for differences in the purchasing power of different national currencies in 1985 using estimates contained in the Penn World Tables 5.6.

The single most important manifestation of poverty is hunger. The inadequacy of food is revealed in the average per capita food consumption of less than 2,200 kcal per day (96% of the daily minimum requirement) in developing countries, compared to the average diet in industrialised countries of 3,350 kcal per day (129% of the daily requirement). These averages do not reflect the fact that the impact of malnutrition is not uniform even amongst the people living in poverty, because women and children are particularly prone to malnutrition.

The condition of nutritional vulnerability is aggravated by the lack of adequate housing. Typically available construction materials and techniques often fail to provide either permanent or satisfactory protection against the sun, rain and winds—nor do most homes have connections to adequate water supplies or sanitation facilities. Housing conditions such as these allow for the spread of disease, lead to high infant mortality rates, and to low life expectancies.

2.1.1.1 The energy-poverty nexus [4]

Poverty has received scant attention from an energy perspective. This is remarkable given that energy is central to the satisfaction of basic nutrition and health needs, and that energy services constitute a sizeable share of total household expenditure in developing countries.

Observations across countries reveal that low-income households tend to rely on a significantly different set of energy carriers than do the rich. People living in poverty primarily use wood, dung, and other biomass for their energy services, and tend to use less electricity and liquefied petroleum gas (LPG) than do those who are better-off. Approximately two billion people continue to depend on traditional fuels, such as biomass, for cooking. This finding is significant in part because indoor air pollution is a major by-product of the traditional use of biomass, which diminishes the quality of life, especially for women and young children (see Section 2.2.1).

Households use fuel for a variety of purposes including cooking, water heating, lighting and space heating. Firewood, dung, charcoal, coal, kerosene, electricity, and LPG can be used for cooking; and kerosene and electricity for lighting. Together, these energy carriers form what is commonly referred to as an "energy ladder". Each rung of the ladder corresponds to the dominant fuel used by a particular income group, and different income groups use different fuels and therefore occupy different rungs of the energy ladder (Hosier, 1994). For example, wood, dung, and other biomass represent the lowest rung on the energy ladder for cooking, with charcoal, coal, and when available, kerosene, representing the next rungs up the ladder to the highest rungs, electricity and LPG.

The order of fuels on the energy ladder corresponds to their efficiency (i.e., the fraction of energy released from the carrier that is actually turned into an energy service by the end-use device) and their "cleanliness". For example, the cook stove efficiencies of firewood, kerosene, and gas are roughly 15%, 50%, and 65% respectively. Therefore, moving up the energy ladder results in declining emissions of carbon dioxide, sulphur dioxide, and particulates.

Households make choices among the energy carrier options presumably on the basis of both the household's socio-economic characteristics and the attributes of the alternative energy carriers. Income is the main driver in choosing an energy carrier (Leach, 1992; Reddy and Reddy, 1994). Relevant attributes of the energy carriers that are important to the consumer are accessibility, convenience, controllability, cleanliness, efficiency, current cost, and the expected distribution of future costs.

Fuel costs have fixed and variable components. The division of costs into fixed, quasi-fixed, and variable components is relevant to household decisions about fuel choice. The outcome of these decisions depends upon the household's preparedness to forego present consumption for future benefits (i.e., upon the rate at which a household discounts future benefits). This discount rate is determined in part by the household's level of wealth and the liquidity of its assets. For example, households that apply high discount rates to fuel consumption decisions, either because of the high cost of diverting resources from other uses or of borrowing funds to cover up-front capital costs, will

---

[4] See also (World Bank, 1996).

tend to prefer fuel carriers that involve lower up-front costs. People living in poverty tend to use much higher discount rates than do the rich when making decisions about energy carriers (Reddy and Reddy, 1994). They think primarily in terms of the first cost, rather than the life-cycle cost. Since efficient devices tend to have higher initial costs, poor households typically end up with less efficient devices consuming more energy for a given level of energy services. Fuel costs may be determined either in a market or implicitly in terms of the opportunity cost of time spent gathering the fuel (e.g., firewood).

2.1.1.2 Cross-country data on the energy-poverty nexus

Recent cross-country data for 114 countries shows the linkages between energy consumption and the distribution of income. First, total energy consumption per capita, measured in kilograms of oil equivalent, increases with the per capita GDP. Second, the mix of energy carriers varies with income and its distribution (Leach, 1992). In particular, reliance on biomass is greater among countries with lower incomes, among countries with more unequal income distributions, and among countries with relatively small urban populations. The income level and inequality/poverty effects are also quite sizeable in magnitude.[5]

The cross-country data is thus consistent with the notion of an energy ladder. Both poor countries, and the people living in poverty within countries, are disproportionately positioned on the lowest rung (i.e., biomass). Insofar as total energy use increases sharply with income, the ladder may also be thought to widen as one climbs its rungs.

Household survey data reveal the connection between energy consumption patterns and poverty status. Table 2.1 compares energy consumption and fuel sources of extremely low-income households (those in the lowest income quintile) with much wealthier households (those in the highest income quintile) in Pakistan and Vietnam. The energy carriers evaluated are biomass, kerosene, electricity, and gas; and the household activities examined are cooking, space heating, water heating, and lighting.

The results confirm the existence of an energy ladder in Pakistan and Vietnam. People living in poverty are far more likely to use biomass rather than gas or electricity for cooking, and they are more inclined to use kerosene rather than electricity for lighting. This result is due to the fact that about 1.5-2.0 billion people are without electricity, thus limiting their energy choices. On the other hand, the wealthier households consume more energy overall and are far more likely to consume energy carriers at the upper end of the energy ladder (e.g., electricity and gas).

Table 2.2 compares household expenditures for those people in Pakistan living in poverty (i.e., in the first quintile) and those with higher incomes (i.e., in the fifth quintile). The results show that very low income households devote 5.4% of their total household expenditures to energy services, whereas those in the highest income quintile allocate 22.2% for this purpose. This substantial difference reflects in part the fact that people living in poverty use energy primarily only for cooking, while wealthier households use energy for many of tasks, including cooking, space heating, and lighting. Other studies indicate that people living in poverty spend a relatively higher fraction of their income on cooking than well-to-do households.

Most estimates of household expenditures on fuel are substantially understated for very low income households because people living in poverty devote a larger portion of their most important asset, their time, to the production of energy services. Table 2.3 indicates that there is a striking difference between allocations of time and money for people living and poverty and the wealthy. For example, very low income households devote roughly 100 more hours per year to the collection of biomass than do the rich households. However, the rich households spend about 30 times more money per year on fuel than those living in poverty. The fact that the people living in poverty spend more time for energy services, has a powerful implication. The economic hardship endured by very low-income households is understated when their incomes

---

One standard deviation increase in income per capita and in inequality translate, respectively, into a 12% point decrease and an 8% point increase in the biomass share of total energy consumption (44% and 30% of the average country biomass share).

Table 2.1: Household (HH) Energy Consumption and Poverty Status

Fuel and Uses	Pakistan		Vietnam	
	% of Poor HH	% of Rich HH	% of Poor HH	% of Rich HH
Cooking				
Gas (Natural Gas/LPG)	3.1	36.4	0.0	0.1
Electricity	0.0	2.3	0.0	6.9
Kerosene	6.7	18.7	0.0	13.7
Charcoal and Coal			1.9	28.2
Biomass Fuels	91.4	60.9	52.7	60.3
Cooking inside the house	34.3	27.8		
Inside with no chimney	87.9	74.6		
Space Heating				
Gas (Natural Gas/LPG)	0.1	3.8		
Electricity	0.1	4.4		
Kerosene	0.7	0.5		
Biomass Fuels	27.4	19.6		
Water Heating				
Gas (Natural Gas/LPG)	2.3	22.4		
Electricity	0.0	1.6		
Kerosene	1.4	5.6		
Biomass Fuels	23.0	25.9		
Lighting				
Electricity	57.4	80.9	35.1	74.7
Kerosene	81.2	55.5	65.0	26.2

1. Biomass is wood, dung, wheat, straw, coconut shell, cotton sticks, rice hull, corn husk, bagasse, tobacco husk and other biomass.
2. Poor households are households in the lowest quintile of the distribution of household expenditure (1st quintile). Rich households are households in the highest quintile of the distribution of household expenditure (5th quintile).
   Source: (Pakistan LSMS, 1991; Vietnam LSMS, 1992-93)

or consumption expenditures are evaluated in terms of their command over the basket of goods and services typically consumed by households with average incomes or consumption expenditures.

2.1.1.3 Considerations on alleviating poverty

Current patterns of energy consumption among people living in poverty tend to further increase their poverty (Leach, 1992 and Dasgupta, 1993) for the following reasons. First, people living in poverty pay more for energy, they are less likely to accumulate the wealth needed to make the investments that are necessary to make use of higher quality fuels. Second, the use of biomass has a negative impact on the health of household members, especially when it is burned indoors without either a proper stove to help control the generation of smoke, or a chimney to draw the smoke outside. There are a number of studies of the health effects of indoor air pollution which demonstrate a positive correlation between indoor pollution generated by the use of traditional fuels and the incidence of respiratory illness or congestive heart failure[6, 7]. Thus, the use of biomass as a source of energy may also promote higher medical care expenditures and diminish the ability of the people living in poverty to work productively (see Section 2.2.1 for the health

---

[6] See also (Smith, 1987) for a thorough review; and (Mumford, et al, 1990; Chen, et al., 1990; Van Horen, et al., 1993; and Sims, 1994), for examples of recent studies.

[7] It is, however, difficult to infer a causal link from these correlations given the fact that respiratory illness often develops over a long period of time and also given the possible existence of compounding influences on the prevalence of respiratory illness such as smoking and levels of outdoor air pollution. Indeed, some studies have failed to find evidence of a connection between indoor air pollution and ill health; see (Ellegard and Egneus, 1993).

Table 2.2: Household Expenditure Shares by Quintile in Pakistan

| | Total Population | | Urban Population | |
	1st Quintile	5th Quintile	1st Quintile	5th Quintile
Food	57.5	29.1	51.5	25.6
Housing	9.6	13.6	14.9	19.0
Clothing	8.4	5.3	6.8	5.4
Health	6.8	9.8	5.8	7.7
Fuel	5.4	22.2	8.4	20.3
Education	2.7	3.4	3.9	4.5
Transport	0.8	1.8	0.8	2.3
Other Expenditures	8.8	14.4	7.9	15.1
Total	100.0	100.0	100.0	100.0

Note: Other expenditure share includes (in order of size) marriage, birth and funeral ceremonies, toiletries, dowry, recreation and travel, and others.

Source: (Pakistan Living Standard Management Study (LSMS), 1991)

implications of biomass use). These effects are reinforced to the extent that users of biomass are less likely to boil the water they drink, for reasons of either cost or custom. Insofar as the use of biomass in urban areas promotes deforestation, reliance on biomass may also tend to increase its future cost, further diminishing the living standards of people living in poverty.

The linkages between energy and poverty have implications for the development of strategies to alleviate poverty. The standard poverty-alleviation strategies—macroeconomic growth, human capital investment, and income redistribution—do not address directly the energy-poverty nexus. If patterns of energy use result in adverse effects on nutrition, health, and productivity, the benefits of economic growth are likely to be absorbed only very slowly by the people living in poverty. For instance, schooling will continue to promote earning capacity, but by less when biomass is the dominant energy carrier because of poor lighting, limited access to knowledge via radio and television, and poor school attendance due to respiratory illness. In contrast, policies and programs that focus directly on creating opportunities for the people living in poverty to improve their energy services by increasing their use of energy carriers other than biomass, or by using biomass in modern ways, can enable poorer households to enjoy both short-term and self-reinforcing long-term improvements in their standard of living.

2.1.1.4 The Social Summit and energy

The World Summit for Social Development held in Copenhagen in March 1995 focused on poverty and sustainable development and also made reference to the role of energy in poverty alleviation. The Social Summit Programme of Action represents a global effort to address issues related to social development and the negative impacts of underdevelopment and poverty. Global consensus was reached on the need to create an enabling economic environment aimed at promoting more equitable access to sustainable development and resources, and the goal of eradicating poverty.

Chapter II of the Programme for Action recognises that improving the availability and accessibility of transportation, communication, power and energy services at the local and community level is a way of improving access to productive resources and infrastructure, especially for isolated, remote and marginalised communities. Like the other global conferences, Copenhagen emphasised that the major cause of the continued deterioration of the global environment is unsustainable patterns of consumption and production, particularly in industrialised countries.[8] The participating governments committed to strive to ensure that international agreements relating to trade, investment, technology, debt and official development assistance (ODA) are implemented in a manner that promotes social development.

Chapter III of the Platform for Action makes the case for the expansion of produc-

---

[8] Copenhagen Declaration on Social Development, para 15 (d), p.4.

Table 2.3: Household Fuel Expenditure by Quintile in Pakistan

	1st Quintile	5th Quintile
Money[1]	1,348	40,132
Time[2]	164.5	61.4

1. Money is 1991 Pakistani Rupees per year.
2. Time is the average number of hours per year spent collecting wood or dung.
    Source: (Pakistan Living Standards Management Study (LSMS), 1991)

tive employment and reduction of unemployment. The energy-poverty nexus is raised in this context. Among patterns of growth that would maximise employment creation is included "encouraging the utilisation of renewable energy, based on local employment-intensive resources, in particular in the rural areas."[9] This refers to the labour intensive nature of commercial biomass production to generate energy as well as the ready availability of renewable resources in areas which are often poor and uniquely agriculturally-based. Renewable energy development, whether the development of commercial biomass, agricultural residue processing for energy, the development of wind farms, or the marketing of renewables generated energy services, requires human input and generates new jobs and means of livelihood based on existing resources. The Social Summit clearly placed energy concerns within the productive realm, as part of sustainable livelihoods, especially for rural development. This is in addition to earlier environmentally driven concerns that have been consistently expressed at, and since, Rio.

2.1.2 Gender Disparity
2.1.2.1 Trends[10]

Despite robust economic growth over the past five decades, gender disparities have continued:

- Poverty has a woman's face. Of the approximately 1.3 billion people living in poverty, 70% are women. Increasing poverty among women has been linked to their unequal situation in the labour market, their unequal treatment under social welfare systems, their lack of access to health and education services, and their lack of status and power in the family.

- Women's participation in the labour force has risen by only four % points, from 36% to 40%, despite a 60-70% increase in female adult literacy and school enrolment between 1970 and 1990.

- Women have access to a disproportionately small share of credit from formal banking institutions. In Latin America and the Caribbean, women constitute only 7-11% of the beneficiaries of credit programmes; in Africa only about 10% of small-scale credit is accessed by women.

- Women in general receive much lower average wages than men. In part this is because many women work in the informal sector or in inherently low-paying jobs, but also because women are often paid less than men for equal work. The average female wage is only three-fourths of the male wage in the non-agricical sector.

- In developing countries, women still constitute less than a seventh of administrative and managerial positions. Globally, women occupy only 10% of all parliamentary seats and only 6% of cabinet positions. In 55 countries, there are either no women in parliament or fewer than 5%.

- Throughout the world women face unequal treatment under the law, and often face violence and abuse as both girls and women.

The undervaluation of women is reflected in the undervaluation of their work and in the absence of recognition of the contribution that they make (see Figure 2.1). On average women work longer hours than men in nearly every country. Moreover, women support 53% of the total burden of work in

---

[9] Copenhagen Programme of Action of the World Social Summit for Social Development, Ch. III, para 50, p.57

[10] Section 2.1.2.1 is based on (HDR, 1995).

Figure 2.1: Most of Women's Work Remains Unpaid, Unrecognized and undervalued

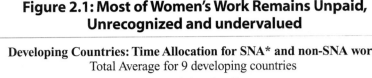

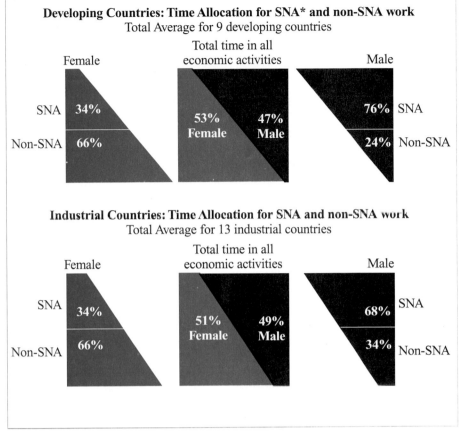

*   SNA (System of National Accounts) corresponds, in this case, to work recognised and included in official national statistics.
Source: (HDR, 1995)

developing countries, and 51%, in industrialised countries. About half of the total work time of both men and women is spent in economic activities in the market or in the subsistence sector. The other half normally is devoted to unpaid household or community activities. In industrialised countries men's total work time is spent roughly two-thirds on paid activities and one-third on unpaid activities. For women, the situation is reversed. In developing countries, more than three-quarters of men's work is in market activities. As a result men receive a much larger share of cash income and recognition for their economic contributions. Conversely, most of women's work remains unpaid in non-marketed or subsistence activities and is thus unrecognised and undervalued. If unpaid activities were treated as market trans-

actions at prevailing wages, global output would increase by US$16 trillion. This represents a 70% increase in the officially estiamted global output of US$23 trillion. US$11 trillion of this increase would correspond to the non-monetised, "invisible" contribution of women.[11]

Despite such gender disparities, there has been significant progress in recognising women's contributions in society and the economy, in building women's capabilities, and in closing gender gaps in education and health over the past two decades. Female life expectancy has increased 20% faster than male life expectancy. High fertility rates, which have direct and often negative effects on women, have fallen from 4.7 live births per woman in 1970-75 to 3.0 in 1990-95. Women's literacy increased from 54% of the

---

[11]   For an explanation of the methodology for this calculation see Chapter 4 of the Human Development Report (HDR, 1995) "Valuing women's work".

male rate in 1970 to 74% in 1990, and combined female primary and secondary enrolment increased from 67% to 86% of the male rate in this period. Significant advances are being made and there is heightened awareness of the negative impacts on society generally when women are accorded low status.

In 1995, UNDP's Human Development Report introduced a new "Gender-related Development Index (GDI)" to reflect gender disparities in basic human capabilities ranking 130 countries on a global scale. Although in no society do women enjoy the same opportunities as men, a comparison of the GDI ranking of countries of different income levels demonstrates that the magnitude of effort needed to remove gender inequalities does not require high national income levels. Across all countries, decisions to invest in the education and health of people, irrespective of gender, seem to cut across income levels, political ideologies, cultures, continents, and stages of development. In many cases, a strong political commitment has driven efforts to improve women's human development despite a shortage of resources. Underdevelopment does not implicitly predispose women's inequality.

2.1.2.2 Energy and women's work[12]

Energy is both necessary for survival and a critical factor affecting economic and social development. As such, energy can contribute to widening opportunities and empowering people to exercise choices. Conversely, its absence can constrain both men and women from contributing to economic growth and overall development.

Energy's relationship to women's work and well-being in particular is evident in women's roles as:

- users of energy resources (both traditional biomass and modern fuels) for household, subsistence and income-earning activities;
- producers of traditional biomass fuels and providers of "human energy" services;
- those most vulnerable to energy scarcity, environmental damages from energy production and use, and adverse impacts of technological changes in the energy sector; and
- educators concerning the collection,

management and use of fuels, and activists in energy and environmental debates and action.

Women are the major users of traditional and biomass energy resources for household and income-earning activities, and they also play major roles in the use of modern energy by households:

- Biomass fuels account for 80% of all household fuel consumption in developing countries, mostly for cooking, which is done primarily by women. Women have practical interests and applied expertise in the burning properties of different fuels, fire and heat management, fuel-saving techniques, and the advantages and disadvantages of different fuels and stoves.
- Women do most of the cooking when using modern fuels as well, and purchase, or influence the purchasing patterns, for fuels, stoves and other energy-using appliances. Perhaps even more important, women influence the direct and indirect energy consumption patterns of their households, the use of heating and air conditioning, hot water and electrical appliances as well as the time of use, and therefore peak energy use. Household consumption and purchasing patterns for products and services which may be more or less energy-intensively produced, as well as the transport systems used by households are directly influenced by the gendered division of labour and the decisions of women.
- Many income activities of women in the informal sector are fuel intensive, and the viability of these activities is affected by energy prices and availabilities (see Table 2.4). Examples include food processing industries, kiln-using manufacturing activities and numerous service-sector activities. Women often participate on a seasonal or part-time basis in many income-earning activities, providing off-farm income that is essential for ensuring family food security, especially for very low-income and landless households.
- Women walk and take public transport more frequently than men. In many countries there are large differences be-

---

[12]   The subsequent 2 sections are based on (Cecelski, 1995).

Table 2.4:
Sample Energy-Intensive, Small-Scale Enterprises Operated by Women

Enterprise	Comments
Beer brewing	25% of fuelwood used in Ouagadougou; main source of income for 54% of women in surveyed Tanzanian village/ 1kg wood/1 litre beer
Rice parboiling	15-20% of firewood in some districts of Bangladesh
Tortilla making	1 kg wood/0.4 kg tortillas
Bakeries	Wood is 25% of bread production costs in Kenya; 80% in Peru 0.8-1.5 kg wood/1 kg bread
Shea butter production	60% of cash income for women in parts of cash
Fish smoking	40,000 tonnes wood/year in Mopti, Mali; 1.5-12 kg wood/kg smoked fish; fuel is 40% of processing costs
Palm oil processing	Extremely arduous, requiring lifting and moving heavy containers of liquid; 0.43 kg wood/1 litre oil; 55% of income of female-headed households in Cameroons study
Gari (cassava) processing	Women in 2 Nigerian districts earned $171/year each; 1kg wood/4 kg gari
Hotels, restaurants, guest houses, tea shops	816,865 tonnes wood annually in Nepal
Food preparation and processing	13% of total household income in Nepal; 48% of mothers in Dangbe district in Ghana engaged; 49% of women in one village in Burkina Faso
Pottery making	Men and women both have distinctive roles in different processes
Soap making	Fuel is high percentage of production

Sources: (BEST, 1988; Gordon, 1986)

tween men and women in automobile ownership and access as well as in possession of driver's licences. Women tend to make a number of shorter and more complex daily trips for shopping, schools, part-time employment and volunteer work. Current urban transport systems are not only energy-intensive, but can often restrict the mobility of those who do not use them (e.g. pedestrians, cyclists and users of public transport) (Spitzner, 1993).

Women also have large roles as producers of traditional biomass fuels and providers of "human energy" services:

- Women and children are the primary collectors of fuelwood, other household fuels, and other forest products for household consumption as well as for sale to urban markets. For example, 48% of women in Fazoum Province, Egypt, work in minor forest industries, and some 250,000 women are employed in collecting forest products in Manipur, India (FAO, 1992). Women fuelwood carriers surveyed in Gujarat, India use most of their income for buying food (FAO, 1989). The management and conservation of these depletable forest resources are critically important to women, who are the chief repositories of knowledge concerning the use and management of trees and other forest products.

- Home-based industries depend on biomass supplies. Studies in Uttar Pradesh, India found that nearly 50% of poor women's incomes originates from common land, compared to about one-eighth of the incomes of poor men (FAO/SIDA, 1981). Women comprise a large share of the labour force in forest industries, nurseries, plantation establishment, logging and wood processing, and depend on these activities for their livelihoods.

- Compared to men, women in developing countries spend long hours working in survival activities such as firewood collection, water hauling, food processing, and cooking (see Table 2.5). Women's time spent on these survival tasks is largely invisible

Table 2.5: Time Allocations to Survival Activities (hours/day)

Survival Activity	Indonesia[1]	Burkina Faso	India	Nepal[1]
Firewood Collection				
Women	0.09	0.10	0.65	2.37
Men	0.21	0.03	0.57	0.83
Water Hauling				
Women	0.00	0.63	1.23	0.67
Men	0.00	0.00	0.04	0.07
Food Processing				
Women	2.72	2.02	1.42	0.70
Men	0.10	0.17	0.27	0.20
Cooking				
Women	-	2.35	3.55	2.10
Men	-	0.01	0.03	0.38
Average Total Work Time/Day				
Women	11.02	9.08	9.07	11.88
Men	8.07	7.05	5.07	6.53

1. For Indonesia, cooking is included in food processing. For Nepal, firewood collection includes leaf fodder collection.
Sources: (Tinker, 1990; Kumar and Hotchkiss, 1988)

in current methods of reporting energy patterns and statistics. For example, while the energy used by an electric pump that transports drinking water can be easily measured and reported, the human energy expended by a woman carrying water goes unmeasured, unmonetised and unrecorded in energy statistics. Although the energy expended for a water-mill grinding grain is accounted for in industrial energy balances, the human efforts of women doing the same task with mortar and pestle are not. Trucks transporting crops consume fossil fuels that are traded and valued through market mechanisms, while women headloading the same maize to market in baskets walk outside the quantified energy balances.

- An analysis of rural "total transport demand" in Sub-Saharan Africa (i.e. all movement of people and goods by any conceivable means, including women headloading water, pack animals moving relief supplies, and non-motorised vehicles on footpaths and trails) indicates that total transport requirements in agricultural production and to meet essential domestic needs (water and fuel collection for example) are much more significant there than those of crop marketing. Most of this internal transport

burden falls on women: 70% of the time and over 80% of the effort (tonnes km) (see Figure 2.2) (Urasa, 1990).

- Because such non-monetised "human energy" services are not included in national energy accounts, a misleading picture of the real economic importance of informal production is given, under-representing women's muscle as an energy source. This omission in the statistical accounts tends to support an investment bias towards large-scale, energy infrastructure projects. For example, new energy technologies for agricultural irrigation and pumping and large infrastructure are primarily within the domain of men. These have received far more energy policy attention than technologies for pumping and transporting drinking water, which falls, almost exclusively, within the domain of women's work in the informal sector.

There is considerable evidence that women are often the most vulnerable to energy scarcity, environmental damages from energy production and use, and adverse impacts of technological changes in the energy sector:

- Based on FAO estimates of the percentage of household energy provided by fuelwood, the proportions of rural women

16

Figure 2.2: Rural Transport Activities by Males and Females in Tanzania

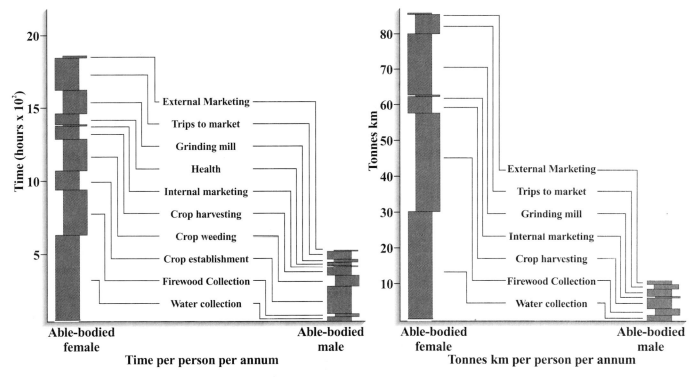

Source: (Makete, 1987)

affected by fuelwood scarcity are estimated to be 60% in Africa, nearly 80% in Asia, and nearly 40% in Latin America and the Caribbean (HDR, 1995). Time spent in fuel collection in fuel-scarce areas can range from 1 to 5 hours per household per day. Additional impacts include less water heating and washing, decreased time and fuel used for cooking, declining nutritional status, and less time for agricultural work and food production. There can also be direct negative impacts on children's participation in education as they are increasingly drawn into fuel-gathering activities. To the extent that girls are more often involved than boys, gender disparities in literacy and subsequent status will result. In some developing countries girls spend more than 7 times as many hours in wood and water collection as compared to adult males, and 3.5 times as many hours as compared to boys (HDR, 1995).

- Energy scarcity impinges on the provision of other basic services, such as water, health, and education. For example, the proportions of rural women affected by water scarcity are estimated to be 55%

in Africa, 32% in Asia, and 45% in Latin America, with the median time for collecting water in the dry season about 1.6 hours per day (World's Women, 1995).

- On a global basis, it is estimated that more than half of the world's households cook daily with wood, crop residues and untreated coal, as a result of which women and children have the highest exposures to indoor air pollution. Typical indoor concentrations of important pollutants, such as respirable particulates, carbon monoxide, benzene and formaldehyde, are excessive by comparison to health-based standards. Such exposures are linked to acute respiratory infections, chronic obstructive lung diseases, low birth weights, lung cancer and eye problems (Smith, 1990) (see Section 2.2.1).

- Current energy production and use entails occupational hazards for women. For example, the estimated 10,000 women fuelwood carriers in Addis Ababa, who supply one third of the wood fuel consumed in the city, suffer frequent falls, bone fractures, eye problems, headaches, rheumatism, anaemia, chest, back and internal disorders, and miscarriages, from carrying loads often weighing 40-50 kg—nearly as much as their own body weights (Haile, 1991). The production of palm and other oils in women's informal sector enterprises is extremely arduous, requiring lifting and moving heavy containers of hot liquids and hence exposure to burns and smoke. Women working in the informal sector on Bangkok streets have high exposures to traffic-based lead emissions from gasoline fuels and have given birth to newborns with dangerously high blood lead levels as a result.

- In some circumstances, physical and psychological violence against women can be related to energy systems. Where fuel must be collected in areas of contested access or civil disturbances, women may face violence. There have been hundreds of documented cases of Somali refugee women raped while gathering fuelwood around camps bordering the Somali-Kenyan border (The Economist, 1993) while women in Sarajevo often faced sniper fire while gathering fuel. Bride suicides in India related to women's inability to meet their family's wood fuel needs have also been documented (Agarwal, 1986).

Women, especially poor women, are more vulnerable than men to changes in energy availabilities and prices, in light of the relatively high proportion of households headed by females (30% in most regions), the global feminisation of poverty, and the fact that women typically are responsible for household fuel and food expenditures. The average urban household consumption and expenditure on energy ranges from 6.5 to 24% of total monthly income (see Table 2.6). Even in rural areas, fuel can be 5-10% of non-food cash expenditures. In rural India, as much as 50% of the non-food expenditure of the lowest expenditure groups is on energy, compared to 10% or less for the highest expenditure groups (ILO,1987).

Women are often vulnerable to adverse impacts of technological changes, including energy-related technological changes, even when such changes appear to be "gender-neutral." A classic example is the displacement of landless women in rice hulling in South and South East Asia. In Indonesia, on governmental initiative, mechanised rice

hullers replaced 90% of hand rice-hulling between 1970 and 1978, with estimated resulting job losses as high as 1.2 million in Java alone and 7.7 million in all of Indonesia. Losses in earnings to women handpounders arising from the use of hullers were estimated US$50 million annually in Java, representing 125 million women days of labour (UNIFEM, 1988). In Ghana, a feasibility study on improving the efficiency of charcoal making from sawmill residues found that small-scale itinerant producers (mostly women) were unlikely to be able to secure land tenure for fixed kilns, to invest in the new equipment or to purchase the now more valuable residues (Cecelski, 1990a). In Nigeria, the introduction of modern power-driven palm oil mills resulted in women demonstrating against them because the women lost valuable by-products and income to their husbands (UNIFEM, 1987). While technological changes always involve dislocations of those using existing technologies, so that initiatives to introduce such changes should be accompanied by measures to minimise the hardships on all who are adversely affected and to help them find ways to be engaged in more productive activities, these examples highlight the importance of understanding in particular the gender biases of technological change, even for seemingly gender-neutral energy-related technological changes.

There are several aspects to women as educators and activists in energy and environmental debates and action:

- Women are educators of young people in the collection, management and use of fuels and other natural resources which has implications on how energy-use patterns are replicated over time and passed on to future generations;
- Women often are the primary educators of children concerning sanitation, consumption habits, waste disposal, natural resources use and interaction with the environment in general;
- Patterns of water use for food preparation, cooking, washing, laundry and irrigation, activities which are often in the domain of women, will be passed on through this process of education to subsequent generations of adults through women. The same is true for the collection, management and use of traditional

Table 2.6: Urban Household Energy Consumption and Expenditures in Relation to Monthly Income, 11 Countries, 1988

Country	Income/person (US$/month)	Energy consumption (kgoe/month)	Energy expenditures (US$)	As % of total income
Bolivia	68.33	10.79	4.43	6.48
Haiti	65.08	12.57	11.04	16.97
Yemen	87.89	7.78	10.07	11.46
Indonesia	24.45	8.51	2.40	9.81
Philippines	60.10	6.92	4.93	8.21
Thailand	117.50	10.82	8.85	7.53
Cape Verde	56.05	7.03	9.29	16.57
Mauritania	25.34	10.83	6.18	24.40
Burkina Faso	35.12	10.48	4.39	12.51
Zambia	23.04	16.48	3.76	16.31
China	17.92	21.16	1.44	8.05
Average	**41.82**	**11.41**	**4.93**	**11.78**

Source: (Cecelski, 1995)

fuels for these activities.

- Because of the importance of energy to women's roles and activities, energy policy debates have often elicited women's strong interests and distinct perspectives. Women and their organisations have been active and effective in changing some energy and environmental policies. Women have been especially vocal in anti-nuclear and peace movements.
- When convinced of the utility and practicality of an energy technology or forestry scheme, women or women's groups have been effective in persuading households and communities to invest the resources necessary to make the scheme work. The Vietnam Women's Union, for instance, is at the forefront of a revolving credit project to install the first household and community photovoltaic systems in that country.
- When convinced of the negative effects and costs to their livelihoods, on the other hand, women have been equally forceful in blocking changes advanced as "improvements." The Chipko movement to protect forests on which women's livelihoods depend in northern India is a well-known example. More subtle but no less effective was Sahelian women's rejection in the 1970s of so-called improved stoves designed without their consultation and whose laboratory savings were not borne out in actual use (Baldwin, 1984).

2.1.2.3 New energy paradigms and new opportunities

The effective incorporation into energy decision making of women's concerns, with attention to gender disparity in general and gender biases in particular, requires both new analytical approaches to the energy problem and a new energy paradigm, as women's concerns are typically given inadequate attention or neglected at present (Cecelski, 1992).

Under a new energy paradigm based on the energy technologies and strategies needed to meet sustainable development objectives, as discussed in subsequent chapters, it would be much easier to deal with such gender concerns in energy decision making than under the current energy paradigm. Sustainable development objectives cannot be realised without giving close attention in energy analysis, as prelude to energy policy, to the services that energy provides and to the total impacts of producing and using energy in providing these services, and thus to the users and providers of these energy services, both men and women. The enactment of policies to achieve sustainable development objectives cannot be realised without the participation of a wide range of stakeholders, including women and women's groups.

At the same time, new gender-focused analytical approaches provide a better basis than ever before for strengthening women's roles in sustainable energy development. Research on women, environment and development has identified women's special relationships with the environment and has shown that the burden of environmental degradation and energy shortages often falls disproportionately on women (see Section 2.1.2.2). Gender analysis shows that women and men often relate to the resources of the natural environment differently. Their knowledge bases are different, and hence, their respective needs and interests distinct. Gender analysis also has demonstrated that women are not a homogeneous category. Their interests in energy and environmental issues vary by class, race, caste and other variables and must be addressed based on the specific circumstances of the group and location under discussion (Jackson, 1993 and Agarwal, 1992).

Effective gender analysis tools and proven participatory approaches for strengthening women's roles in sustainable development, including natural resource management, are available for the forestry and water and sanitation sectors (FAO, 1996 and Wakeman, 1995) and are beginning to be developed for the energy sector (RWEDP, 1996 and Skutsch, 1996) .

Another recent change is that today there are many more women working in energy-related professions than only a few years ago. Women are participating not only as sociologists (already fairly common a few years ago), but also increasingly as engineers, economists, and biological and physical scientists. Although women are still under-represented in energy policy-making, planning and research, there is a critical mass of women professionals scattered throughout energy organisations that can provide critical role models, advice and contacts to promote women's roles in sustainable energy development.

Increasingly men are becoming more involved in gender-relevant energy research and policy. This includes such important areas as household energy strategies, indoor air pollution from biomass fuel combustion, the inclusion of human energy in analysis and the compiling of statistics on energy balances, and the measurement of production in the informal sector.

In sum, the adoption of a sustainable energy development paradigm would facilitate the inclusion of women's concerns in energy

decision-making, and would support and build on gains that are already beginning to be made. The interests of women in these issues have direct impacts on the course of sustainable energy development and the lives of women.

2.1.2.4 The Beijing Conference[13]

The Fourth World Conference on Women held in Beijing in September 1995 was the largest United Nations global conference ever convened. It looked at the role of women in development and how gender issues affect the development process and vice versa. Energy was considered in the context of gender, science and technology. The conference marked a shift away from viewing women as only passive recipients of science and technology. Rather women were viewed as active participants in the innovation process, through their knowledge of their own material reality and through their demonstrated innovative capacities. Further, the incorporation of women (and their values) into the practice of science and technology is expected to help shift the mainstream of science and technology in the direction of meeting the needs of people living in poverty, people in the South and women (UNIFEM, 1994).

Energy is dealt with in several sections of the Beijing Conference documents though like Agenda 21, there is no cohesive approach put forward with regards to energy. In the Platform for Action, Chapter C "Women and Health", specific reference is made to inadequate access to fuel supplies, particularly in rural areas, as one of the factors (together with water) which overburden women and their families and has a negative effect on health.[14] This impact is due not only to the long hours spent in the collection and carting of energy inputs, but also to the adverse health effects and respiratory disease associated with the combustion of traditional fuels during the food preparation process, which disproportionately impacts women.

In Chapter K "Women and the Environment" women's multiple roles in the management and use of natural resources, as providers of sustenance for their families and communities, as well as women's needs and requirements as users, consumers, manag-

---

13   This section is based on the Beijing Platform for Action.

14   Beijing Platform for Action, Chapter C, para 92, p. 57.

ers and decision-makers is discussed. The need to integrate gender concerns and perspectives in all programmes for sustainable development is stressed. The fact that over 70% of those living in poverty world-wide are women is but one reason why gender issues are directly relevant to concerns regarding sustainable development. As is the case in Agenda 21, Chapter K of the Beijing Platform for Action includes as a premise that women have an essential role to play in the development of sustainable and ecologically sound consumption and production patterns as well as natural resource management.

The deterioration of natural resources displaces communities, especially the women within them, from income-earning activities while greatly adding to unremunerated work.[15] This problem is particularly important with regard to land degradation due to fuelwood collection and to the ever lengthening time spent on these subsistence activities as population increases and resources continue to erode. Strategic objective K.2 aims to "integrate gender concerns and perspectives in policies and programmes for sustainable development,"[16] and, with regard to energy, requests governments to promote knowledge and sponsor research on the roles of women, particularly rural and indigenous women, in forest conservation, and new and renewable sources or energy.[17] Governments are called on to support women's equal access to "sustainable and affordable energy technologies, such as wind, solar, biomass and other renewable sources, through participatory needs assessments, energy planning and policy formation at the local and national levels."[18] From this it is clear that there is a gender dimension to energy production and use, especially but not exclusively, in poor and rural populations.

2.1.3 Population
2.1.3.1 Population trends

Many of today's global problems depend upon the availability and use of natural re-sources, which in turn must be seen in relation to the magnitude of human populations depending and exerting pressure on these resources. This pressure has been escalating rapidly, to a large extent as a result of the dramatic increase in the world population over the last century:

"It took the world population millions of years to reach the first billion, then 123 years to get to the second, 33 years to the third, 14 years to the fourth, 13 years to the fifth billion."[19]

Additions to the population have been unprecedented:

"During the last decade, between 1980 and 1990, the number of people on earth grew by about 923 million, an increase nearly the size of the total world's population in Malthus's time."[19]

This growth led to fears of a continuously growing population that would lead humanity to its doom. However, these predictions have generally assumed the persistence of the very high population growth rates of the 1950s, which correspond to a doubling approximately every 23 years.

It is now clear that the tremendous recent increase in the world's population is associated with what is known as a demographic transition. In such a transition, the population moves from an old balance characterised by high mortality and high fertility rates to a new balance with low mortality and low fertility rates. Demographic transitions have occurred in the past, in Western Europe in the 19th century, and in Southern and Eastern Europe in the first quarter of this century. They are now taking place all over the developing world. In some countries, they are just starting; in others, they are well under way; and in the remaining countries, they are over or almost over.

The demographic transition currently taking place in the developing countries has been initiated by the rapid decline in mortality in these countries brought about by improvements in public health and advances

15 Beijing Platform for Action, Chapter K, para 247, p.138.

16 Beijing Platform for Action, Chapter K, para 256, p.142.

17 Beijing Platform for Action, Chapter K, para 256(f), pp.142-143.

18 Beijing Platform for Action, Chapter K, para 256(k), pp.142-143.

19 The quotes in this section are from (Sen, 1994).

in medical technology. For example, an increase in life expectancy from 40 to 50 years was achieved in developing countries in only 15 years from 1950 to 1965. In comparison, a similar increase in life expectancy required 70 years (from 1830 to 1900) in Western Europe and 25 years (from 1900 to 1925) in Southern and Eastern Europe.

If a large reduction in mortality rates is not accompanied by a fall in fertility rates, the population will increase indefinitely. In the industrialised countries, the low value of mortality has been balanced by new, lower fertility rates. Thus, the population growth rate is low both before and after demographic transition, while population grows rapidly during the transition:

"The rate of the world population growth is certainly declining, and even over the last two decades, its percentage growth rate has fallen from 2.2% per year between 1970 and 1980 to 1.7% between 1980 and 1992. This rate is expected to go steadily down until the size of the world's population becomes nearly stationary."[19]

The crucial question is whether the reduction in mortality that took place in the developing countries between 1950 and 1965 has been followed by a fall in fertility. The evidence seems clear. Until the mid '60s, there was no sign of this fertility decline, but since then, fertility has begun to fall in almost all the developing countries except those in Sub-Saharan Africa. The average "total fertility rate"[20] in the developing countries has fallen from about 5.9 to about 4.7 (i.e., by about 20%, in the 15-year period from 1965 to 1980).

It can be concluded that a demographic transition is taking place and that the population of developing countries and of the world as a whole is likely to stabilise eventually. The world will have a growing population for quite some time, however, because of "population momentum." What is extremely important is that the response of fertility is not as rapid as the decline in mortality, and the delay in fertility decline leads to a "bulge" in the time variation of population It is this "bulge" that

gives rise to the problems associated with population size, such as the implications for energy and natural resources use.

This population momentum has important geographical, location and age dimensions. First, there is an uneven geographical distribution of population growth; 90% of the additions to the world's population are taking place in the developing countries. Current additions to population are primarily in the people-abundant countries with low average incomes. Second, the locational distribution of population growth is such that the urban share of population growth has increased, and will continue to do so. Third, the age distribution of the population is changing in all countries, but the nature of the change is different across countries. The population is becoming older in the rich countries because life expectancy is increasing when infant mortality is relatively stable. In the poor countries, the population is becoming younger because infant mortality is declining much more than the increase in life expectancy.

A recent World Bank base case projection of the world's future population is that the world's population will increase from 5.69 billion in 1995, to 9.58, 10.96, and 11.40 billion by 2050, 2100, and 2150, respectively (Figure 2.3) (Bos et al., 1994). The bulk of the population increase is expected to take place in the developing countries, where the population increases from 4.45 billion in 1995 to 8.22 billion in 2050, 9.59 billion by 2100, and 10.01 billion by 2150.

2.1.3.2 The energy-population nexus

An assumed exogenous impact of population on energy is the conventional, and obvious, aspect of the population/energy connection. Population levels influence energy demand in a straightforward way; the larger the population, the more the total energy required, with the magnitude of this total energy depending on the per capita energy consumption.[21] This is the conventional approach to the energy-population nexus: population is an external factor influencing energy consumption.[22]

---

[20]   A measure of the average number of children a woman will bear throughout her child-bearing years if at each age she has the average fertility corresponding to that age group.

[21]   Total Energy Demand = Population x Per Capita Energy Consumption.

[22]   While many believe that population growth in developing countries represents the most serious threat to the global atmosphere via global warming, the continued high and/or growing levels of fossil fuel con-

Figure 2.3: Population Projection to the Year 2150

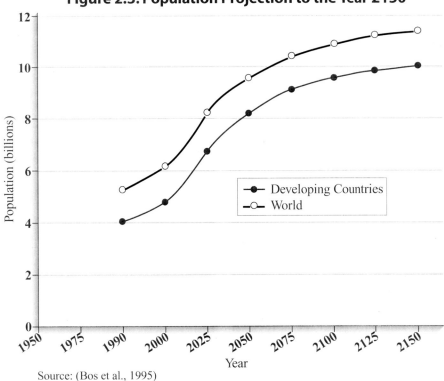

Source: (Bos et al., 1995)

There can be another connection in which energy strategies contribute to a reduction of the intensity of the population "burden." If energy consumption and population growth are a dialectical pair-each transforming the other, and each being the effect when the other is the cause-then the pattern of energy consumption could also have an effect on population growth. This is an alternative perspective in which energy consumption patterns influence the rate of population growth through their effect on the desired number of births in a family and the relative benefits and costs of fertility. Ultimately, these patterns can retard or accelerate the demographic transition (Goldemberg et al., 1988).

This dimension of the energy-population nexus will be illustrated through the influence of energy consumption on population growth at two levels: the micro-level of villages in developing countries and the macro-level of the world. The implication is that an important task for energy is to help accelerate the demographic transition, particularly by achieving dramatic reductions in fertility to stabilise global population as quickly as possible and at as low a level as possible.

2.1.3.3 Rural energy consumption patterns

There are several noteworthy features of patterns of energy consumption in rural areas of developing countries. Though these features vary with country and agro-climatic conditions, a few numbers typical of South Indian villages (ASTRA, 1982) are presented to give an idea of the magnitudes involved.

- What is conventionally referred to as commercial energy (e.g., kerosene, electricity) accounts for a very small percentage of the energy used in villages, the remaining energy coming from fuelwood.[23]
- Animate energy sources, derived from human beings and draught animals (for example, bullocks), account for less than 10% of the total energy but represent the bulk of the energy used in agriculture.
- Virtually all of the energy consumption

sumption in the industrialized countries and among the rich in developing countries are making far greater impacts on the global atmosphere than the poor in developing countries, even though the populations of the industrialized countries and the rich in the developing countries are growing very slowly.

[23] In one of the villages studied, fuelwood consumption amounted to about 217 tonnes of firewood per year, i.e., about 0.6 tonnes/day for the village, or 0.6 tonnes/year/capita.

comes from traditional renewable sources: agriculture is largely based on human beings and bullocks, while domestic cooking (which utilises most of the total inanimate energy) is based entirely on fuelwood.[24]

- The environmental soundness of this pattern of dependence on renewable resources is achieved at a high social cost: levels of agricultural productivity are very low, and large amounts of human energy are spent on fuelwood gathering (for example, about 2 to 6 hours and 4 to 8 km per day per family to collect about 10 kg of fuelwood).
- Fetching water for domestic consumption also utilises a great deal of human energy (an average of 1.5 hours and 1.6 km per day per household) to achieve an extremely low per capita water consumption rate of 17 litres per day.
- Almost half of the human energy is spent on grazing livestock (5 to 8 hours/day/household), a crucial source of supplementary household income.
- Children contribute approximately one-third of the labour for gathering fuelwood, fetching water and grazing livestock respectively. Their labour contributions are vital to the survival of families, a point often ignored by population and education planners.

The end-uses of human energy in villages show that the inhabitants, particularly its women and children, face burdens (e.g., gathering fuelwood and fetching water) that have been largely eliminated in urban settings by the deployment of appropriate forms of inanimate energy. There are also serious gender and health implications arising from rural energy consumption patterns (Batliwala, 1982; Batliwala, 1987; and Batliwala, 1984).

2.1.3.4 Population implications of village energy consumption patterns

To understand the population implications of these features of energy consumption in villages, it is necessary to consider how these features influence the desired number of births in a family and the relative benefits and costs of fertility. Coale (1983) delineates some of the key preconditions necessary for a decline in fertility:

- Fertility must be within the calculus of conscious choice. Potential parents must consider it an acceptable mode of thought and form of behaviour to balance advantages and disadvantages before deciding to have another child.
- Reduced fertility must be advantageous. Perceived social and economic circumstances must make reduced fertility seem an advantage to individual couples.
- Effective techniques of fertility reduction must be available. Procedures that will in fact prevent births must be known, and there must be sufficient communication between spouses and sufficient sustained will, in both, to employ them successfully.

The exercise of choice in matters of fertility is a complicated issue, varying across cultures. The awareness and availability of fertility-reduction techniques depends upon specific technologies and the success with which they are spread. The desired number of births, and therefore the relative benefits and costs of fertility, depend upon socio-economic factors such as:

- Infant mortality and the probability of offspring surviving—the lower this probability, the larger the number of children aspired for and the greater the exposure of the mother to the possibility of additional pregnancies,
- The role of women in arduous time-consuming household chores—the greater this role. The less the scope and emphasis on women's education and the lower the age of marriage,
- The use of children for the performance of essential household tasks—the greater the use of children for these tasks, the more they become essential for the survival of the household,
- The opportunities for children to earn wages—such wage-earning children become desirable and wanted as economic assets.

---

[24] Unlike some rural areas of India, dung cakes are not used as cooking fuel in the region studied. In situations where agro-wastes (e.g., coconut husks) are not abundant, it appears that, if firewood is available within some convenient range (determined by the capacity of head-load transportation), dung-cakes are never burnt as fuel; instead dung is used as fertilizer.

These are only a few of the factors that enter the perceptions of advantages and disadvantages of fertility and family size. Nevertheless, it is clear that the reduction of fertility, and therefore the acceleration of the demographic transition, depends upon crucial developmental tasks such an increase of life expectancies, provision of water, sanitation, housing, and health services, improving the environment, educating women, and diverting children away from life-support tasks and employment to schooling. Further, almost every one of these socio-economic preconditions for smaller family size and fertility decline depends upon energy-utilising technologies.

- Infant mortality has much to do with adequate and safe supplies of domestic water and with a clean environment.
- The conditions for women's education become favourable: if the drudgery of their household chores is reduced, if not eliminated; with sufficient access to energy supplies, efficient energy sources and/or devices for cooking; and with energy-utilising technologies for the supply of water for domestic uses.
- The deployment of energy for industries that generate employment and income for women also can help in delaying the marriage age which is an important determinant of fertility.
- If the use of energy results in child-labour becoming unnecessary for crucial household tasks (such as cooking, gathering fuelwood, fetching drinking water, and grazing livestock), an important rationale for large families is eliminated.

From this standpoint, it is obvious that the prevailing patterns of energy consumption in villages do not emphasise energy inputs for providing safe and sufficient supplies of drinking water, the maintenance of a clean and healthy environment, reduction of the drudgery of household chores traditionally performed by women, the relief of menial tasks carried out by children, and the establishment of income-generating industries in rural areas.

Thus, current energy consumption patterns tend to exclude the type of energy-utilising technologies necessary to satisfy the socio-economic preconditions for fertility decline. In fact these energy use patterns encourage an increase in the desired number of births in a family and an increase in the relative benefits of fertility.

2.1.3.5 The energy-population nexus at the global level

The September 1994 Cairo Conference on Population and Development looked at how population size and rate of growth impact, and are related to, the process of economic growth and sustainable development. The Programme of Action adopted at the Cairo Conference emphasized the need to integrate population concerns into all aspects of economic and social activity. Chapter 3 of this Programme addresses the interrelationships between population, sustained economic growth and comprehensive sustainable development, particularly for the implementation of effective population policies and meeting basic human needs. The Cairo Conference recognized poverty as a major obstacle to solving population problems.

The Preamble of the Programme of Action noted that around the world many basic resources on which future generations will depend for their survival and well-being are being depleted and that environmental degradation is intensifying, driven by unsustainable patterns of production and consumption. The current large global population (approximately 5.7 billion in 1995), its rapid growth (at present some 83 million people are added to the current population each year), and the strong urbanisation trend in nearly all countries, pose daunting challenges to realisation of the goal of a sustainable future. Indeed the Cairo Programme noted that "demographic factors, combined with poverty, and lack of access to resources in some areas, and excessive consumption and wasteful production pattern in others, cause or exacerbate problems of environmental degradation and resources depletion and thus inhibit sustainable development."[25]

The implementation and follow-up of recommendations from Cairo and Copenhagen related to health, education, safe food, potable water and sanitation, transportation, employment and poverty eradication, as well as the needs of special groups such as the aged,

---

[25] This paragraph is based on: Cairo Programme of Action, Chapter 1, Preamble, para 1.2, p.6

handicapped, victims of natural disasters, children, refugees and displaced, will all require a substantial increases in energy services.

As is discussed in Chapters 3 and 4, large increases in energy services can be provided in ways that are consistent with sustainable development, via emphasis on energy-efficient end-use technologies and modern energy carriers, based on both renewable and improved fossil energy technologies. Accelerating the pace at which such technologies are made available to improve the living standards of those living in poverty in developing countries would help slow the rate of population growth. Insofar as current energy strategies do not sufficiently emphasise increasing energy services with such technologies, they are not directly addressing the population problem.

2.1.4 Undernutrition and Food[26]

2.1.4.1 Undernutrition

The United Nations Food and Agricultural Organisation (FAO) estimated that, in the period 1990 to 1992, nearly 840 million people were undernourished. This figure accounted for approximately 20% of the 1990-1992 developing country population of 4.2 billion (FAO, 1995). The definition of an inadequate diet is based on an intake of less than 2,160 calories per day (Schrimshaw, 1980) which is only 1.55 times the Basal Metabolic Rate. Thus, this criterion of undernourishment only reckons with the energy required for minimal physical activity.

Estimates such as these, however, present only gross averages. In fact, the percentage of undernourished people varies widely, depending on factors such as:

- Geographic region. The countries with the highest percentage of undernourished people are in regions where the staple foods are either millet and sorghum or roots and tubers;
- Distribution of income. Both the consumption of protein and the total calories intake increase with family income (Schrimshaw and Taylor, 1980);
- Gender effects. Due to cultural intra-family factors women in many developing countries "eat last and least," even though studies are revealing that they work harder and expend more energy

than men (ASTRA, 1982 and Batliwala, 1982); also boys are often given a better diet than girls; and

- Seasonal variations. For instance, food consumption in the Sahelian countries can average 25-30% less before the harvest than soon after it (IDRC, 1980).

The occurrence of undernutrition has a number of serious implications. As noted in Hube (1982):

"Though for the poorest, undernutrition is a condition close to starvation, undernutrition in its broadest sense results from a diet inadequate to maintain satisfactory physical and mental development. Undernutrition impairs the capacity for work output and lowers resistance to infection. Infection, in turn, increases the food nutrient demand to repair the damage wrought by disease. Undernutrition and chronic infection impair learning ability which further reduces the capacity for effective work. Consequently, undernutrition begins a vicious circle broken only by provision of an adequate diet."

With more than 800 million people undernourished at the beginning of the decade, undernutrition is a grave problem even at present population levels. By the end of this century the world may have to feed as many as 800 million additional people (compared to 1990 levels). This leads to the question as to whether food supplies are and will be adequate for the world's population.

The level of undernutrition is not as much a function of the adequacy of global food production as it is a function of the distribution of food supplies. This can be illustrated with a few simple figures. The caloric yields of approximately 45 million tonnes of cereals would suffice to meet the requirements of the undernourished population today. This amount represents only 2.6% of the actual 1989-91 world production, 35% of the industrialised countries grain trade, or a 13% diversion of the total cereal output now being fed to animals. Moreover, if the 1989-91 global production of about 1,727 million tonnes grain were to become uniformly accessible to the world's population of 5.7 billion, the per capita availability of food would be an adequate supply of about 2,460 calories per day for everyone in the world.

One important cause of undernutrition is

---

[26]   This section is based on (FAO, 1995 and FAO, 1979).

the non-uniformity of foodgrain production and food availability in various parts of the world. The developing countries, with about 73% of the world's population, produce only about 50% of the global grain supply. In contrast, the industrialised countries with only about 22% of the global population, produce about 35% of the world's cereal output.

The quantity of grain entering into world trade is only 7.5% of total grain production. Despite this, the grain trade is associated with a number of important logistical, balance-of-payments and political challenges that affect the self-reliance of countries. It follows that serious attempts must be made to achieve self-sufficiency in food production at regional and national levels.

2.1.4.2 Prospects for increasing food production

This dispersal of food production requires a special emphasis on increasing food production and availability in the developing countries—particularly because it is these countries that will have to absorb the bulk of future population increase. One key question is whether the developing countries, individually and collectively, can increase their food production to feed their additional population.

From the nutritional point of view, developing countries would have to increase their plant-derived nutritional energy by 170%. While countries of Latin America and Asia would have to roughly double their plant-derived energy, Africa would have to increase its plant-derived energy five-fold (seven-fold for the root and tuber-consuming countries). For Asia or Latin America, achieving this goal would require a lower rate of productivity growth than was seen in the last 15 years, However, Africa would have to accelerate its productivity growth.

The FAO study, Agriculture: Towards 2010 (FAO, 1995), addresses a possible future outcome of a 70% increase over the 1989-91 actual food production in developing countries by the year 2010. This increase would require
- a greater intensity of cropping,
- higher crop yields, and
- bringing new land into agricultural production.

The area of land under cultivation is a crucial factor, but it is under severe threat from several pressures particularly population in-creases and land degradation. In 1990, the developing country population of about 2.9 billion had 757 million hectares of arable land in use, i.e., an average of approximately 3.9 people in developing countries were dependent on each hectare of arable land. It is estimated that in 2010 about 4.5 billion people in developing countries will have available to them 850 million hectares of arable land; this corresponds to about 1 hectares of arable land for food production for every 5.3 individuals. The total world area available for cropping, counting more than once those areas where multiple crops are grown, is much larger. Thus, there is room for expansion of cropped area, provided capital is available for land reclamation and irrigation.

However, the bulk of the increase in food production is expected to come from higher yields, as has been the case from 1950 to 1980—when 70-90% of the increase in output in the developed and developing countries came from gains in yield. Even greater increases in yield may be necessary if the projected 12% increase in arable land cannot be realised.

Nevertheless, it must be noted that whereas significant increases can be achieved in the yields of wheat and rice, corresponding successes have not been attained with legumes even though "the protein in food legumes is nutritionally complementary to that of cereal grains" (Hube, 1982). The nutritionally desirable ratio is one tonne of legume for every two tonnes of cereal, but the Asian legume harvest is only about one-tenth of that of cereal production.

2.1.4.3 Increasing access to and consumption of food

Increasing food production, particularly in the developing countries, is a necessary condition for solving the problem of under-nutrition, but it is not a sufficient condition. Even if food supplies were adequate, the issue of distribution remains and is related to income inequalities and the inadequate purchasing power of the poorest households.

The fundamental cause of undernutrition is poverty. Even when food is available, the people living in poverty, particularly (but not solely) in developing countries, cannot afford to buy adequate food for themselves. If the poor do not have the purchasing power, they cannot articulate their demands through the market and gain access to food which is today a commodity. This requires an increase in the purchasing power of the people living in poverty through access to assets and/or employment leading to enhanced incomes.

However, such purchasing-power augmenting programmes are often not enough to tackle undernutrition, for poverty is also associated with poor health. Gastro-intestinal parasites, for instance, can undermine nutritional status by consuming perhaps as much as 10-15% of the food intake. This has to be tackled by health care and the provision of safe water and a clean environment.

Also, the incidence of undernutrition tends to be non-uniform even within a family: children (0 to 5 years) and expectant and nursing mothers tend to be more vulnerable. This situation may require programmes of supplementary nutrition for the vulnerable sections of society.

2.1.4.4 Water, food and energy

Energy-efficient technologies and sources of energy that are sustainable are needed for irrigation, the second most energy-consuming activity in agriculture, following fertilisation.

World-wide, some 250 million hectares receive irrigation. Irrigation serves 29% of all land under agricultural use. There are, however, wide regional variations, with Asia at 38%, sub-Saharan Africa at 4% and Latin America at 15%. New irrigation has been added at an average rate of 3 million hectares annually over the last two decades, of which 87% is in Asia. At present, irrigation development has slowed substantially relative to the 1960s. Internationally-funded irrigation development also has declined. For example, World Bank lending to irrigation projects fell from US$2 billion in 1980 to US$1 billion in 1993.

Irrigated lands occupy only 15% of all arable land, but they produce 36% of all crops and more than half the total grain produced in developing countries. There will most probably have to be a substantial increase in irrigated land area if food production is to be increased dramatically.

Any retrenchment in irrigation, or even a failure to expand it in line with the proven potential, inevitably will lead to further expansion of rain-fed agriculture. Much of this

expansion would take place under risky rainfall regimes. Moreover, expansion of the area of rain-fed agriculture will result in deforestation, and increase cultivation on slopes and close to stream banks, with a consequent increase in soil erosion and the accelerated sedimentation of river beds, estuaries and reservoirs.

In Sub-Saharan Africa, less than 20% of the theoretical irrigation potential has been realised. The low economic feasibility of irrigation is the greatest obstacle to its expansion. This is due to higher initial investment costs than in other regions, low cropping intensities, market limitations for high-value crops, competition from low-cost imported rice, high transport costs due to poor roads (major consumption centres are often supplied more cheaply from abroad), and the lack of an irrigation tradition.

In Asia, the average investment cost for new irrigation has doubled in the last ten years, during which time international rice prices have declined. Rates of return to new irrigation infrastructure have fallen as a result. In some cases, irrigation investment can be justified partly by the development of hydro-electricity or aquifer replenishment which benefit water users outside the affected land areas. Nonetheless, despite the multipurpose nature of some irrigation investments, the opportunities for new large-scale irrigation development have diminished. Further, the continuing downward price trend of basic staples has made irrigation increasingly uneconomic for many crops.

The advent of cheap, dependable motors and pumps, and the increasing availability of fuel or electric power, has revolutionised irrigation more than any other technological or managerial innovation. In many parts of the world, large areas of land cannot be irrigated economically by gravity flow techniques. A case in point is land located on the banks of large rivers where construction of diversion structures is not feasible for technical and economic reasons. Such land is now available for pump irrigation. Pump irrigation is suitable for those areas where water supplies require only a few meters of pumping from a canal or another water source.

Small pump sets, individual or communal, have begun to play important roles in augmenting food production. They are widely used as a means to supplement irregular canal water supply, particularly in the river deltas of Asia, but increasingly also in Africa. The traditional notion that pump irrigation is bound to fail in Africa has definitely been proven wrong. Pump sets are easy to install and simple to operate. Experience has shown that pump sets with a small number of farmers having small land holdings are more productive in terms of yield per hectare and more efficient in terms of water use than are large gravity schemes. Joint energy and water management techniques should lead to the use for water pumping using renewable energy supplies such as biomass producer-fueled, mini-hydro plants, wind turbines, and photovoltaic units.

Revolutionary developments have taken place in the last decades in the science and art of irrigation. Among them are: technical innovations on water control allowing nearly optimal soil moisture conditions on a continuous basis; techniques for high frequency, low volume applications of water (and nutrients) in precise and timely response to changing crop needs; and new water application systems which allow irrigation of steep, sandy or stony lands. Many of these developments are highly energy-intensive, and rarely are based on renewable energy sources. For example, the literally thousands of wind-mill water pumps which existed many decades ago should be revived in the form of decentralised new wind, mini-hydro, solar and biomass-powered water lifting and pumping devices. Technologies are ready. A market needs to be created.

2.1.4.5 The energy dependence of food security

Food security can be defined as a situation in which all households have both physical and economic access to adequate food for all members, and where households are not at risk of losing such access. There are three dimensions implicit in this definition: availability, stability and access. Adequate food availability means that, on average, sufficient food supplies are available to meet consumption needs. Stability refers to minimising the probability that, in difficult years or seasons, food consumption might fall below nutritional requirements. Access draws attention to the fact that, even with bountiful supplies, many people still go hungry because they do not have the resources to produce or purchase the food they need. In addition, if food needs are met through exploitation of non-renewable natural resources or degradation of the environment, there is no guarantee of food security over the long term.

Most factors which effect food security are energy-dependent. It is impossible to envisage an effective food production system, or an efficient food processing and distribution system, without the necessary energy inputs that make them operate. There is a close correlation between the quality and quantity of food produced, transformed and consumed and the quality and quantity of energy used to "turn the wheels" of food security. In many cases, it is precisely the low quality and the meagre amounts of energy available for the food system, which are at the base of unattainable food security.

Many areas of developing countries are characterised by a lack of sufficient energy inputs to satisfy the minimum requirements to reach the potential food security level. Agricultural practices, to a large extent, remain based on human and animal power; little, if any indirect energy inputs such as for irrigation or fertilisation are at hand. Food losses are very high due to the lack of energy for processing or storing, or for transportation to markets. The use of locally available energy sources, such as solar, wind, biomass or hydropower is minimal, as is the access to conventional energy sources such as hydrocarbons or electricity.

Energy requirements at all points of the food cycle (from production to consumption) need to be fulfilled in the most socio-environmentally sound manner. Emphasis is needed on the elimination of human drudgery and on efficiency of energy use in agricultural mechanisation (land preparation, planting, fertilising, harvesting, transport, processing, conservation), irrigation, agro-industries (including forest and fisheries) and rural services (lighting, health and education).

Energy is also important for the storage and preservation of food. Food losses between production and retailing in developing countries can be as high as 10% to 20% for cereals and legumes because of rodents, insects, and molds. These problems demand new techniques of food storage and preservation which in turn require energy inputs. But the corresponding expenditure of energy could be well worth it if the cost of reducing food losses is less than the cost of producing needed staples and marketable food products.

In addition, it has been pointed out that the nutritional status of women in particular may be worsened not only because they tend to eat last and least, often for cultural reasons, but they also tend to expend more energy in work than do men. Part of this greater labour may be on account of domestic chores such as gathering firewood or fetching drinking water—tasks which are uncommon in more industrialised countries and even in the urban centres of developing countries. These burdens may be alleviated through inputs of inanimate energy; for example, through the provision of cooking fuel and/or efficient stoves and of water for domestic purposes.

Thus, apart from efforts to increase the production and supply of food in developing countries, many related measures are warranted to enhance food security, such as: *i)* raising incomes through employment generation; *ii)* providing healthy environments; *iii)* implementing programmes of supplementary nutrition for vulnerable groups; and *iv)* increasing supplies of cooking fuel and/or efficient stoves and of domestic water. Several of these measures are strongly energy-related, and therefore if energy is to contribute to the solution of undernutrition, the energy components of these measures must be reflected in energy strategies. Such considerations, however, only rarely have been incorporated into conventional energy strategies.

2.2 Energy and the Environment

Energy conversion significantly impacts several areas of concern from a health and environment point of view, including indoor and urban air pollution, acidification, climate change, and land degradation. The situation in each of these areas implies a need for fundamental change of the energy system to reach the goals and objectives of the major conferences and environment-related conventions.

2.2.1 Health

The energy-health nexus arises from the fact that, without proper control, the production and use of energy can be accompanied by adverse impacts on the environment, and

ultimately on human health. Indeed, as shown in Table 2.7, the amount and type of energy use is itself a useful general indicator of the potential for a number of important environmental health risks. It shows that across many energy sectors, there are profound influences on environmental parameters due to human activities.

Fundamental to an evaluation of the environmental and health impact of energy is the concept of fuel (or flow) cycle; that is, the chain of activities that extend from energy source extraction, through processing, transport, and storage, to the end use. In such a fuel cycle, the ultimate demand and consumption of energy comes at the end of the cycle as shown in Figure 2.4.

In cases such as the gathering of agricultural wastes for fuel in a Bangladeshi village, the spatial domain and time period over which the fuel cycle operates is short. What is gathered today is burned nearby tomorrow. At the other end of the spectrum, however, are the large-scale fuel cycles for conventional energy, which link activities occurring over many parts of the globe extending over months, years, or even centuries in the case of waste disposal.

In each case, however, full understanding of the impacts of energy use is achieved only by tracing the fuel cycle from end-use of the fuel cycle to its source (origin) so as to examine impacts at every stage. Conceptually, evaluation is done by assuming that, for example, a litre of petrol burned in a vehicle not only causes local air pollution, but also adds incrementally to the impacts associated with petroleum recovery, transport, processing, and storage at various sites before the fuel is ultimately consumed.

Many stages of the major world fuel cycles have important direct environmental health implications. Broadly these can be categorised as follows:

- human exposures to chemical or radioactive pollution from routine operations;
- accidents and diseases in work related to the fuel-cycle;
- shifts in disease-vector distributions from hydropower development;
- physical injury or pollutant contamination from major accidents.

In addition, there are other indirect health impacts that may be significant. Shifts

Table 2.7: Human Impact on the Global Environment—Portion Attributable to Energy Supply*

Affected Quantity	Natural Baseline	Human Disruption Index**	Portion of Human Disruption Caused by:			
			Industrial Energy	Traditional Energy	Agriculture	Manufacturing, Other
Lead Flow	25,000 tons/yr	15	63% fossil fuel burning including additives	Small	Small	37% metals processing, manufacturing, refuse burning
Oil Flow to Oceans	500,000 tons/yr	10	60% of oil harvesting, processing, transport	Small	Small	40% disposal of oil wastes
Cadmium Flow	1,000 tons/yr	8	13% fossil fuel burning	5% burning traditional fuels	12% agricultural burning	70% metals processing, manufacturing, refuse burning
SO_2 Flow	50 million tons/yr	1.4	85% fossil fuel burning	1% burning traditional fuels	1% agricultural burning	13% smelting, refuse burning
Methane Stock	800 parts per billion	1.1	18% fossil fuel harvesting and processing	5% burning traditional fuels	65% rice paddies, domestic animals, land clearing	12% landfills
Mercury Flow	25,000 tons/yr	0.7	20% fossil fuel burning	1% burning traditional fuels	2% agricultural burning	77% metals processing, manufacturing, refuse burning
Nitrous Oxide Flow	10 million tons/yr	0.4	12% fossil fuel burning	8% burning traditional fuels	80% fertilizer, land clearing, aquifer disruption	small
Particle Flow	500 million tons/yr	0.25	35% fossil fuel burning	10% burning traditional fuels	40% fertilizer, land clearing, aquifer disruption	15% smelting, non-agricultural land clearing, refuse burning
CO_2 Flow	280 parts per million	0.25	75% fossil fuel burning	3% net deforestation for fuelwood	15% net deforestation for land clearing	7% net deforestation for lumber, cement manufacturing

*   Energy systems account for a significant portion of the human impact on the environment through emission of toxic and other pollutants in amounts rivaling or exceeding natural flows.

** The human disruption index is defined as the ratio of human-generated flow to the natural (baseline) flow.

Source: (Holdren, 1990)

of climate patterns due to formation of greenhouse gases from energy systems, for example, may have major impacts on human health because of changing temperatures, sea-levels, and disease-vector ecology. Damage to biodiversity through acid rain or local deforestation from fuel harvesting are other examples of energy-related environmental hazards with potential grave health consequences.

Two criteria commonly used to judge the relative importance of environmental health hazards are population impact and individual risk. The first measure is an evaluation of how much the environmental hazard adds to the total disease burden or loss of healthy life years in society. The second criterion evaluates whether a particular group, coal mine workers for example, suffers an unacceptably high risk, even if the total societal impact is low because the total number in that group is relatively small. Other criteria, such as whether an impact seems to be on the rise, or affects a particularly important population group such as children, also play roles in assessing environmental health hazards.

2.2.1.1 Environmental pathway

Conventional energy production invariably results in the formation of toxic residuals with potential health impacts. To determine the health impacts, it is necessary to understand not only the potential environmental hazard of the pollutant, but also how it is transported through the ecosystem. In areas that are sparsely populated, producers of large amounts of pollution might have a smaller impact on health; whereas sources releasing relatively small amounts of pollution in densely populated areas may cause significant health impacts. This is illustrated in Figure 2.5, which shows the environmental health pathway which leads from the pollution sources through the environment and finally to humans. Also shown are some of the factors influencing the passage of the pollutant from one stage to the next.

For air borne pollution, which is the most important component of energy-using facilities, the emissions that reach people can vary dramatically, depending on the source of pollution. Figure 2.6 shows estimated dose effectiveness for a range of energy-using activities in relation to the dose effectiveness of other polluting activities. Dose effectiveness is simply the fraction of the pollutants released that is eventually breathed in. At the top of the scale, for comparison, is active cigarette smoking which, by definition, has a dose effectiveness of 100% (i.e., for every one ton of air pollution, one ton is breathed in). At the other end of the spectrum shown is the average United States coal-fired power plant, where the dose effectiveness is one million times lower (i.e., only one gram out of every ton (one million grams) emitted is inhaled). Along the spectrum are shown other major sources, including vehicles and household stoves.

As a result, the health impact of pollutant releases may be quite different from their other environmental impacts. In the case of

climate change, for example, the location of release and the location of release in relation to human population is irrelevant because climate change is a global problem.

2.2.1.2 Fossil fuels

Coal mining, particularly underground, results in accidents and health-related illnesses from the inhalation of coal dust. Processing of coal for the production of processed fuels and coke also is associated with occupational disease and risks. Hazards associated with petroleum and natural gas industry are less extensive than coal and are seen mostly in exploration and development phases of new oil fields.

Combustion of fossil fuels is the largest source of atmospheric pollution. This process gives rise to large quantities of sulphur and nitrogen oxides, heavy metals, hydrocarbons, particulates, and carbon monoxide, among other directly health-damaging pollutants. Fossil fuel combustion processes also are the chief sources of human-generated greenhouse gases in the form of carbon dioxide and methane. Such pollution has arisen, not only as a result of fossil fuel combustion in power plants and industry, but also from motor vehicles and households.

In general, the potential air pollution from fossil fuels depends on the level of non-combustible material in the fuel, and in the carbon-hydrogen ratio. Thus, natural gas burns cleaner than oil which burns cleaner than coal. A similar ranking is found for production of solid wastes, water pollution, and occupational hazards among the three fuel cycles.

An indicator of pollution potential, therefore, can be derived in what might be called the coal-equivalent index, which is simply the pollution potential of the mix of fuels used by a country, city, or industry, compared to the potential it would have if it used 100% coal. Although this index could be extended to biomass, nuclear, and other sources, here it is applied only to the fossil fuel mix. By this index, therefore, the world fossil fuel mix has a 48% coal equivalence (i.e., the mix of coal, oil, and gas used by the world has a pollution potential as if it were 48% coal and 52% (relatively) clean sources). The extent to which pollution potential is translated to actual pollution releases, of course, depends on the quality of the particular fuels used and the types of tech-

Figure 2.4: Sample Fuel Cycle Flow Chart for Coal Showing Point of Potential Environmental Problems

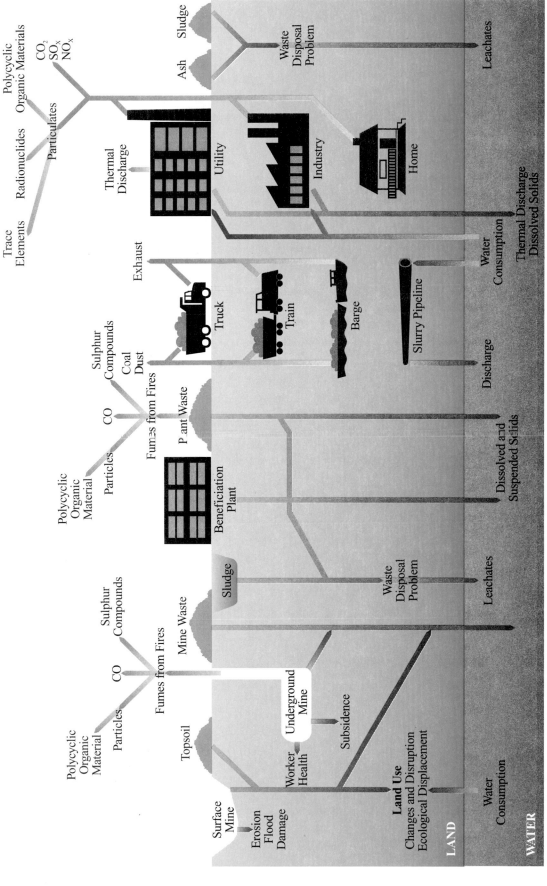

Modified from (OTA, 1979)

Figure 2.5: Example Environmental Pathway for Combustion-derived, Health-damaging Air Pollution

SOURCE ➤ EMISSIONS ➤ CONCENTRATION ➤ EXPOSURE ➤ DOSE ➤ HEALTH EFFECTS

Quantity and quality of fuel gives some idea of potential harm.	Emissions of air pollutants depend on how much of which type is burned in what way.	The concentration of air pollutants in the air depends not only on the emissions but also on the atmospheric conditions (or ventilation conditions inside a building if the concern is indoor pollution).	Exposure depends on how many people breathe certain concentrations and for how long.	Dose measures how much pollutant is actually deposited in the body and depends not only on exposure but also factors such as the rate of breathing and the size of the particles.	Health effects depend not only on dose but also on factors such as age, sex, whether the person smokes, and the existence of other diseases.

Measurement and control can be initiated at any stage.

nology and pollution control equipment that are employed. In general, the index gives an idea of the relative pollution under uncontrolled situations and the relative cost and effort required to obtain pollution control.

Contamination of waters and land can occur during the disposal of fly-ash and scrubber sludge from flue-gas desulphurisation equipment. Of particular concern are the trace elements such as arsenic, beryllium, cadmium, chromium, lead, and selenium that are found in coal ash. The deposition of air pollution on land or in waterways can further pollute the environment, thereby increasing risk for human health.

2.2.1.3 Transport

Fossil fuel use for transport has increased dramatically over the past three decades. There has been a 3% annual growth rate in the world vehicle fleet leading, in 1996, to some 800 million vehicles on the world's roads. This growth rate is faster than that of either the world population or economy. For example, in 1965 there were fewer than 60 vehicles per 1,000 people in the world; today there are more than 140.

Transportation is a major cause of air pollution in urban areas. The major air pollution concerns are carbon monoxide (CO) emissions, photochemical smog, toxic emissions, and particulate emissions. Given the high growth rates of vehicle fleets in many developing countries, vehicle-generated environmental problems have the potential to increase steadily over the next decade.

Vehicles can have a large effect on human exposure to pollutants, because their emissions are released close to the ground. For example, vehicles are the dominant source of CO emissions, and they are likely to contribute to high CO concentrations at street level. At moderate concentrations, CO impairs motor skills, and at higher concentrations it significantly impairs the bloodstream's oxygen-carrying capacity.

Additionally, vehicles are important contributors to the formation of secondary (photochemical) pollutants, such as ozone, which are becoming a widespread urban problem. Photochemical smog involves the production of oxidising agents (e.g. ozone), which, at sufficiently high concentrations, impairs breathing capacity, causes eye irritation, and damages materials, vegetation, and crops. Photochemical smog is especially serious in Buenos Aires, Los Angeles, Mexico City, Sao Paulo, and Tokyo (see Figure 2.7) and is likely to become an ever more serious problem if current trends in urban transportation persist. The seriousness of the problem is shown in Mexico City, where smog

Figure 2.6: Nominal Dose Effectiveness

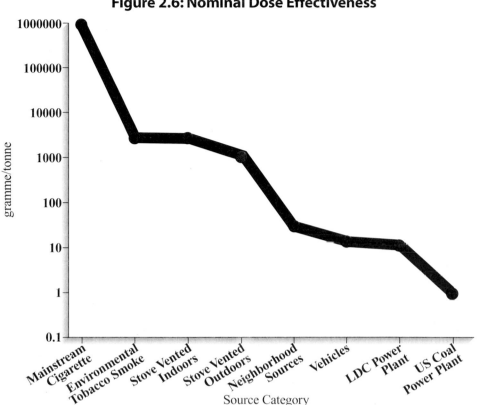

Rough estimates of nominal dose effectiveness of a range of energy-using technologies. Note the log scale and the consequent great variation across a great range of devices, ranging from one million grammes per tonne of mainstream tobacco going into the lungs (i.e., 100% dose effectiveness) to one gram per ton reaching people's lungs from a typical U.S. power plant. The term "nominal" indicates that the amount actually deposited in the lungs is not determined. Sources are generic and estimates are uncertain, as indicated by the broad continuous line.

Source: (Smith, 1993)

officials ordered 40% of the city's vehicles off of the roads in mid-October 1996, after ozone levels had risen to 2.5 times the World Health Organisation's health guideline levels. It is estimated that about 70% of the city's smog is due to the its 3.5 million vehicles.

Emissions of benzene, a carcinogenic compound that makes up 1-2% of gasoline by weight, is a major concern. It is given off as a vapour by hot engines and fuel tanks and is present in auto exhausts (partly from the combustion of other aromatic compounds in gasoline).

Particulate pollution, which has been linked to pulmonary diseases and lung cancer, has become the leading public health concern relating to urban air pollution. The relatively high particulate emission levels from diesel engines, the relatively large diesel shares in the motor vehicle populations, and the rapidly growing demand for urban transportation in developing countries indicates that this situation is likely to get much worse unless fundamental changes can be made in the transport system.

The decision to allow lead to be used as a petrol additive to enhance performance has been called one of the worst environmental health mistakes of the century, primarily because of its effect on mental development in children, although other ill-effects have been found as well[27]. Lead is a highly toxic octane-boosting gasoline additive that is still widely used in many

---

[27] In recent years, however, there has been gratifying progress in removing lead from vehicle fuels around the world. Compared to 100% in the early 1970s, not much more than one-quarter of the petrol burned globally in 1995 contained lead as an additive. Although representing a large improvement, there is urgent need to eliminate all lead as soon as possible. Unfortunately, there are several large countries that have not yet made strong commitments to a speedy shift to unleaded fuels.

Figure 2.7: Overview of Air Quality in Twenty Megacities*

City	SO$_2$	SPM	Pb	CO	NO$_2$	O$_3$
Bangkok						
Beijing						
Bombay						
Buenos Aires						
Cairo						
Calcutta						
Delhi						
Jakarta						
Karachi						
London						
Los Angeles						
Manila						
Mexico City						
Moscow						
New York						
Rio de Janeiro						
São Paulo						
Seoul						
Shanghai						
Tokyo						

 Serious problem, WHO guidelines exceeded by more than a factor of two

 Moderate to heavy pollution, WHO guidelines exceeded by up to a factor of two (short term guidelines exceeded on a regular basis at certain locations)

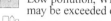 Low pollution, WHO guidelines are normally met (short term guidelines may be exceeded occasionally)

No data available or insufficient data for assessment

* Based on a subjective assessment of monitoring data and emissions inventory.
Source: (UNEP/WHO, 1992)

parts of the world, although its use has been largely phased out in many countries both because of its toxicity and because its presence in gasoline makes it impossible to use catalytic converters for controlling tailpipe emissions. Developing countries tend to suffer more, not only because of less stringent environmental standards and weaker enforcement, but also because urbanisation trends are largest in these countries[28].

Considering six indicators of air quality: sulphur dioxide, solid particulate matter, lead, carbon monoxide, nitrous oxide, and ozone, the air pollution situation in twenty megacities (of which sixteen are in developing countries) is such that 38% of the indicators register as either "serious problems"[29] or "moderate to heavy pollution"[30] (see Figure 2.7). In fact, most developing country megacities have air pollution levels well above WHO guidelines, and the situation is getting worse.

2.2.1.4 Household use of biomass and coal

In developing countries, biomass accounts for about one-third of all energy and nearly 90% in some of the least-developed

---

[28] Most megacities will be found in developing countries in the next ten to twenty years.

[29] Defined as exceeding WHO guidelines by a factor of more than two.

[30] Defined as exceeding WHO guidelines by a factor of up to two, with short-term guidelines exceeded on a regular basis.

countries. About two billion people rely mainly or exclusively on traditional fuels (mostly biomass) for their daily energy needs (see Figure 2.8).

In rural or peri-urban areas in developing countries, an open fire inside the dwelling is commonly used for cooking and heating. The fire may be set in a hole in the ground, among stones on which the cooking-pot is placed, in a three-sided brick or stone platform, or in a simple clay or metal stove. The stove is often at floor level, adding to the risk of accidents, and jeopardising food hygiene. In many instances, there is no chimney to remove the pollutants.

Solid fuels such as biomass are quite difficult to burn completely in simple household-sized stoves. As a result, even though biomass does not contain many non-combustible contaminants, the emissions of health-damaging pollutants in the form of incomplete combustion products are quite high per unit of energy as shown in Table 2.8.

The use of solid fossil fuels for space and water heating in the home, or for cooking, is also widespread in many countries. Bituminous coal, or lignite for domestic use, is particularly problematic since it burns inefficiently and thus has high emissions of health-damaging air pollutants. Indeed, small-scale coal burning produces all the same pollutants as biomass, and in addition, sulphur oxides (see Table 2.8) and other toxic elements such as arsenic, fluoride, and lead. The use of unprocessed solid fuels, coal and biomass, in large furnaces and boilers achieves more complete combustion and thus lower pollution levels than in the case of household appliances.

Typically emissions are high and ventilation is poor in households that use coal and biomass. Because occupants usually are indoors when they are using coal and biomass, they tend to be exposed to significant amounts of particulate pollution, as indicated in Figure 2.9. Because a large portion of the population is exposed, the total indoor air pollution exposure is likely to be greater for most important pollutants than from outdoor urban pollution in all the world's cities combined.

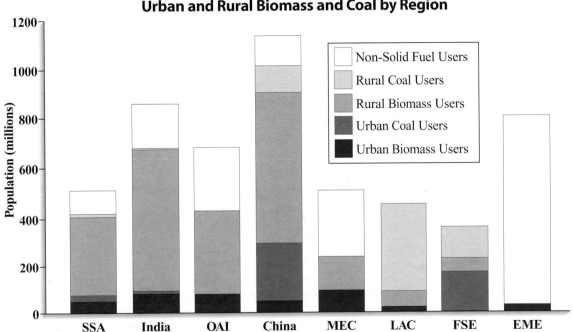

Figure 2.8: Global Population Using Solid Household Fuels, Urban and Rural Biomass and Coal by Region

This figure represents the approximate situation in the early 1990s. Most use in FSE and EME is for household heating only.

Distribution of household use of coal, biomas and other fuels according to region and urban/rural location. Regions: SSA=Sub-Saharan Africa; OAI=Other Asia (mainly southeast) and Pacific Island; MEC=Middle-East Crescent (from Algeria to Pakistan); FSE=Former Soviet Union and Eastern Europe; LAC=Latin America and Caribbean; EME=Established Market Economies (Japan, North America, Western Europe).

Source: (WHO, 1997)

Table 2.8: Comparison of Air Pollutant Emissions in Kilograms per Unit of Energy Delivered

Use and Scale Fuel (Efficiency)		Amount equivalent to one million MJ delivered	Particulates*	Sulphur Oxides**	Nitrogen Oxides	Hydro-Carbons	Carbon Monoxide
Industrial (>20KW)							
Wood (70%)	tonnes	89	500	53	400	400	450
Bituminous (80%)	tonnes	43	2,800	820	320	22	46
Residual oil (80%)	liters	33,000	94	1,300	240	4	20
Distillate oil (90%)	liters	31,000	8	1,100	83	4	19
Natural gas (90%)	m³	28,000	7	neg	99	2	8
Residential Heating Stoves (<5kW)							
Wood (50%)	tonnes	130	2,700	30	100	6,800	17,000
Anthracite (65%)	tonnes	49	48	200	250	100	1,000
Bituminous (80%)	tonnes	53	550	1,100	270	530	5,300
Distillate oil (90%)	liters	33,000	11	1,200	71	4	20
Natural gas (90%)	m³	30,000	7	neg	38	4	10
Cooking Stoves							
Tropical wood (15%)	tonnes	420	3,800	250	300	3,200	34,000
Cow dung (15%)	tonnes	530	10,000	3,200	7	?	44,000
Indian Coal (20%)	tonnes	220	280	2,200	460	2,200	27,000
Coconut husk (15%)	tonnes	480	17,000	?	7	?	54,000
Natural gas (80%)	m³	32,000	1	neg	10	5	250

* Particulates from coal, and to a much lesser extent, oil can contain toxic metals and other hazardous elements such as flourine.

** Sulphur emissions from fossil fuels vary widely depending on fuel quality.

Source: (Smith, 1987)

Health effects from biomass can be seen throughout the world. The largest direct impacts would seem to be respiratory infections in children (the most significant class of disease in the world) and chronic lung disease in non-smoking women. There are also a range of other health problems associated with this fuel cycle, some direct such as the impacts on women and children of gathering heavy loads of biomass in distant and sometimes dangerous areas (see Section 2.1.2).

In addition, indirect health impacts from lack of fuel for proper cooking (malnutrition) and boiling water (diarrhoea and parasites) may be significant, although difficult to document. The household use of solid fuels, therefore, is a useful indicator of potential environmental health hazard, although the degree of impact will depend on ventilation and other factors.

Today, widespread household use of coal is limited to a few countries; however, some countries are proposing to promote coal use as a substitute for dwindling supplies of biomass and to avoid increased demand for petroleum-based fuels, kerosene and LPG. Given the high emissions associated with small-scale combustion of coal and the documented health effects due to household use of coal in China, South Africa, and elsewhere, this alternative should be carefully examined because of its adverse effects on health. In many countries of Europe, the transition from household coal use in recent decades was a primary means of controlling air pollution.

One solution to the emissions problems associated with biomass and coal is to process them to make them cleaner, for example as charcoal and biogas or smokeless coal and coal gas. In general, the environmental pollution from final use of processed solid fuel is less than from the raw forms; however, the limitation is that new sources of pollution are created during processing (e.g., at the kiln or the coal processing facility).

Figure 2.9: Approximate Distribution of Human Exposure to Particulate Air Pollution

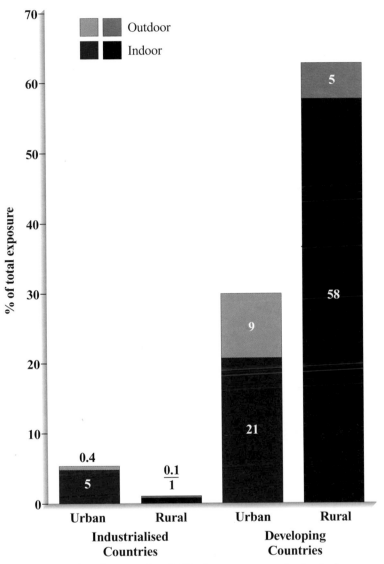

Note that more than 90 % of exposure occurs in developing countries; furthermore, two thirds of human exposure seems to occur indoors in rural areas.

Source: (Smith, 1993)

2.2.1.5 Hydropower

Hydroelectric power currently accounts for nearly 20% of the world's electricity output. The world-wide technically usable potential is estimated to be seven times greater than today's generation (Moreira and Poole, 1993). However, development of potential capacity entails a number of hazards.

The process of generating hydropower does not produce wastes or other harmful by-products. At the same time, the accumulation of a large, almost stationary body of water

sets in motion a train of events, particularly in tropical areas, that may enhance the spread of infection and disease, including filariasis and schistosomiasis. Shallow waters associated with the shores of reservoirs can provide suitable breeding places for mosquito vectors of malaria. Dams also create new and favourable habitats for various kinds of vegetation, which in turn may render sizeable areas more attractive to disease vectors. In addition, dissolved minerals, silt, and organic matter brought by in-flowing rivers, may alter the aquatic ecosystems and possibly cause algae blooms, and foster growth of snails, midges, and mosquito larvae. Dams also pose accident risks when sited upstream from large populations. Important indirect health effects can be created in populations forced to leave their lands because of large hydropower development (IPCC, 1996b).

2.2.2 Acidification

2.2.2.1 Introduction

Acidification is a process by which soils and surface waters are depleted of bases and consequently suffer an unnatural increase in acidity. Acidification of soils and waters results in damage to both terrestrial and aquatic ecosystems. Emissions of sulphur dioxide, nitrogen oxides and ammonia give rise to acidifying deposition after chemical transformation and transport in the atmosphere. Sulphur and nitrogen oxides mainly are formed during the combustion of fossil fuels in the power and transport sectors. Acidification is influenced by transformations of deposited sulphur and nitrogen compounds in soil and surface waters. This process is the energy-acidification nexus.

The impact of acidifying deposition depends on the sensitivity of the ecosystem. Many lakes and small streams have become acidified during this century in Europe and North America, dramatically altering the flora and fauna in these lakes. These changes have been so significant that many surface waters are entirely devoid of fish, amphibians and other creatures. Soil pH[31] has dropped over large areas, affecting the nutrition of plants and the diversity of vegetation. Acidification has been implicated as one of the major factors that has led to a substantial decrease in forest vitality in large areas of both Europe and North America. Acidification, therefore, has the potential to disrupt ecosystem structure and function over widespread areas. Once acidification damage has occurred, the ecosystems tend to have a slow recovery time (related to the deposition reduction achieved and ecosystem characteristics); therefore, problems associated with acidifying deposition have become one of the most pressing regional environmental issues faced today.

Damage to surface waters was observed in Europe in the early 1900s. The rate of acidification damage accelerated after the Second World War, due to the exponential increase in the use of fossil fuels from 1950 through the 1970s. Steps now are being taken to reduce these impacts. The Sulphur Protocol under the Convention on Long-Range Transboundary Air Pollution in Europe (LRTAP) entails a reduction in sulphur emissions of between 50 and 60% by 2010. The progress in environmental protection that this envisions may be illustrated by the excess of deposition above critical loads (thresholds for damage). Compared to 1990, emissions levels for 2010 show the areas of the more sensitive ecosystems across Europe in which deposition exceeds critical loads contracting by about 50% (Posch et al., 1995). Nevertheless, the deposition of sulphur still would be twice as high as the critical loads in southern Scandinavia and up to 5 times the critical load in parts Central and Eastern Europe.

In contrast, there are many developing countries where the emissions are now increasing and, in some areas, are projected to continue increasing at an exponential rate over the next decades. This suggests that acidifying deposition is likely to become an important regional issue, particularly in Asia, but also in parts of South and Central America and in southern Africa.

Emissions into high levels of the atmosphere from large stationary sources through tall stacks are transported over large distances and can give rise to problems far from the pollution source, sometimes many kilometres away. Therefore, acidifying deposition constitutes a transboundary problem and for this reason, it is necessary for emission reductions to be carried out as international efforts, in conjunction with national measures.

2.2.2.2 Currently impacted areas

In Europe, the highest deposition is found in parts of Central Europe and in the United Kingdom. Many sensitive ecosystems have been impacted in these areas. Forest decline has been greatest in the most heavily impacted areas of Central Europe, in the so-called "Black Triangle" covering parts of Germany, Poland and the Czech Republic. The acidifying deposition rate is lower in

---

[31]   Substances with a low pH are acidic while substances with a high pH are termed basic.

Scandinavia, but the sensitivity is very high over a widespread area due to the geology and soil characteristics of the Scandinavian Shield. In addition, there are many more lakes in the Nordic countries (more than 100,000), several thousand of which now are heavily acidified. Soil pH has dropped all over Europe, as has been shown in Scandinavia, Central Europe and in the United Kingdom. In Eastern Canada and the Northeast region of the United States, many lakes also have been impacted. The Canadian shield is as sensitive as the Scandinavian shield and also has numerous lakes.

The consequences of soil acidification are not always easy to observe but include changes and reductions in nutrient availability which affect fertility of the soil. This can affect the growth rates of forests, their resilience to stresses, and to changes in species composition with impacts on diversity.

The impacts in both Europe and North America have led to a number of policy responses that have already resulted in emission reductions, and there are further agreements in place that will lead to substantial reductions in sulphur over the next few decades. The policy responses have been made at both national and regional levels and under the auspices of different organisations.

The European Union Large Combustion Plant Directive, agreed upon in 1988, set emission standards for units of greater than 50 MW. The main regional policy initiative is under the auspices of the United Nations Economic Commission for Europe (UN ECE). A framework for compiling the necessary background material for the protocols on sulphur and nitrogen reductions has been developed. Critical load figures (thresholds for damage) have been determined and the use of Integrated Assessment Models has been co-ordinated through the UN ECE Working Groups and Task Forces. The Sulphur Protocol under the LRTAP Convention was signed in 1994, and countries have agreed to varying degrees of abatement with an overall reduction of between 50 and 60% of their 1983 levels in Europe by the year 2010 (UN ECE, 1994).

In North America, an agreement between Canada and the United States has been developed to address the emissions issues. In the United States, mechanisms such as the bubble concept and emissions trading will continue to be used to achieve the required reductions in emissions (these mechanisms are defined in the Clean Air Act Amendments of 1990) (Kete, 1992; Sorrel, 1994).

The agreements for nitrogen reduction in these regions are less well-developed. The Nitrogen Protocol will be designed and adopted over the next few years in Europe. The major sectors contributing NO_x emissions are the transport and power generation sectors. For ammonia emissions the agricultural sector is the largest contributor. For NO_x emissions, European Union directives encourage the production and use of low NO_x emission vehicles and low-NO_x burners in power stations. Despite such efforts, the increasing numbers of vehicles has obviated reductions in NO_x emissions. Little has occurred at an international level to secure ammonia emission reductions. Therefore, nitrogen emissions form the next challenge in acidification for both Europe and North America.

The effects of acidification on the environment create the need for fundamental changes in the energy sector. Alternatives for alleviating the problems associated with acidification are related to reducing emissions across all energy sectors. These emissions reductions can be achieved in a variety of ways, including supply-side measures and demand-side measures. Near-term supply-side measures include fuel switching to less polluting fuels (such as the switch from coal to gas), fuel modification (such as coal washing) and the development of bolt-on technologies (such as the installation of flue gas desulphurisation). New fossil fuel conversion technologies offer a variety of technological improvements as well reduced emissions (see Chapter 3). Demand-side measures include the use of more efficient end-use technologies (see Chapter 3) and changes in consumer habits and lifestyles.

2.2.2.3 Areas at risk in the future

Deposition of sulphur already has increased to significant levels in China and parts of Southeast Asia, and it is projected to triple in many parts of Asia, giving rise to a situation similar to that in the more polluted parts of Europe and North America. It is therefore anticipated that damage is likely to occur in these areas in the future. The tropical and subtropical ecosystems in these areas are different from the mainly temperate ecosystems that have been impacted in Europe and North

America. Despite this difference, the same processes are operating in both types of ecosystems, although differences in soils and vegetation for these regions will result in varying types of damages.

Emissions are projected to increase in many parts of Asia, Africa, South and Central America, creating potential for serious damage in many parts of the world that have not experienced this type of pollution problem before. Figure 2.10 illustrates that the projected world-wide deposition of sulphur in 2050, according to emissions levels projected under an IPCC scenario. Figure 2.11 shows a preliminary estimate of world-wide sensitivity to acidifying deposition. Under this scenario it can be seen that high depositions are expected to occur in sensitive areas of Asia, South America and Africa. The potential seriousness of the Asian situation is illustrated in Figure 2.12, which shows the risk of acidification damage represented as the excess of deposition above critical loads (thresholds for damage). The figure highlights large areas at risk in the year 2020.

One major difference between the impacts on Europe and North America and on the developing countries is that in many areas agriculture is carried out on marginal soils which have a low buffering potential. It is possible that anticipated depositions will have serious impacts on the soil quality and yields. In Europe, agricultural soils are limed and acidification of arable land doesnot represent a serious problem. However, liming is not carried out to any great extent in many countries of the developing world due to its high costs.

The emission abatement situation also is different in developing countries because the problems are expected to occur in the future due to the projected increases in emissions. This is in contrast to Europe and North America, where the policies reflect response to a problem that had already occurred. Therefore, the emissions being dealt with in many developing countries are for installations that are either in the planning phase or under construction. This situation creates different emissions abatement opportunities and rational siting of emission sources. Currently, most abatement policies are being developed on a national basis only.

A problematic aspect of acidification is that the recovery process is quite long. Therefore, it is preferable to try to prevent damages at the outset rather than ameliorate them once they have occurred. It is technologically possible to avoid projected emissions, particularly at the planning stage of large industrial projects. For this new approach to be taken, an understanding of the underlying scientific evidence of acidification is required. In light of the uncertainties, precautionary actions may be preferable. Meeting emissions abatement goals with promising new technologies that offer multiple benefits in addition to low-cost opportunities for emissions reduction (see Chapter 3) is a promising approach for taking precautionary action.

2.2.3 Climate Change

Despite remaining uncertainties, there is a growing consensus in the scientific community that "the balance of evidence suggests a discernible human influence on global climate."[32] Since 1990, several major scientific studies of climate change have been carried out by the Intergovernmental Panel on Climate Change (IPCC), which was jointly established in 1988 under the auspices of the World Meteorological Organisation and the United Nations Environment Programme to: *i)* assess available scientific information on climate change; *ii)* assess the environmental and socio-economic impacts of climate change; and *iii)* formulate response strategies.

The First Scientific Assessment of the IPCC (IPCC, 1990) concluded that the increase in atmospheric concentrations of greenhouse gases since pre-industrial times had altered the energy balance of the Earth and that global warming would result. It also argued that continued increases in greenhouse gas concentrations as a result of human activity will lead to significant climate change in the coming century. The projected changes in temperature, precipitation, and soil moisture were not expected to be uniform over the globe. Anthropogenic aerosols also were recognised as possible sources of regional cooling.

The 1992 Supplementary Report of Working Group I of the IPCC (IPCC, 1992) confirmed the initial findings and conclusions

32   This is one of the main conclusions of the Second Assessment Report (SAR) of Working Group I of the Intergovernmental Panel on Climate Change (IPCC, 1996a).

Figure 2.10: Annual Total Deposition (Wet & Dry) of Sulphur, Calculated by the MOCGUNTIA Model*

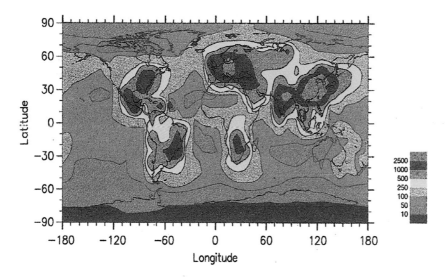

* Based on a 10 x 10 degree resolution, for the year 2050 using the IPCC IS92a scenario. Isolines are 10, 250, 1000 and 2500 mg Sm-2 yr-1 [to the fourth degree]. Source: (Rodhe et al., 1995)

43

Figure 2.11: Preliminary Map 0f the Relative Sensitivity of Terrestrial Ecosystems to Acidfying Deposition

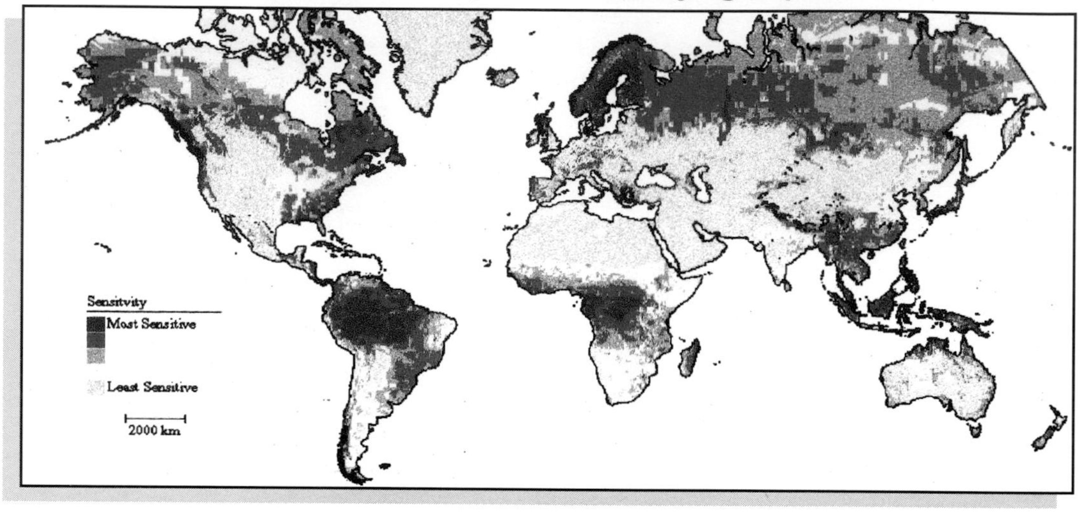

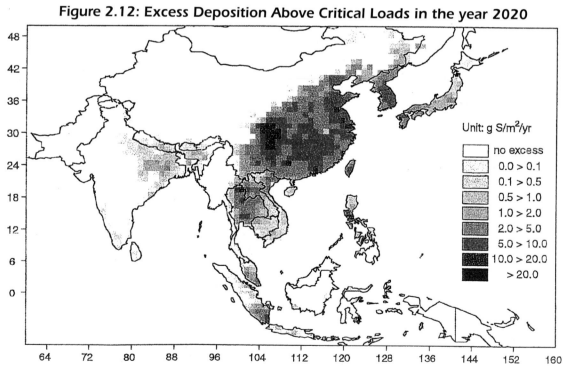

Darker colors indicate more sensitive ecosystems. Source: (Kuylenstierna et al., 1995)

Figure 2.12: Excess Deposition Above Critical Loads in the year 2020

Unit: g S/m²/yr

	no excess
	0.0 > 0.1
	0.1 > 0.5
	0.5 > 1.0
	1.0 > 2.0
	2.0 > 5.0
	5.0 > 10.0
	10.0 > 20.0
	> 20.0

Reference scenario assumes no emission control beyond current legislation. Data from RAINS-ASIA project. Source: (Foell et al., 1995) of the First Assessment and produced range of global mean temperature projections. These were based on a new set of IPCC scenarios (IS92, a to f), with greenhouse gas emission profiles made under alternative assumptions about future energy and other greenhouse gas-emitting human activities. For all the IS92 scenarios, it was assumed that governments take no action to deal with climate change issues. These findings spurred governments to sign the United Nations Framework Convention on Climate Change in Rio (1992)(UNFCC). Article 2 of the UNFCCC states that the ultimate objective of the Convention is to: "achieve...stabilisation of the greenhouse gas concentrations in the atmosphere at a level that would prevent dangerous anthropogenic interference with the climate system. Such a level should be achieved within a time frame sufficient to allow eco-systems to adapt naturally to climate change, to ensure that food production is not threatened, and to enable economic development to proceed in a sustainable manner."

The convention does not specify what the maximum levels of CO_2 and other greenhouse gases should be, because society must ultimately decide the levels that are acceptable and pursue economic futures that are consistent with these ceilings.

2.2.3.1 IPCC Second Assessment Report

The Second Assessment Report (SAR) of IPCC involved more than 2,000 scientists from all over the world, included updates of relevant material in all the preceding IPCC reports. The main findings of SAR Working Group I (IPCC, 1996a) are that:

- Greenhouse gas concentrations [mainly carbon dioxide (CO_2) and methane (CH_4)] have grown significantly since pre-industrial times. Since the eighteenth century, the atmospheric concentration of CO_2 has risen from 280 to 360 parts per million by volume (ppmv), and that for CH_4 from 700 to 1720 ppbv.
- Anthropogenic aerosols tend to produce negative radiative forcing (perturbation to the energy balance of the earth-atmosphere system).
- These increases in greenhouse gas concentration have perturbed the energy balance of the earth-atmosphere system, tending to warm the earth's surface and to produce other climate changes.

- The world surface temperature rose by 0.3°C to 0.6° C within the last 100 years.
- Global sea level has risen by between 10 and 25 cm over the past 100 years, and much of the rise may be related to the increase in the global mean temperature.
- While scientists' ability to quantify the human influence on global climate is currently limited because the signal is difficult to differentiate from natural variability, and because there are uncertainties in key factors, the balance of evidence suggests a discernible human influence on global change.
- Climate is expected to continue to change in the future. For the IS92a scenario (the IPCC reference scenario), the global mean surface air temperature would increase about 2°C by 2100. The expected temperature increases by 2100 for the other IS92 scenarios range from 1°C to 3.5°C. Such a rapid rise has been unprecedented over the last 10,000 years.
- Important uncertainties related to future climate change still exist, including the magnitude and patterns of long-term natural variability.

Working Group II (WG II) of IPCC examined the impacts, adaptations, and mitigation of climate change (IPCC, 1996b). Its assessment provided scientific, technical and economic information for use in evaluating whether the projected range of plausible impacts constitute "dangerous anthropogenic interference with the climate system..." as referred to in Article 2 of the United Nations Framework Convention on Climate Change. The report looked at both natural and human systems and highlighted the state of knowledge about the vulnerability of ecosystems and human communities to climate change, based on the range of sensitivities to increases in greenhouse gas concentrations and plausible ranges of emissions (IS92 scenarios) and concluded that:

- Many trees, plants and species, vulnerable to temperature changes, will become extinct.
- The compositional diversity of the world's forests is likely to change, and entire forest types may disappear.
- Natural disasters, such as droughts and forest fires, will continue the destruction of existing forested areas of the world and will aggravate biodiversity damages.

- Biogeographical shifts in deserts are likely to take place.
- Rising sea levels (15 to 95 cm in 2100) and extreme weather events will cause migrations, placing additional stress on social and political systems.
- A one meter rise in sea level would threaten half of the world's coastal wetlands of international importance for biodiversity, and would provoke huge population movements and destruction of human settlements and infrastructure.
- Wide-ranging and mostly adverse impacts to human health due to pollution, scarcity of clean water, and spread of infectious diseases are expected.

For planning purposes, analyses are needed that relate alternative ceilings on atmospheric concentrations to emission profiles over time. Carbon cycle studies carried out under the auspices of the Intergovernmental Panel on Climate Change have done this (IPCC, 1994). These studies have shown that, according to the present state of knowledge:

- If the current level of CO_2 emissions were to persist, the atmospheric CO_2 concentration would continue to linearly increase over time for at least two centuries, reaching a concentration of 500 ppmv by 2100, which is 1.4 times the present concentration (360 ppmv) or 1.8 times the pre-industrial levels (280 ppmv).
- A stable level of CO_2 concentration up to 750 ppmv can be achieved only if the CO_2 emission rate drops below the 1990 rate.
- The stabilised concentration of CO_2 in the atmosphere depends primarily on the cumulative CO_2 emission between now and the time of stabilisation and less on the exact path taken to realise stabilisation.

Table 2.9, developed by the IPCC (IPCC, 1994), shows the quantities of cumulative emissions, 1990-2100, that are consistent with stabilising the atmospheric CO_2 concentration at various levels ranging from 350 to 750 ppmv. Cumulative emissions associated with the IS92 scenarios of the IPCC are also shown in this table. For IS92a, the IPCC reference scenario, cumulative emissions of CO_2, 1990-2100, reach 1500 GtC, which is consistent with stabilisation at an atmospheric CO_2 concentration in excess of 750 ppmv (see Table 2.9). The table indicates how fast and how deep emissions reductions would have to be in order to achieve stabilisation of atmospheric

CO_2 concentration at different levels. The level at which stabilisation will be required is ultimately dependent on an interpretation of Article II of the FCCC and an understanding the effects of due to greenhouse gas emissions and accumulations.

2.2.3.2 The energy origins of the threat of climate change

Current energy systems are based largely on the combustion of fossil fuels, which accounted for 87% of the world's primary commercial energy consumption in 1992 (EIA, 1994). Carbon dioxide is released to the atmosphere as a product of fossil fuel combustion. Fossil fuel combustion accounts for the bulk of the annual anthropogenic emissions of CO_2, the most important greenhouse gas. During the 1980s fossil fuel combustion contributed, on average, 5.5 gigatonnes C per year out of a total global CO_2 emission rate of 7.1 gigatonnes C per year-i.e., 77% of total annual emissions. During the 1980s, some 46% of total CO_2 emissions accumulated in the atmosphere. The 1500 GtC of cumulative CO_2 emissions, 1900-2100 for the IS92 Scenario (see Table 2.9) arise largely from the burning of fossil fuels. In this reference IPCC scenario CO_2 emissions from fossil fuel burning increase from 6 GtC/year in 1990 to 20 GtC/year in 2100; during this period, total annual energy use, fossil fuel use, and coal use increase 4.2-fold, 2.7-fold, and 7.0-fold respectively.

Because an increased CO_2 concentration in the atmosphere leads to global climate change, current energy patterns are taking the world on a path that is unsustainable. This process forms the energy-climate change nexus.

2.2.4 Land Degradation

The total land surface on the Earth is just over 13 billion hectares. Of this land, roughly one-third is under forest and woodlands, one-third under grassland and arable, and the remaining one-third includes deserts, stony, steep (mountains) and/or ice-covered land. Increases in cropland have come mainly at the expense of forests and woodlands. Arable land is estimated to have increased from 860 Mha in 1882 to 1,477 Mha in 1990 (11.3% of the world's surface). At the same time, forested land has decreased from 5,200 Mha to

**Table 2.9: Cumulative Emissions of CO$_2$
to the Atmosphere, 1900-2100**

Stabilization Case	Gt C
350 ppmv	300-430
450 ppmv	640-800
550 ppmv	880-1060
650 ppmv	1000-1240
750 ppmv	1220-1420
IPCC IS92 Emission Scenarios	**Gt C**
e	2190
f	1830
a (the IPCC "reference scenario")	1500
b	1430
c	980
d	770

Note: The range of uncertainty for the alternative atmospheric CO$_2$ stabilisation cases arises from the spread of carbon cycle modeling results.
Source: (IPCC, 1994)

4,087 Mha (31.2% of the world's land area).

Land degradation—the process by which land loses some of this natural productivity as a result of crop production activities, overgrazing, and deforestation—is taking place at rates that are high by historical standards (WRI, 1992). Some 6 to 7 Mha are lost annually due to soil erosion, and up to 20 Mha of irrigated land are affected by salinity. Globally, about 2,000 Mha of land has been degraded since 1945. Of this some 750 Mha is lightly degraded and can be restored by good conservation practices. Over 1200 Mha (an area approximately the size of China and India combined, 80% of which is in developing countries) is moderately, severely, or extremely degraded. Restoring the more than 900 Mha that is moderately degraded requires more resources than an average farmer can provide. The 300 Mha of severely degraded land can in principle be restored but requires a restoration effort that is beyond the capacity of most developing countries. Land that requires expensive restoration is often abandoned. The 9 Mha that is extremely degraded is considered impossible to restore.

Nearly half of the degraded land total is on drylands, where water erosion is the dominant cause of degradation. The most severe human-induced degradation occurs on the wetter margins of the drylands.

Typically land degradation takes place over a number of years and proceeds through phases. As degradation of cropland proceeds, crop yields fall. Eventually arable land can become pasture, pasture can become scrub, and finally the scrub can become barren.

2.2.4.1 Mechanisms of land degradation

Land degradation occurs as the result of many factors, the most influential of which include:

- *Human Intervention in Forest Lands:* Human intervention in forest lands for agricultural and industrial activities has resulted in large-scale deforestation and soil degradation. Even construction of roads and highways has deleterious consequences leading to the destruction of forests and degradation of land. One recent estimate is that net global cropland will have to expand at an average rate of 2.6 Mha/year, 1989-2050, in order to meet future food requirements (Leach, 1995). If the rate of abandonment of productive cropland due to degradation is 7 Mha/year, some 340 Mha of additional forest land would have to be cleared by 2025 to meet food requirements. The additional clearing of forested land for crop production would be even greater if other higher estimates of the cropland abandonment rate (~ 10-12 Mha/year) prove to be more accurate. Moreover, even higher rates of forest clearing would be required to provide for net pasture area expansion and to replace any loss of pasture land to degradation, and also to compensate for loss of cropland and pasture to non-agricultural uses.

- *Conversion of Land to Non-agricultural Uses:*
  Much good crop land is currently being converted to non-agricultural uses. Urban expansion and road building are the biggest culprits, but mining, industry and recreation also play a part. Unfortunately, it is the best crop land that usually disappears.
- *Unsuitable Land Management Practices:*
  Wasteland also has been created through changing methods of management, often towards more intensive and unsuitable forms of land use. A prime example is fallow land in shifting agriculture, where fallow periods previously lasted 30 or more years and may now be as little as 1 to 5 years.
- *Biomass Extraction for Energy Purposes*
  The consumption of biomass for cooking and heating has contributed to land degradation. This is the case especially when trees are felled for fuelwood and charcoal delivery to cities and when scarce biomass is over-exploited for cooking fuel. In addition, the use of non-woody biomass, such as stalks, husks, and other agricultural residues, contributes to loss of agricultural productivity through the reduction of nitrogen in the soil cycle.
- *Build-up of Salts*
  If topsoil becomes too saline or too alkaline, its productivity falls. This can happen when poorly drained land is irrigated in hot climates. The sun evaporates the surface water, leaving behind the salts. At the same time, inadequate drainage causes the water table to rise, bringing salt water into contact with plant roots. Salinity problems are often associated with water-logged soils. The area of land currently being abandoned every year owing to salinization and waterlogging is roughly equal to the amount of land being reclaimed and irrigated. World-wide, about 40 million hectares out of a total of 200 million irrigated hectares are either waterlogged, affected by salt, or both.
- *Physical and Biological Damage*
  Soil may be physically damaged when it is repeatedly worked with heavy equip-

ment in wet weather, or when it is compacted around water holes in pasture land. It is difficult to return compacted soil to full productivity and deep-rooting crops may have to be planted selectively. Biological damage occurs when soils are deprived of their essential fertilisers, organic matter or humus content. The former can be replaced by artificial fertiliser, the latter cannot. Crop rotation and good farming practices are the solution.

- *Wind Erosion*
  Large areas of the world are affected by wind erosion, one of the key causes of desertification. Wind erosion occurs when soil is left bare of vegetation and is particularly severe in arid and semi-arid areas following over-stocking and overgrazing. According to an FAO/United Nations Environment Programme (UNEP) study on soil degradation, 22% of Africa north of the Equator and 36% of the Near East are affected by wind erosion. Not only can the wind strip topsoil from good land but it causes extra damage by burying land, buildings, machinery and fences with unwanted soil. Under the worst conditions, as much as 150 tonnes of soil can be blown off one hectare of land in an hour.
- *Water Erosion*
  Water erosion is the commonest form of erosion, causing massive damage in nearly all developing countries. It is found where steep land is being unwisely farmed and where gently sloping land is left exposed to the effects of heavy rain for any length of time. World-wide, about 25,000 million tonnes of soil are being washed away each year, ending up in the rivers and finally the oceans. It is estimated that 12% of Africa north of the Equator and 17% of the Near East are subject to water erosion. So are 74 million of India's 297 million hectares.

  In the United States, the annual loss of topsoil from crop land averages 12 tonnes/hectares, and some 50 million tonnes of plant nutrients are lost every year, nutrients which must be replaced with artificial fertilisers. The United States has lost about one-third of its topsoil since farming began.

2.2.4.2 Bioenergy production as a response to land degradation

While the unsustainable harvesting of biomass for energy purposes (e.g., fuelwood for cooking) has been one of many contributors to land degradation (see Section 2.2.4.1), the sustainable production of biomass via energy-efficient conversion processes for the production of modern energy carriers (electricity, liquid and gaseous fuels) can be a powerful mechanism for stemming and reversing land degradation. This process can make it feasible to restore degraded lands in areas where the rainfall and soil quality are adequate to support high-yielding energy crops after land restoration (see Section 4.2.7.2). Biomass-derived energy carriers have good prospects for competing with electricity and synthetic fluid fuels derived from coal (see Sections 3.3.2.6 and 3.3.5.6). Moreover, sustainably grown biomass fuels are CO_2 neutral[33] and low in sulphur. And, returning the ashes created as a residue of biomass fuel processing to the land reduces the need for fertilisers in the growing of new biomass.

If biomass is grown for the production of such modern energy carriers, the biomass would command a much higher market price than would be the case if the biomass were grown to serve traditional fuelwood markets, such as cooking, which are so energy-efficient that only low market prices can be supported. At the much higher biomass market prices that the production of modern energy carrier can support, it becomes feasible to provide the inputs to the biomass production process needed to make production sustainable, while creating major new employment-generation opportunities for rural regions.

Well-conceived and politically committed national programmes supported by policies and programmes at the international level could lead to significant biomass energy production on such land and thereby contribute positively towards improving farmers' income and employment opportunities, promoting rural industrialisation, reducing urban migration, and reducing poverty and insecurity of food supplies, while rehabilitating abandoned and marginal lands

2.2.4.3 The Convention to Combat Desertification

Land degradation, especially the process of desertification, was the subject of a United Nations global convention. The United Nations Convention to Combat Desertification (CCD) is the result of a long intergovernmental, negotiated process and was adopted in Paris on 17th June 1994. Signed by over 100 countries, the Parties to the CCD noted that desertification is caused by complex interactions among physical, biological, political, social, cultural and economic factors. The objective of the CCD is to mitigate the effects of drought and desertification, especially in the hardest hit countries in Africa, by developing integrated strategies to promote sustainable land management consistent with Agenda 21. In Article 10, the CCD recommends that affected countries develop national action programmes that would address priority activities to combat desertification, including promotion of sustainable livelihoods, sustainable management of natural resources, sustainable agricultural practices, the development and efficient use of various energy sources, as well as capacity-building, education and public awareness.[34]

In Article 19 the role of energy is further elaborated in recommendations for the promotion of specific measures, including "providing appropriate training and technology in the use of alternative energy sources, particularly renewable energy resources, aimed particularly at reducing the dependence on wood for fuel."[35] The measures to conserve natural

---

[33]   Growing trees to sequester carbon is an alternative strategy for using degraded lands to help cope with climate change. The growing of biomass for carbon sequestration might be preferable to growing biomass for energy purposes in those regions where potential annual yields are so low or which are so remote from prospective energy markets that biomass production for energy cannot be done cost-competitively, or in regions (e.g. wilderness areas) where industrial activity such as biomass energy farming is regarded as undesirable (Hall et al., 1991a; Hall et al., 1991b).

[34]   CCD, Article 10, p.14.

[35]   CCD, Article 19 (f), p.22.

resources that are recommended in Article 8 of Annex I include "ensuring the development and efficient use of diverse energy sources, the promotion of alternative sources of energy, particularly solar energy, wind energy and bio-gas, and specific arrangements for the transfer, acquisition and adaptation of relevant technology to alleviate pressure on fragile natural resources."[36] With respect to the preparation of subregional action programmes, Article 11 of the same Annex recommends that some issues be addressed at the subregional level, including the co-ordination of programmes to develop alternative energy sources.[37]

Throughout the CCD emphasis is placed on the importance of including local community participation, especially women, in the development and implementation of these action plans, the creation of an enabling environment for improved land use management, and the use of appropriate technologies. Energy, women, land management and new technologies to develop alternative energy sources are explicitly linked in the CCD.

2.2.5 Energy and Environment at the Rio Conference and in Agenda 21

Energy and environment were much discussed at the June 1992 UN Conference on Environment and Development in Rio de Janeiro. Agenda 21, produced at the Rio Summit, reached the conclusion that the present energy course is unsustainable. Chapter Nine of Agenda 21, "Protection of the Atmosphere" begins:

"Energy is essential to economic and social development and improved quality of life. Much of the world's energy, however, is currently produced and consumed in ways that could not be sustained if technology were to remain constant and if overall quantities were to increase substantially. The need to control atmospheric emissions of greenhouse and other gases and substances will increasingly need to be based on efficiency in energy production, transmission, distribution and consumption, and on growing re-liance on environmentally sound energy systems, particularly new and renewable sources of energy."[38]

Agenda 21 called upon governments, working in concert with United Nations agencies, non-governmental organisations, and the private sector to undertake a series of specific activities to promote sustainable energy (see Box 2.1).[39]

Greenhouse gas emissions and their relation to climate change were dealt with extensively at the Rio Conference and in Agenda 21. The climate change issue was given prominence by the Framework Convention on Climate Change (FCCC), which was a result of long and complex negotiations between various groups of countries having very different perceptions of what was at stake. Signed at the Rio Conference and entered into force in 1994, the FCCC has now been ratified by more than four fifths of the United Nations member states (164 as of June 1996). Unlike the earlier Montreal Protocol on ozone depleting substances, the FCCC includes neither binding stabilization commitments, nor quantified targets and timetables for emissions reduction. However, following the adoption of the FCCC several industrialized countries announced that they would pursue CO_2 emission limits on a voluntary basis. Moreover, the Global Environment Facility (GEF) has been established to provide financial support for developing country projects that offer global benefits relating to climate change, as well as biological diversity, and international waters (i.e., the three focal areas of GEF activity).

In April 1995, Germany hosted the first Conference of the Parties of the FCCC (COP 1) in Berlin. Although the Parties had divergent opinions about future directions, there was overall consensus on the necessity of strengthening the FCCC, and the Berlin Mandate was agreed upon as the basis for negotiations to this end. The second Conference of the Parties (COP 2, July 1996, Geneva) endorsed the 1995 IPCC Second Assessment Report "as currently the most comprehensive assessment of the sci-

---

36   CCD, Annex I, Article 8 (b) iii, p.46.

37   CCD, Annex I, Article 11 (b), p.49.

38   Agenda 21, Chapter 9, B.1. "Energy Development, Efficiency and Consumption", para 9.9, p.113.

39   Agenda 21, Chapter 9, B.1. "Energy Development, Efficiency and Consumption," para. 9.1,pp. 114-115.

Box 2.1: Agenda 21 Recommendations for Energy

Agenda 21 recommends a series of concrete actions to promote sustainable energy. Governments, working in concert with United Nations agencies, non-governmental organisations, and the private sector, were called upon to:

"Co-operate in identifying and developing economically viable, environmental sound energy sources to promote the availability of increased energy supplies to support sustainable development efforts, in particular in developing countries;

Promote the development at the national level of appropriate methodologies for making integrated energy, environment and economic policy decisions for sustainable development;

Promote the research, development, transfer and use of improved energy-efficient technologies and practices, including endogenous technologies in all relevant sectors, giving special attention to the rehabilitation and modernisation of power systems, with particular attention to developing countries;

Promote the research, development, transfer and use of technologies and practices for environmentally sound energy systems, including new and renewable energy systems, with particular attention to developing countries;

Promote the development of institutional, scientific, planning and management capacities, particularly in developing countries, to develop, produce and use increasingly efficient and less polluting forms of energy;

Review current energy supply mixes to determine how the contribution of environmentally sound energy systems as a whole, particularly new and renewable energy systems, could be increased in an economically efficient manner, taking into account respective countries' unique social, physical, economic and political characteristics, and examining and implementing, where appropriate, measures to overcome any barriers to their development and use;

Coordinate energy plans regionally and sub-regionally, where applicable, and study the feasibility of efficient distribution of environmentally sound energy from new and renewable energy sources;

In accordance with national socioeconomic development and environment priorities, evaluate and, as appropriate, promote cost-effective policies or programmes, including administrative, social and economic measures, in order to improve energy efficiency;

Build capacity for energy planning and programme management in energy efficiency, as well as for the development, introduction, and promotion of new and renewable sources of energy;

Promote appropriate energy efficiency and emission standards or recommendations at the national level, aimed at the development and use of technologies that minimise adverse impacts on the environment;

Encourage education and awareness-raising programmes at the local, national, sub-regional and regional levels concerning energy efficiency and environmentally sound energy systems;

Establish or enhance, as appropriate, in co-operation with the private sector, labelling programmes for products to provide decision makers and consumers with information on opportunities for energy efficiency.

---

ence of climate change, its impacts and response options now available." The conference placed particular emphasis on IPCC's assertion that "the balance of evidence suggests a discernible human influence on global climate". The Ministerial Declaration expressed the agreement "to strengthen the process under the Convention for the regular review of the implementation of present and future commitments" (FCCC/CP/1996/ L.17). Within the same Declaration, the Ministers and other heads of delegations at COP 2 instructed their representatives to accelerate negotiations on the text of a "legally-binding protocol or another legal instrument" to be completed in due time for adoption at the third session of the Conference of the Parties (COP 3, Kyoto-Japan, December 1997).

Despite the recognition of the present energy course as unsustainable and the setting of ambitious goals relating to sustainable energy in Agenda 21, little has been done since Rio in terms of the development of coordinated action plans to address the identified challenges. Even in the area of climate change, which received focused attention in Rio, little has been accomplished. It is now generally recognized that most industrialized countries will be unable to meet the voluntary targets they set for limiting their own emissions. Moreover, support for research and development on and commercialization of new sustainable energy technologies has been low and declining in the industrialized countries (see Section 5.4.5). While the establishment of the GEF represents a concrete course of action for helping bring sustainable energy technologies to developing countries, its resources available for addressing climate change are very modest in relation to the challenge.

2.3 Energy and the Economy
2.3.1 Investment Requirements of Energy

In 1990 global capital investments in energy supply were a little less than US$400 billion—nearly 2% of world GDP. At present, more than half of energy supply investments are made by OECD countries; there, environment-related investments account for about 25% of total annual capital expenditures by many leading energy companies (WEC, 1993). Energy-related investments in developing countries and economies in transition presently account for, respectively, 25-30% and less than 15% of the global total. Although investments in energy supply as a percentage of total investments vary greatly across countries, average values have been relatively stable. Historically, energy supply investments have accounted for 15% to 20% of total investments—10% for the power sector plus 5% to 10% for coal, oil, and natural gas (WEC/IIASA, 1995).

Forward projections of energy investment requirements are very uncertain. For the period 1990-2020, the World Energy Council estimated in 1993 that global investment requirements for the energy sector in its Reference Scenario for world energy would amount to US$30 trillion at 1992 prices, including US$7 trillion for energy-efficiency and environment-related investments (WEC, 1993). A more recent estimate from a joint study by the World Energy Council and the International Institute for Applied Systems Analysis (IIASA) estimated capital investment requirements for 1990-2020 in the range US$13 to US$20 trillion for alternative scenarios of energy supply, including US$16 billion for the WEC/IIASA Reference Scenario (WEC/IIASA, 1995). This is lower than the earlier WEC estimate both because it does not take into account investments requirements for energy efficiency and because it estimates learning effects that lead to lower capital requirements.

A more recent projection of capital requirements for energy supply (very similar to the WEC/IIASA estimate for its Reference Scenario) is shown in Table 2.10. A noteworthy feature of this projection is the large role projected for developing countries. The developing countries, which account for 75% of the world population and 35% of the world gross domestic product, are expected to account for about half of the total capital investment requirements (double their present share). While, as at present, the global investment in energy supply would average about 2% of world GDP over the period 1990-2020, there would be marked differences among regions: developing countries and economies in transition would spend, respectively, 4.5% and 9% of their GDP on energy supplies, compared to only 1% in OECD countries.

The uncertainty of estimates of future capital investment requirements is indicated further by the findings of yet another WEC study (WEC, 1995). This study estimated energy capital investment needs for developing countries to be US$4.1 trillion, 1990-2020, for the WEC Reference Scenario A—less than half the estimate presented in Table 2.10, but with a slightly larger capital investment requirement (US$3.2 trillion) for the electric power sector.

Even the lowest of these estimates will be challenging for developing countries, especially in the power, sector where annual investment requirements are projected to increase from US$65 billion per year, 1990-1995, to US$170 billion per year, 2015-2020 (WEC, 1995). Historically, overseas investments in coal, oil and natural gas, which have been nearly comparable to those for electric power, primarily have been undertaken by well-established international companies with proven track records in financial markets. In contrast, for many power sector investments, both in economies now in transition and in developing countries, financing has become increasingly problematic.

The early 1980s represented the high point of ratios of investment to GDP in developing countries. With the international debt crisis that began in 1982, the investment ratio began to fall. Public sources traditionally have provided the capital for the power sector in developing countries. However, increasing fiscal constraints on public funds are limiting the continuity and expansion of this source of capital. External financing also dropped, and although the level of domestic savings in many developing countries is substantial, there have been widespread political, institutional and cultural barriers to the successful harnessing of domestic savings for energy and many other investment purposes. It was only in Asia that the 1980s were marked by an increase in the investment ratio.

A significant part of the capital problem is due to widespread subsidies that distort energy prices. On average electricity and natural gas prices would have to be raised 60% and 25%, respectively, for electric and gas utilities to generate enough revenues to cover costs in developing countries.[40] The financial burden of underpriced electricity in developing countries has been estimated to be US$90 billion per year.[41] Underpricing weakens market power in capital markets (STAP/GEF, 1996), leads to new capacity requirements in excess of true needs, and makes it difficult to make the system more efficient.[42] A number of developing countries and transitional economies recognize the problems posed by underpricing energy and are moving away from heavy subsidies to a system where pricing is more reflective of costs. However, few steps have been taken to reflect all costs including externalities such as adverse environmental and other societal impacts (see Chapter 5 for a further discussion of this topic).

If these externalities are not addressed adequately, the consequences often could be grave. Consider, for example, emissions of oxides of sulfur. In the absence of abatement measures, high coal-consumption scenarios imply both significant deterioration in ambient air quality in South and East Asia, and acid deposition levels exceeding by factors of up to 10 what soils that provide economically important food crops in Asia could sustain (see Section 2.2.2.3 and WEC/IIASA (1995)). Fortunately, costs of abating emissions of oxides of sulfur will not be prohibitive. Costs for flue gas desulfurization have fallen from about US$225 per kW in 1993 to about US$100 per kW in 1996. Moreover, advanced coal conversion technologies that are both highly efficient and low-polluting are expected to be cost-competitive within a decade's time (see Sections 3.3.2.2 and 3.3.2.3).

Major challenges for developing countries and for the economies in transition are to establish strong domestic capital markets and to attract more private capital to the energy sector, especially the power sector. One of the difficulties is that, in the absence of economic development, increased levels of privately financed energy investment are unlikely. Private investment in the energy sector has been greatest in several of the Asia/ Pacific countries and some Latin American countries, which have been able to move away from use of heavy energy subsidies. Such investments have by-passed those countries that have had difficulty in stepping up the pace of economic development.

Despite the many problems, energy investments can bring about extremely rapid changes in energy supply and consumption patterns when the economic and/or political climate is suitable. The growth of North Sea natural gas in the United Kingdom is a good example. First used in 1963, consumption had grown by 1973 from near zero to 25 million tonnes of oil equivalent (Mtoe) or 12.6% of total energy supply in the United

---

[40]   See Figure 2.2, page 47 in World Bank (1994).

[41]   See Table 6.7, page 121 in World Bank (1994).

[42]   For example, it is estimated that reducing transmission, distribution, and generation losses would lead to savings of $30 billion per year in developing countries [see Table 6.8, p. 122, in World Bank (1994)].

Table 2.10: A Projection of Capital Spending for Energy Supplies, 1990-2020*

	Electric Utility	Gas Utility	Oil and Gas	Coal	Biomass	Totals
Developing Countries	3000	660	4500	240	390	8790
OECD Countries	4500	600	1200	180	90	6570
Economies in Transition	990	330	900	90	30	2340
Totals	8490	1590	6600	510	510	17,700

*   Billions 1990 US$
      Source: (Hyman and O'Neill, 1995)

Kingdom. By 1983, natural gas use had almost doubled again to provide 24.1% of primary energy in the United Kingdom, mainly at the expense of coal and other solid fuels. More recently, natural gas has replaced coal at very rapid rates in the United Kingdom power sector, due to price differentials and market-oriented government policies. Between 1990 and 1994 this "dash for gas" saw gas consumption by power stations rise 18-fold, from 0.5 to 9.0 Mtoe, while coal use declined by 16.1 Mtoe or 31%.

Quantitatively, capital requirements for the energy sector are not large in comparison to what is potentially available from global financial markets. However, bringing about the flow of capital from financial markets to needed energy investments will require a set of conditions that make such opportunities attractive to prospective investors. Thus, significant legal, institutional, and economic changes are required if energy is not to become, or remain, a constraint on development.

2.3.2 Foreign Exchange Impacts of Energy Imports

The foreign exchange required for fossil fuel imports, usually oil, has been a heavy burden on the balance of trade of many countries, especially as a result of the high oil prices in the 1974-86 period.

In the short-term, since oil imports tend to account for a significant portion of total imports, and since oil consumption is deeply rooted in the energy systems of many oil-importing countries, an increase in oil prices leads to a significant increase in the total cost of imports. In the absence of an equivalent increase in exports, trade balances deteriorate sharply. In such situations, decision-makers generally are compelled to finance the resulting deficit either by borrowing or by running down foreign exchange reserves.

During the five years following the 1973-74 crisis, the external borrowings of non-oil-producing countries rose sharply, tripling in nominal terms (excluding private non-guaranteed debt). This increase occurred despite the fact that most of these countries took exceptional measures to hold down import levels and to increase the volume of exports. Moreover, the economies of several developing countries also suffered from effects of oil-induced inflation and recession in the industrialized countries to which they exported, as well as from the direct effects of oil price increases on their economies. Directly linked to the balance of trade, the burden of indebtedness increased. This burden remains a major problem in many developing countries.

In 1992, the world oil price (in constant dollars) was less than a third of the peak price in 1981. Yet many developing countries are still spending significant portions of their convertible currency earnings on energy imports. At present over 30 countries have energy imports exceeding 10% of the value of all exports, and for some countries net energy imports as a percentage of total merchandise exports is much higher (e.g., 18% for India, 58% for Nicaragua, and 71% for Uganda in 1992) (World Bank, 1994). Such energy import requirements are a heavy burden on the balance of trade, often leading to debt problems. In about 20 developing countries, including Ethiopia, Cambodia and Lebanon, payments for oil imports exceed payments for external debt servicing. (World Bank,

1994). These are the important aspects of the energy-foreign exchange nexus.

2.4 Energy and Security
2.4.1 Energy Trade and National Security

There are several national security issues related to energy trade. On a regional scale, conflicts potentially could arise from the harnessing of rivers for hydroelectric power in watersheds covering several countries. Energy security concerns are raised when natural gas pipelines that cross national borders are built or proposed. But oil trade has raised the greatest concerns about national security.

On a global scale, oil accounted for approximately 40% of commercial energy use world-wide in 1990—some 66 million barrels of oil per day. The industrialized countries of the Organization for Economic Co-operation and Development (OECD), principally the United States, Western Europe, and Japan, together consumed 57% of the world total, or 38 million barrels per day. Of this consumption, nearly 60% was imported (EIA, 1994). By far the greatest source of imported oil is from the Middle East. In 1991 the Middle East exported 13 million barrels per day, two-thirds of which were imported by the OECD countries (EIA, 1994).

The dependence of the United States, Western Europe and Japan on oil imports from the Middle East represents one potential source of conflict in the world today. The point was well illustrated by the Gulf War in 1990.

The global dependence on Middle East oil is not likely to change soon. The United States Geological Survey estimates that 65% of the world's oil reserves are located in the Persian Gulf—approximately 80% of the reserves of all the oil-exporting states (Masters et al., 1994). However, it is likely that there will be a shift in the mix of oil importers. In the WEC/IIASA Reference Scenario it is projected that world oil demand will increase by nearly 1/4, 1990-2020, and that oil demand in developing in developing countries will more than double in this period, while demand will decline by nearly 1/5 in OECD countries (WEC/IIASA, 1995). According to this projection, the developing world would be consuming 1.4 times as much oil as OECD countries by 2020, compared to 0.5 times as much in 1990. Much of this increased demand by developing countries would be met by imports. Thus in the future national security concerns about oil trade might be more widely held than at present.

2.4.2 Nuclear Energy and Nuclear Proliferation

In the text agreed to by Government delegations at the final plenary session for Working Group II of the Intergovernmental Panel on Climate Change, it is stated that "nuclear energy could replace baseload fossil fuel electricity generation in many parts of the world if generally acceptable responses can be found to concerns such as reactor safety, radioactive waste transport and disposal, and nuclear proliferation" (IPCC, 1996c). The nuclear proliferation concern is a security issue that will be discussed here.

Nuclear power programs require national cadres of nuclear scientists and technicians, a network of research facilities, research reactors, and laboratories—each being indispensable to a nuclear weapons program. The most direct connection between nuclear power and nuclear explosives, however, is through the production and use of fissile materials, plutonium and highly-enriched uranium, which could be used in nuclear explosives. For example, the spent fuel from all power reactors contains large quantities of plutonium. A one gigawatt-electric (GW_e) light water reactor (LWR), the dominant type in most of the world, discharges approximately 200 kilograms of plutonium annually in its spent fuel—enough for more than 20 nuclear explosives. In 1995, the total discharge of plutonium world-wide from civilian power reactors exceeded 60 tonnes (a nuclear explosive requires less than ten kilograms of plutonium). Although countries that have produced plutonium explosives have produced weapons-grade plutonium in dedicated reactors, the difference in proliferation risk posed by separated weapons-grade plutonium and separated reactor-grade plutonium is small[43] (CISAC, 1994). This is recognized by the safeguards system established by the International Atomic Energy Agency (IAEA), which does not distinguish

---

[43] The plutonium discharged from power reactors contains a higher fraction of the isotope plutonium-240 than plutonium produced directly for weapons in so-called production reactors in the nuclear

between different plutonium grades.[44]

The Nuclear Non-Proliferation Treaty (NPT) was developed to provide a system of safeguards aimed at assuring that civilian nuclear power programmes not be used to divert nuclear materials to weapon usage. The NPT went into force in 1970 and as of 23 January 1997 there are 185 signatories and parties to the treaty (ACDA, 1997). The treaty requires that all non-nuclear parties to the treaty accept international safeguards on their civilian nuclear activities. The treaty assigned the IAEA the role of implementing the NPT safeguards, which involve both monitoring of records and on-site inspections at reactors and other fuel cycle facilities. The NPT and its associated safeguards have been very effective in the sense that nearly all non-nuclear states with nuclear power programs are now parties to the treaty and thus under safeguards obligations.

Changes already underway in the nuclear fuel cycle world-wide will make the safeguarding task markedly more difficult and expensive, however. For the current generation of nuclear powerplants operating on a "once-through" fuel cycle, the risks of proliferation and criminal or terrorist diversion of nuclear explosives-usable materials are limited by the fact that such material is never isolated. The fresh uranium fuel is dilute in the fissile isotope, uranium-235 (about 4%), and the plutonium produced in the reactor is not separated from the spent fuel. As long as the plutonium remains mixed in the spent fuel, it is protected against diversion to nuclear explosives use by the intensely radioactive products of nuclear fission contained in the spent fuel.

Several countries are now looking beyond the once-through fuel cycle to nuclear power systems that separate the plutonium in the spent fuel and then recycle it into fresh fuel for reactors. Initially, it was hoped by the nuclear industry in many countries that the recycled plutonium would be used in "plutonium breeder" reactors, which could produce more plutonium than they consume. In once-through fuel cycles based on LWRs, only a small fraction of the natural uranium is exploited for energy. In contrast, in a breeder fuel cycle, 50 times as much energy can be derived from the equivalent amount of natural uranium. However, because uranium prices have been relatively low and breeder reactor capital costs are projected to be relatively high, programs to develop commercial breeder reactors have been ended in most countries and the commercialization of breeder reactors is now many decades away. Despite this, a few industrialized countries have begun commercial-scale reprocessing to recover plutonium from spent fuel and have also begun to recycle plutonium in mixed-oxide uranium-plutonium (MO_x) fuel for light water reactors. By the end of the century, approximately 20,000 kg of plutonium will be separated annually world-wide (Berkhout et al., 1993).

The challenges to safeguards will be made more severe by an inexorable growth in the amounts of plutonium that will have to be monitored. This will be the case even if nuclear power does not grow much beyond the present installed capacity of 350 GW_e. In 1990, approximately 530 tonnes of plutonium were contained in spent fuel discharged from civilian reactors and about 120 tonnes had been separated from spent fuel. The separated plutonium was about one-half of the 250 tonnes plutonium that had been separated for military purposes. By 2010, looking only at spent fuel discharged from already operating nuclear power reactors, the relative sizes of the civilian and military stockpiles will be dramatically reversed. At

weapon states. Plutonium-240, for various reasons, complicates bomb design—a fact that once led some observers to argue that the "reactor-grade" plutonium is unsuited for weapons. However, it has been convincingly shown that it is quite possible for a potential proliferator to make a nuclear explosive from reactor-grade plutonium. Theft or diversion of separated plutonium, whether weapon-grade or reactor-grade, would pose a grave security risk. In the view of the recently published U.S. National Academy of Science study on plutonium disposition (CISAC, 1994): "... it would be quite possible for a potential proliferator to make a nuclear explosive from reactor-grade plutonium using a simple design that would be assured of having a yield in the range of one to a few kilotons, and more using advanced design."

[44] International Atomic Energy Agency, INFCIRC/153. This system establishes safeguards on all plutonium in excess of one kilogram, with the exception of "plutonium with an isotopic concentration of plutonium-238 exceeding 80%."

that time, it is expected that there will be approximately 1550 tonnes of plutonium in unreprocessed spent fuel from civilian reactors; and there will be 546 tonnes separated from civilian spent fuel[45]—more than twice the amount of weapons plutonium, the production of which is now frozen.

Unfortunately, safeguards are an imperfect barrier to proliferation, as has been understood since the dawn of the nuclear era[46] and shown by the fact that there has been at least one country that had an extensive nuclear weapons programme underway while subject to full-scope IAEA international safeguards (United Nations, 1995b).

In the long-run, if nuclear power comes to produce a significant fraction of world energy, the challenge of safeguarding explosives-usable materials will become still more daunting. Consider the implications of expanding nuclear capacity ten-fold, to 3,000 GW_e during the next century. Such an expansion could be helpful in dealing with the challenge of climate change, reducing cumulative CO_2 emissions, 1900-2100, by about 200 GtC (equivalent to 10 to 25% of total cumulative emissions for the IS92 scenarios presented in Table 2.9), if the elctricity produced were to displace electricity that would otherwise be generated from coal. However, in current reactors, a nuclear capacity of this magnitude would generate over 500,000 kg of plutonium per year in the spent fuel discharged. Concerns about uranium supply at such a high level of nuclear power would lead to pressures to deploy plutonium breeder reactors. A 3000-GW_e system based on breeder reactors would place into global nuclear commerce approximately 3-5 million kilograms of plutonium per year.[47] It is difficult to imagine human institutions capable of safeguarding such plutonium flows against occasional diversions of quantities that are significant compared to what is needed for nuclear explosives.

It might turn out that in the future nuclear power systems can be developed that are significantly more diversion resistant than the current ones—for example, systems in which very little plutonium is produced in the spent fuel (Williams and Feiveson, 1990). So far, however, generally acceptable solutions to the problem of nuclear proliferation have not been identified. The continuing concern of many members of the general public and many policymakers with regards to proliferation as well as safety issues may remain a severe constraint on nuclear power generation in many countries (WEC, 1993).

2.5 The United Nations Conferences on Small Island Developing States and Habitat II

In contrast to the United Nations conferences discussed above in conjunction with the issues of poverty, population, and women, the multi-faceted nature of the energy-development nexus was evident at two of the United Nations conferences held after UNCED. The Global Conference on Small Island Developing States (SIDS) was held in Barbados in the spring of 1994 and the Habitat II Conference on Human Settlements in Turkey in June 1996. Both United Nations conferences ac-

---

[45]   This assumes a discharge of plutonium of approximately 70 tonnes per year, roughly the current rate, and a separation rate of about 20 tonnes per year, most of this from reprocessing plants in France, the UK, Russia, and Japan. (See, for example, Nuclear Control Institute, "Plutonium on the Internet", April 1996.)

[46]   The question of the adequacy of international inspections in preventing nuclear proliferation was first considered in the Acheson-Lilienthal Report that became the basis of the Baruch Plan for international control of nuclear weapons that the United States submitted to the United Nations in 1946 (Lilienthal et al., 1946). The report stated:

"We have concluded unanimously that there is no prospect of security against atomic warfare in a system of international agreements to outlaw such weapons controlled only by a system which relies on inspection and similar police-like methods. The reasons supporting this conclusion are not merely technical but primarily the inseparable political, social, and organizational problems involved in enforcing agreements between nations, each free to develop atomic energy but only pledged not to use bombs...So long as intrinsically dangerous activities may be carried on by nations, rivalries are inevitable and fears are engendered that place so great a pressure on a systems of international enforcement by police methods that no degree of ingenuity or technical competence could possibly hope to cope with them."

[47]   While in light water reactors about 200 kg of plutonium are generated per gigawatt-year, several times as much plutonium would be recycled per gigawatt-year in a breeder reactor.

tively debated the role of energy in development especially as it relates to the unique conditions in island states and urban development respectively. Energy was taken up not as a sectoral issue, but as a barrier affecting numerous elements of the development process including health, transportation, environment, women, foreign exchange, urban health conditions, land degradation and economic growth—many of the same issues which have been reviewed in this chapter.

Although no consolidated approach to energy was advocated at either conference, the same common elements of a sustainable energy strategy emerged at both SIDS and Habitat: emphasis on energy efficiency; the adoption of renewable energy; dissemination of modern, clean energy technologies; and the need to reorient policy frameworks toward end-use energy services to the populations in question. The main recommendations concerning energy are reviewed here and point to the need to fundamentally reorient current approaches to energy in order to achieve sustainable development in both the island states and growing metropolis.

The Global Conference on Small Island Developing States produced the Declaration of Barbados which begins by recognising that SIDS want to translate Agenda 21 into specific policies, actions and measures to be taken at the national, regional and international level to enable small island developing states to achieve sustainable development. Starting from the premise that development options for SIDS are more limited than in other countries due to their unique geographic conditions, limited natural resources, and lack of opportunities for economies of scale, the SIDS Programme of Action begins by considering the impact of climate change and sea level rises for sustainable development in SIDS. Sea level rises pose unique and serious threats to the security and long term sustainability of SIDS due not on to the threat to their territorial integrity, but to salinization of water tables, loss of agricultural land, increased vulnerability to the effects of storms and storm surges, and other associated impacts.

The Preamble of the Programme of Action calls for international action to provide access to environmentally sound and energy efficient technology to assist SIDS in conserving energy.[48] The production of adequate energy is a long standing bottleneck to economic and social development in SIDS.

The SIDS Programme of Action includes a specific chapter (7) on energy resources, looking at how energy consumption and production patterns are directly related to sustainable development in SIDS.[49] Chapter 7 begins by profiling the unique conditions of SIDS with respect to energy. They are heavily dependent on imported petroleum products, largely for transport and electricity generation, energy often accounting for more than 12% of all imports. This represents a long-term and growing burden to SIDS under present conditions. SIDS also are heavily dependent on indigenous biomass fuels for cooking and crop drying bringing the associated social and health impacts, especially with regards to the role of women, as discussed in section 2.1.2. A major constraint facing sustainable development in all SIDS countries is the expected continued reliance on imported petroleum fuels and the inefficiency of their use. In fact paragraph 36 argues that "increased efficiency through appropriate technology and national energy policies and management measures will reap financial and environmental benefits for small island developing states".

Renewable energy options are also discussed in Chapter 7.[50] All SIDS have substantial solar resources which have not been exploited fully. Wind, hydro, ocean thermal, geothermal and biomass also are discussed, with the conclusion that such resources are unequally distributed, have widely variable potential, and that these options require more research. More important are the institutional and financial constraints to the widespread adoption of alternative sources of energy. "Several constraints to the large scale use of renewable energy resources remain, including technology development, investment costs, available indigenous skills and management capabilities. The use of renewable

---

[48] SIDS Programme of Action, Preamble, C. (v), p.12.

[49] Report of the Global Conference on SIDS, Programme of Action, Chapter 7, pp.25-26

[50] SIDS Programme of Action, Chapter 7, pp.25-27.

energy resources as substantial commercial fuels by small island developing states is dependent on the development and commercial production of appropriate technologies".[51] It can be concluded that the combination of technology and appropriate enabling conditions, especially human, institutional and financial capacities, remains a key sustainable development issue with regard to energy in SIDS.

At the national level, the Programme of Action calls for public education, consumer incentives for energy conservation, the promotion of efficient use of energy, development of environmentally sound sources of energy and energy efficient technologies. Further it calls for the strengthening of research capabilities in new and renewable energy and technologies for non-renewable energy sources. It also calls for the use of "economic instruments and incentive structures and increasing the economic possibilities of renewable sources of energy".[52] Enhanced national capacity to plan manage and monitor the energy sector is called for in the same chapter.

At the regional level, coordinated action is called for in the formulation of energy policies, standards and guidelines for the energy sector. There are mutual benefits for countries with common conditions to work in a co-ordinated fashion to achieve the economies of scale and critical mass of institutional capacities needed to address the important market and non-market barriers to sustainable energy development.

At the international level, the SIDS Programme of Action encourages "international institutions and agencies, including public international financial institutions, to incorporate environmental efficiency and conservation principles into energy sector related projects, training and technical assistance."[53] As such, the proposed role of multilateral agencies, including those of the United Nations system, is to facilitate SIDS to reach the energy objectives designated in the Programme of Action through the intergovernmental process.

Two years later, many of these themes emerged again when the community of nations met to discuss the impacts of escalating rates of urbanisation, especially within developing countries where urbanisation rates are highest and the impacts on living conditions for the urban poor and sustainable cities development are most dire. The Habitat II Conference on Human Settlements was held in Istanbul, Turkey in June 1996. It included many references to the importance of sustainable energy use. This concern was embodied in the Habitat II statement "Sustainable Human Settlements Development in an Urbanising World" which explicitly deals with sustainable energy use to achieve sustainable human settlements.

Habitat II, like the other United Nations conferences, produced a Global Plan of Action which provides detailed recommendations concerning directions for improving the sustainable use of energy. Energy was discussed in relation to health, shelter, industry, transport, environment and community participation. Energy was described as integral to sustainable development issues, especially in relation to the human habitat and urban environment. Technology transfer, as in all the other platforms for action, was an essential part of the sustainable energy pathway described. Building on the topic of housing and shelter for the urban people living in poverty, the Plan of Action made concrete recommendations concerning the role of energy in Chapter IV, Section C6, entitled "Sustainable Energy Use".

The role of energy as part of the basic infrastructure and services needed at the community level was a key topic in Istanbul. It was argued that lack of basic services (which are a key component of the overall concept of "shelter") exacts a heavy toll on human health, productivity and quality of life, especially for those living in poverty in both rural and urban areas. Paragraph 85 of the Plan of Action called on governments at the appropriate levels to safeguard the health, safety and welfare of all people and to provide affordable basic infrastructure including "access to sustainable sources of energy".[54] Government's role in

---

[51] SIDS Programme of Action, Chapter 7, para.38, p.25.

[52] SIDS Programme of Action, Chapter 7, A (ii), p.26.

[53] SIDS Programme of Action, Chapter 7, C (iv), pp.26-27.

[54] HABITAT Agenda, Chapter IV, B.2, para 85.

assuring enabling conditions for sustainable energy was described as well. Public policy and institutional support in the form of industrial standards and quality control, with particular attention to energy efficiency, were called for.[55] Energy was addressed not only as an input necessary for development, but also as a social issue impacting living conditions, human health, personal security and the quality of shelter.

Chapter IV of the Habitat Agenda stated that the use of energy is essential in urban centres for transportation, industrial production, household and office activities. It asserted that:

"Current dependence in most urban centres on non-renewable energy sources can lead to climate change, air pollution and consequent environmental and human health problems, and may represent a serious threat to sustainable development. Sustainable energy production and use can be enhanced by encouraging energy efficiency, by such means as pricing policies, fuel switching, alternative energy, mass transit and public awareness. Human settlements and energy policies should be actively co-ordinated."[56]

The promotion of efficient and sustainable energy use and of actions by governments, the private sector, non-governmental organisations, community-based organisations, and consumer groups to solve many of the crucial social and economic requirements of sustainable development were recommended. The conference drew attention to the need for all sectors of society, both public and private, to take coordinated action with regard to facilitating the conditions to bring about sustainable patterns of energy production and use.

Section 6 of Chapter IV was based on the premise that human settlements and energy policy should be actively coordinated. It was argued that sustainable energy production and consumption could be enhanced by "encouraging energy efficiency, by such means as pricing policies, fuel switching, alternative energy, mass transit and public awareness."[57] Governments, the private sec-

tor, non-governmental organisations, community-based organisations, and consumer groups were called on to undertake specific policy actions to promote efficient and sustainable energy use. These actions included: promoting urban and rural planning that incorporates energy efficiency design considerations; promoting measures to promote the use of renewable and safe sources of energy to improve the efficiency of energy use in human settlements, while ensuring that the people living in poverty are not disadvantaged; promoting energy efficiency on the supply side in the production and distribution of energy; encouraging the use of low-energy transport systems; instituting user charges to promote household energy efficiency; adopting fiscal incentives to encourage energy efficiency; developing programs to reduce emissions in power generation and transport; and mounting public education campaigns to reduce consumption and promote sustainable energy use.[58] These are among the key issues which would form the basis of a sustainable energy strategy. Like the SIDS Programme of Action and indeed Agenda 21, common themes with regards to energy and sustainable development emerged at Habitat II. These include the need for coordinated action among various sector of society, energy viewed as a complex issue affecting social conditions and quality of life, energy as a development bottleneck in the absence of a coordinated strategy and energy as an area of opportunity to bring about positive and significant changes in conventional approaches to growth and development.

2.6 The Global Implications of Energy

It has been shown that there are linkages between energy and pressing social, environmental, economic and security issues. These linkages and the past development patterns of the world have produced an unsustainable situation. Many of the aspects of the unsustainability of the present course were recognized and highlighted at the 1992 United Nations Conference on Environment

---

[55] HABITAT Agenda, Chapter IV, B.2, para 88.

[56] HABITAT Agenda, Chapter IV, B.2, para 145.

[57] HABITAT Agenda, Chapter IV, C.6, para 145.

[58] HABITAT Agenda, Chapter IV, C.6, para 146 a-l.

and Development (UNCED) in Rio de Janeiro and in subsequent United Nations-sponsored meetings. However, while there are many hopeful technological opportunities for shifting to a more sustainable path (see Chapter 3) and a growing number of experiments with new policy approaches for bringing such technologies to energy markets (see the Appendices to Chapter 5), the world energy system continues to evolve largely according to the trends established before the 1992 UNCED. In other words, the business-as-usual energy patterns and conventional approaches to energy are making the world more unsustainable.

Any coordinated effort to address the social, environmental, economic and security concerns raised at the various United Nations conferences must pay attention to their energy aspects. Energy challenges should be tackled in ways such that these social, environmental, economic and security problems are ameliorated—not aggravated—as is typically the case with conventional energy strategies, which either ignore these global problems or do not deal with them adequately. Energy strategies, policies, programmes and projects should be consistent with, and contribute to, the solutions of the major global problems. The global goal for energy should be to make energy an instrument to help realize the broader goal of sustainable development. In the next chapter, technical options for realizing this goal are discussed.

3 New Opportunities in Energy Demand, Supply and Systems

3.1 Introduction

The adverse impacts of energy production and consumption can be mitigated either by reducing consumption or by shifting energy supplies to options which are better able to support sustainable development objectives.

The objective of the energy system is to provide energy services necessary for all sectors of the economy (residential, commercial, service, industrial, construction, mining, agriculture, and so on). The energy chain to deliver these services begins with the collection or extraction of primary energy supplies from nature. Primary energy sources are converted in one or more steps into energy carriers that are used in energy end-use equipment to provide desired energy services. Figure 3.1 shows the sequence from many energy sources to energy services.

While supply-side activities have attracted the most attention in discussions of the *energy sector,* both energy supply and energy end-use technologies are required to obtain an energy service. This chapter addresses options for improving the efficiency of energy and materials use, as well as for renewable sources of energy, and "cleaner" use of conventional fuels.

3.2 Demand Side: Energy Efficiency and Materials Efficiency

The level of energy demand has a strong influence on the major global issues discussed in Chapter 2: the higher the level of demand, the greater the challenge in providing energy in ways that are consistent with sustainable development goals. Higher demand levels can lead to higher prices both for energy and for the capital needed for energy investments, making it more difficult to provide needed energy services to all in the population. Higher demand levels also can lead to increased levels of air pollution (resulting in global warming, acid precipitation, and smog in the urban and industrial environment), greater waste production (e.g., ashes, slags), and more water and thermal pollution. And higher demand levels reduce

society's energy choices, making it difficult to avoid being overly dependent on problematic energy sources.

The level of demand is determined by a complex set of factors. These include the size and structure of economies, the distribution of income, consumption patterns, the degree and character of urbanisation, and the performance of available technology. Each of these factors provides potential entry points for efforts to reduce energy demand and thereby facilitate the realisation of an energy system compatible with sustainable development. The factor with the largest and most accessible potential is *technological performance*. The potential for reducing energy demand via changes in the patterns of consumption of goods and services is significantly less than via technical measures [see, for example, (DMEE, 1996)], for a discussion of this point in the Danish context). Thus, although changed patterns in the consumption of goods and services could lead to reductions in energy consumption, the emphasis here is on energy conservation measures that result in the use of *less* energy to provide the *same* energy service, or to achieve *more* energy services for the *same* energy input rather than reducing the level of energy use by reducing the level of services provided. Of course, attempts to shift users away from irrational and wasteful patterns of consumption should not be precluded.

The sections below first address methodological issues for assessing opportunities for more efficient use of energy, followed by discussions of the importance of energy efficiency improvements for developing countries, opportunities for energy efficiency improvements in key sectors (industry, commercial and residential buildings, transport and agriculture), and finally opportunities for using energy-intensive materials more efficiently, thereby saving energy in the production of these materials.

3.2.1 Analysing Opportunities for Improving Energy Efficiency

Energy is used in an economy to supply a

Figure 3.1: The Energy System, from Primary Sources of Energy to Energy Services

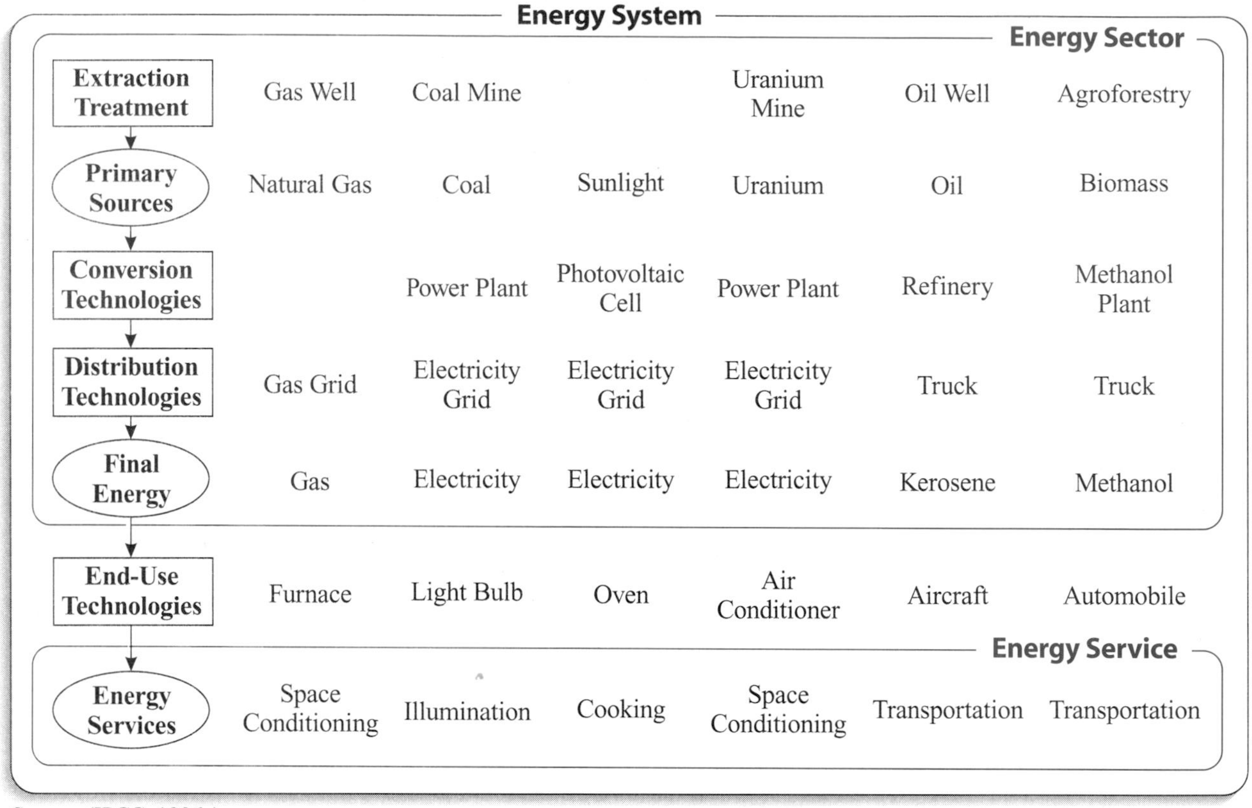

Energy System					Energy Sector	
Extraction Treatment	Gas Well	Coal Mine		Uranium Mine	Oil Well	Agroforestry
Primary Sources	Natural Gas	Coal	Sunlight	Uranium	Oil	Biomass
Conversion Technologies		Power Plant	Photovoltaic Cell	Power Plant	Refinery	Methanol Plant
Distribution Technologies	Gas Grid	Electricity Grid	Electricity Grid	Electricity Grid	Truck	Truck
Final Energy	Gas	Electricity	Electricity	Electricity	Kerosene	Methanol
End-Use Technologies	Furnace	Light Bulb	Oven	Air Conditioner	Aircraft	Automobile
Energy Services	Space Conditioning	Illumination	Cooking	Space Conditioning	Transportation	Transportation

Energy Service

Source: (IPCC, 1996c)

service or to perform a certain activity. Thus energy efficiency improvement means decreasing the use of energy per unit of activity. Two alternative indicators can be used to evaluate changes in energy efficiency—*energy intensity* and *specific energy consumption.*

3.2.1.1 Energy intensity as a measure of energy efficiency

Every economy consists of a number of energy-utilising sectors, each of which makes a value-added contribution to GDP and can be characterised by an *energy intensity,* defined as the energy consumption per unit of value added for that sector. At the national level GDP is the sum over all sectors of the value added from each sector, and the ratio of energy consumption at the national level to GDP is the energy intensity of the economy as a whole.

National energy demand is proportional to GDP *if and only if* the structure of the economy and the energy intensities are constant. If, however, there are changes in energy intensity due to efficiency improvements, process changes or product changes,

and/or there are changes of the contributions of different activities to the GDP, the proportionality breaks down.

The long-term trend for the US (and for many other OECD countries as well) has been a declining energy/GDP ratio (see Figure 3.2). There are three factors responsible for this trend. The first is the improvement over time of the efficiency of production of energy carriers, e.g., the efficiency of electricity generation from fossil fuels increased from an average of 4% in 1900 to 32% in 1960 (Williams and Larson, 1989). Second, there have been improvements in the efficiency of energy end-use technologies. For instance, the average energy efficiency of cars (measured in km/litre) in the US in 1995 was 70% higher than in 1973 (EIA, 1997). Third, there have been structural changes toward less energy-intensive economic activities. At high levels of affluence economic activity tends to shift toward less energy-intensive production, arising as a result of both the shift in consumer preferences to more valuable, less materials-intensive products and the shift in production to better performing materials (Williams et al., 1987; Bernardini and Galli, 1993). As a result, in the United States and other OECD countries apparent consumption of many basic materials is growing only very slowly, not at all, or slowly declining (see Figure 3.3).

Figure 3.4 shows the historical trends for GDP and for commercial energy consumption for OECD and selected countries for the period 1970-1995. For the ten-year period beginning in 1973 energy and economic growth were de-coupled in OECD countries, with no net growth in energy use; for the period 1979-1983 energy use actually declined as GDP continued growing. Since the mid-1980's, energy growth has resumed in OECD countries, although at a slower rate than economic growth.

In China there also has been a substantial decoupling of energy and economic growth. In 1980, China instituted a loan programme and committed around 7-8% of total energy investment to efficiency improvements, primarily in heavy industries (Sinton and Levine, 1994). This programme contributed to a remarkable decline in the energy intensity of China's economy (Figure 3.4). Since 1980, GDP has grown at 9.5%/year while energy consumption has grown half as fast, at an average rate of 4.8%/year (compared to 7.5%/year in the 1970s), mainly due to falling energy intensity in the industrial sector (Sinton and Levine, 1994).

Comparing energy efficiencies of different countries via comparisons of energy intensities is a difficult task. Economic structural differences often account for significant differences among countries. These structural differences can reflect variations in climate, geography, and resource endowments. The stage of economic development is also a major factor shaping the energy intensity of a country. For example, during a country's infrastructure-building period the demand for energy-intensive basic materials often grows faster than GDP. This situation tends to increase energy intensity, even if these basic materials are produced efficiently. Similarly, the dematerialization of affluent countries can contribute significantly to a declining energy intensity (see Figure 3.3). Large differences also arise depending on whether the energy/GDP ratio includes only commercial energy or non-commercial energy as well (see Figure 3.2). Including non-commercial energy is problematic in that good statistics on non-

commercial energy use are often not available. Moreover, alternative measures of GDP also strongly influence comparisons, especially between industrialised and developing countries. For example, if the market exchange rate (MER) is used to measure GDP in India, the total energy intensity (including non-commercial energy) has been falling sharply since the early 1970s but is currently still more than three times the rate for the United States. However, if purchasing power parities are used instead, there has been little change in the energy intensity over this period, and the energy intensity is currently about the same as in the United States (see Figure 3.2).

3.2.1.2 Specific energy consumption as a measure of energy efficiency

In the present analysis emphasis is given to specific energy consumption as an indicator of energy efficiency. Specific energy consumption (SEC) is defined as the amount of energy per unit of human activity measured in physical terms, starting from the primary energy carriers. Examples of a unit

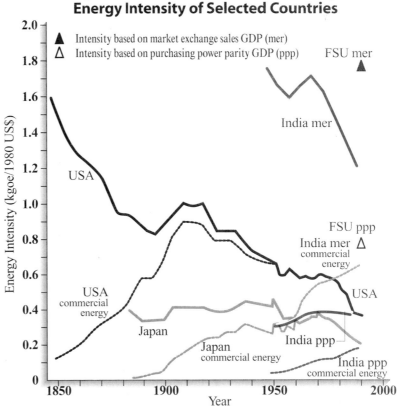

Figure 3.2: Historical Trend for Primary Energy Intensity of Selected Countries

Source: (WEC/IIASA, 1995)

Figure 3.3: Trends in Apparent Consumption of Energy-Intensive Basic Materials for the United States and Western Europe

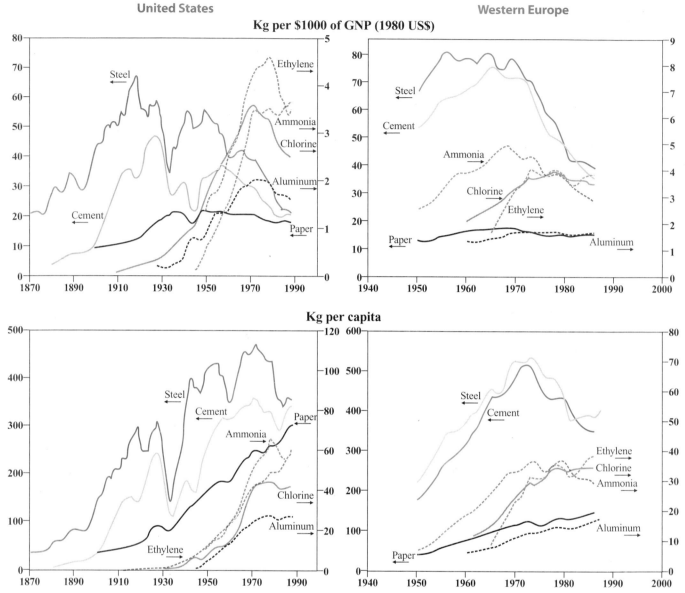

The U.S. data are five-year running averages. The Western Europe data are three-year averages of data for West Germany, France and the United Kingdom. The ammonia data, however, do not include data for the United Kingdom.
Data presented in (Williams et al., 1987) have been updated through 1990.

of activity are a square meter of building area that is heated or a tonne of steel that is produced. In the definition of the SEC, only energy consumed directly for the activity (e.g., a specific industrial process) is taken into account; the energy embodied in the inputs to the process is excluded.

Energy efficiency measures can be classified as: *i*) more efficient end-use of energy in *existing* installations (efficiency retrofits) through improved operation and maintenance and/or replacement of some components; and *ii*) more efficient end-use of energy in *new* installations, equipment, etc., through system-

atic deployment of more energy-efficient systems and technology introduced at the rate of capital turnover and expansion. Specific energy consumption often can be reduced by 20-50% in the case of efficiency improvements in *existing* energy-using installations and 50-90% in the case of *new* installations (with respect to the energy use levels of the present average stock of equipment in industrialised countries). Reductions of such magnitudes can be achieved by using the most efficient technologies that are both available today and that often cost less than increasing energy supply.

Figure 3.4: Trends for GDP and Commercial Energy Consumption for OECD and Selected Countries, 1970-1995

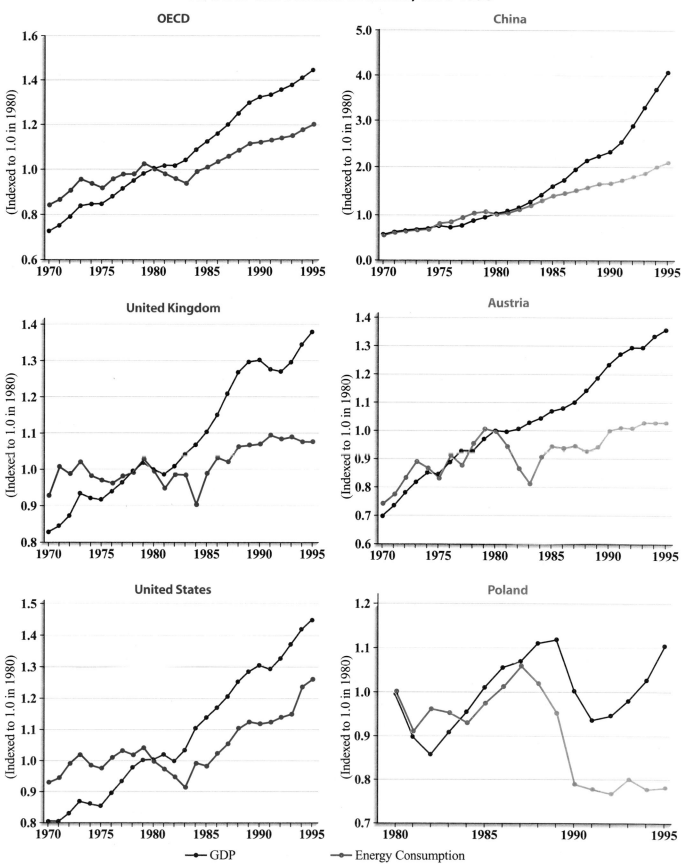

Source: GDP data are from "World Tables 1995" from the World Bank. Commercial energy consumption data are from the Department of Economic and Social Information and Policy Analysis of the United Nations Secretariat, based on various issues of the *Energy Statistics Yearbook*.

The techno-economic performance of energy-utilising equipment (i.e., its energy performance), can be specified in various ways. One indicator of performance is the lifecycle cost; that is, the sum of the present values of all the costs of the equipment throughout its life. The lifecycle costs for different pieces of equipment providing the same energy service can vary considerably. In general, the lifecycle cost of providing an energy service declines initially as a function of energy efficiency, after which it is relatively constant over a considerable range before rising again. Thus, societal interventions aimed at achieving high efficiencies can often be realised at no net extra cost to consumers (in the flat portion of the lifecycle cost versus efficiency plot).

The potential for efficiency improvement of a particular activity can be categorised in several ways. The *theoretical* potential for energy efficiency improvement is determined by thermodynamic laws governing the transformation of primary energy into work. Minimum energy requirements have been estimated from thermodynamic principles for various activities (see, for example, Gyftopoulos et al., 1974; Ford et al., 1975; Szargut and Morris, 1987; Wall, 1988). The theoretical efficiency of energy use for a particular activity is the ratio of the thermodynamic minimum energy required to carry out this activity divided by the actual energy used with existing technology. It has been estimated that the United States uses its primary energy sources to provide energy services with a thermodynamic efficiency of only 2.5% (Ayres, 1989). The theoretical potential for energy savings is the difference between the actual specific energy consumption today and the thermodynamic minimum specific energy consumption.

The concept of minimum energy requirements for energy-utilising tasks takes into account the quality of the energy provided. For example, heat energy at a high temperature has a higher quality than that at a lower temperature, because more work can be performed with high-temperature heat than with low-temperature heat for the same amount of energy (measured as enthalpy) in both cases.

Systems that match the quality of energy provided to the quality of energy needed for a task can lead to significant savings of primary energy inputs. For example, a very wasteful process is one in which the high-quality chemical energy of a fuel is burned to provide low-temperature heat (e.g., for domestic hot water). System designs such as heat-integrated industrial processes that make extensive use of heat exchangers, combined heat and power (CHP) systems, and heat pumps are examples of technologies that provide substantial primary energy savings by matching the quality of the energy provided to the quality of energy needed for tasks. An important strategy for providing high levels of energy services along with major reductions in primary energy inputs in low-polluting ways is a structural change towards a more integrated energy system (WEC/IIASA, 1995).

The *theoretical minimum specific energy consumption* is for processes that reach the final state of equilibrium at an infinitely slow rate. For practical processes, extra energy is needed to drive processes at realistic rates. This extra energy, added to the thermodynamic minimum, defines the *technically achievable minimum energy consumption*. This technical minimum is determined by the technological state-of-the-art, so that the *technical* potential is dependent on the time horizon adopted for a particular analysis. The technical potential is defined as the achievable savings resulting from the most effective combination of the efficiency improvement options available during the period under investigation.

Applying economic constraints, an *economic* potential also can be identified for energy efficiency improvements; namely, the potential savings that can be achieved with a net positive economic return on efficiency investments. However, investors generally demand more rigorous investment criteria, requiring economic returns that are at least as good as those which could be achieved from alternative investment opportunities. To the extent that investors perceive such opportunity costs when evaluating energy efficiency investments, the *market* potential of these investments (i.e., the anticipated potential savings to be realised in practice) is diminished. Policy initiatives can help to reduce the gaps between the technical, economic and market potentials.

Reduced expenditures on energy, resulting from energy efficiency improvements, generate monetary savings that in turn may

68

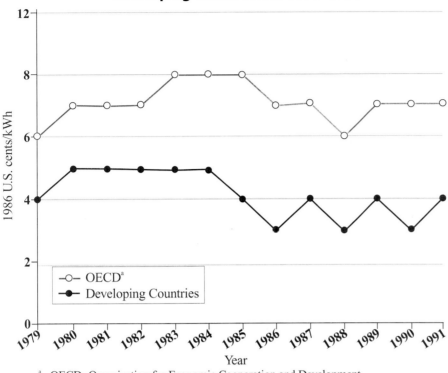

Figure 3.5: Trends in Electricity Tariffs of OECD[a] and Developing Countries for 1979-1991

[a] OECD=Organization for Economic Cooperation and Development
Source: (Heidarian and Wu, 1994)

be spent on additional energy use, thereby reducing the overall impact of the energy efficiency improvement on the energy demand—the so-called *take-back effect*. In general, however, the saved money would be spent not only on energy but on other activities as well, typically reducing the fraction of savings spent on energy to a modest level. Thus, the take-back effect should not be over-emphasized.

A wide body of literature indicates that a considerable energy efficiency improvement potential exists in the short-term to medium-term (for example, WEC, 1995a; WEC, 1995b; Worrell et al., 1997). The potential for further efficiency improvements with future technology through continued research and development also is large because energy efficiencies of current technologies are far from fundamental physical limits (Ayres, 1989). Moreover, there is a wide range of opportunities for reducing energy use via investments in energy efficiency improvement that are typically less costly than providing the same energy services via increasing energy supply. The barriers to seizing these opportunities are mainly institutional rather than technological (Worrell

et al., 1997). For example, capital markets are organised in ways that discriminate against investments in energy efficiency improvement (WEC/IIASA, 1995).

3.2.2 Opportunities for Energy Efficiency Improvement in Developing Countries

In developing countries, the potential for energy efficiency improvement is often much greater than in industrialised countries, for several reasons. First, energy-intensive activities are growing rapidly in developing countries, so that a larger fraction of the opportunities for making improvements in energy efficiency is associated with new installations (rather than retrofits of existing installations) compared to the already industrialised countries. Second, energy prices are typically subsidised and low in many developing countries (as shown in Figure 3.5), so that the market has not encouraged the use of efficient technologies. Third, many commercial technologies for improving energy efficiency have not been readily available in developing countries. Fourth, while capital markets throughout the world tend to discriminate against investments in energy efficiency generally (WEC/IIASA, 1995), the difficulty of financing such investments is compounded in developing countries, where domestic capital markets are not yet as well-established as in industrialised countries.

Particularly important for developing countries is the prospect that emphasis on investments in energy efficiency can speed up the rate of increasing the level of energy services provided. Sometimes a shift to modern efficient conversion and end-use technology will lead simultaneously to increasing the level of energy services and reducing energy use in a single instance (see Box 3.1). More generally, an acceleration in the growth in energy services can be achieved as a result of the freeing up of economic resources from reductions in lifecycle costs and capital investment requirements for providing a given level of energy services, when energy services are provided via the least costly mix of investments in energy efficiency improvements and energy supply expansion. A detailed analysis of such a least-cost approach to providing electricity services for the State of Karnataka in India showed that a substantial fraction of the total investment needed to meet projected demand for energy services would be for energy efficiency improvements; with such investments in energy efficiency, the total cost of providing energy services and the total investment requirements would be considerably less than if only energy supply were made to provide these services (Reddy et al., 1991a; 1991b).

One study (reported in Goldemberg et al., 1985; and Goldemberg et al., 1988) estimated that with wide adoption of modern energy carriers (electricity and liquid and gaseous fuels) and the introduction of efficient energy conversion and end-use technologies, energy service levels equivalent to those in Western Europe in the mid-1970s could be realised in developing countries with primary energy requirements per capita just 20% higher than the actual level in 1990 (see Box 3.2). Another study that assessed potentials for improving the efficiency of energy and materials use found that primary energy use levels per capita in developing countries in 2020 relative to 1990 would

> **Box 3.1: Increasing Energy Services with Energy Efficient Technology: a Lighting Example from South India**
>
> Emphasis on energy services is particularly important in developing countries where the current levels of energy services are low. With modern technologies, energy requirements often can be reduced, even while the levels of energy services provided are increased.
>
> An illustrative example is provided by the switch from kerosene wick-lamps to fluorescent tubelights that took place in Pura village in South India. When this was carried out, the energy input decreased to one ninth compared to the kerosene originally used and the household expenditure for lighting was cut in half, despite the fact that illumination increased by a factor of about 19 (Reddy,1994).

be 1.9. 1.5, 1.15, and 1.0, for, respectively, use of technologies with "business-as-usual" levels of energy performance, use of state-of-the-art technology for efficient use of energy, use of advanced technology for efficient use of energy, and use of advanced technology for efficient use of both energy and materials (Worrell et al., 1997).

3.2.3 Industry

Although there is significant potential for improving energy efficiency in all industries, the greatest opportunities for savings are in the energy-intensive industries. Five of these industries—iron and steel, chemicals, petroleum refining, pulp and paper, and cement—together account for roughly 45% of global industrial energy consumption

Much of the potential for improvement in technical energy efficiencies in industrial processes depends on how closely such processes have approached their thermodynamic limits (see Section 3.2.1.2). For these five industries there are many commercially available technologies for improving energy efficiency and opportunities for further gains with new technologies.[1]

---

[1]   See, for example, (IPCC, 1996a). For particular industries see: (Worrell et al., 1997) and (WEC, 1995a) for steel; (Worrell et al., 1994) and (WEC, 1995a) for chemicals; (WEC, 1995a) for petroleum refining; (WEC, 1995a) for pulp and paper; and (Worrell et al., 1995a) for cement.

**Box 3.2: Energy Services, Modern Technology, and Primary Energy Requirements:
A Thought Experiment**

Analysis has shown that by shifting to high-quality energy carriers and to energy-efficient conversion and end-use technologies it would be possible to satisfy basic human needs *and* to provide considerable further improvements in living standards without significantly increasing the rate of per capita primary energy use in developing countries above their present levels. Per capita final and primary energy requirements needed to provide the West European standard of living of the mid-1970s could be as low as 1.05 kW and 1.27 kW, respectively (Goldemberg et al., 1985; 1988). This level of primary energy use is just 20% more than the actual average for 1990. [In 1990 primary energy use per capita in developing countries was 0.78 tonnes of oil equivalent/yr = 33.4 GJ/year = 1.06 kW (WEC/IIASA, 1995).]

The prospect of achieving such a high living standard at an average final energy use rate of only "1 kW" per capita arises in part as a result of an assumed shift to modern energy carriers (e.g. the supply of final energy in this "1 kW scenario" includes 0.21 kW of electricity, compared to an actual average rate of 0.06 kW in 1990, and 0 kW of non-commercial energy, compared to an actual average rate of 0.30 kW in 1990). The introduction of modern energy carriers makes it possible to achieve much higher efficiencies with commercially available end-use technologies than is possible with traditional energy carriers. Opportunities for improving end-use efficiency are especially high for electricity, the energy carrier of the highest quality.

In 1992 industry accounted for 43% (134 EJ) of global energy use. Between 1971 and 1992, industrial energy use grew at a rate of 1.9%/year, slightly less than the world energy demand growth rate of 2.3%/year. This growth rate has slowed in recent years, falling to 0.3% average annual growth between 1988 and 1992, primarily because of the decline in the industrial output of the economies in transitions. Energy use in the industrial sector is dominated by OECD countries, which account for 45% of world industrial energy use. Developing countries and the economies in transition use 32% and 23% of world industrial energy, respectively.

Most of the future growth in the demand for the products of the basic materials processing industries will come from the developing world. Basic materials such as iron and steel, cement, and chemicals are key inputs to an economy during its infrastructure-building period. Most developing countries are already in this phase of their development or soon will be. Eventually, however, material demand will saturate at stages further along the development path, and there will be an uncoupling of materials demand and economic development (Williams et al., 1987; Bernardini and Galli, 1993). This is the situation for the already industrialised

countries, for which the infrastructure-building era is in the past, and the apparent consumption for most basic materials is stagnating or declining (see Figure 3.3).

Because of the expected rapid growth in the demand for basic materials in the developing countries, innovation aimed at generally improving basic materials and reducing their costs will be important in these countries. Energy purchases represent such a large fraction of production costs in these industries that historically new technologies for making basic materials have been more energy-efficient than the technologies they replaced, a trend that is likely to persist (Goldemberg et al, 1988). Figure 3.6 illustrates how a particular set of advanced technologies can reduce energy requirements while improving the economic and environmental attributes of steel making: with advanced smelt reduction and near net-shape casting technology primary energy requirements per tonne of steel would be only 1/5 as much as at present in China. Such advanced technologies can make it possible to improve substantially the well-being of the majority of the world's population without straining resource bases and with much lower environmental impacts than with existing technologies. Policies aimed at promoting innovation to improve technologi-

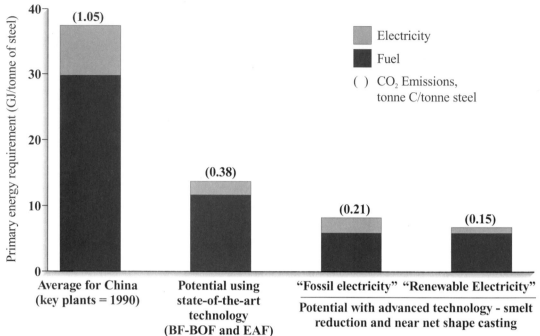

Figure 3.6: Energy Requirements for Producing Steel with Alternative Technologies, Compared to the Current Average Steel-making Technology in China

At present steel-making in China is very inefficient (the average amount of energy used to produce a tonne of steel is nearly twice that used in the United States) and highly polluting. By fine-tuning the most energy-efficient steel-making technology currently available it would be possible to reduce energy requirements for making a tonne of steel in China by more than 60 percent—an option that could be practically realized for new plants by 2000.

With advanced technology (specifically, smelt reduction and near net shape casting) that could become commercially available in the period 2010-2020, unit energy requirements could be reduced by more than 75 percent relative to present practice in China. Despite the dramatic energy efficiency gains made possible by this advanced technology and the associated reduced expenditures on energy, other factors would also be powerful drivers for seeking these improved technologies: (*i*) the process integration made possible by these advanced technologies would lead to lower unit capital costs and would facilitate air pollution control; (*ii*) favorable economics could be achieved at much smaller scales than is feasible with conventional technology, thus expanding market opportunities; (*iii*) the advanced technology makes it possible to use ordinary steam coal instead of the more costly coking coal; (*iv*) the advanced technology makes it possible to use powdered ores directly, without first having to incur the costs of pelletizing or sintering, as is necessary with conventional technology; and, as a "bonus," (*v*) major reductions in CO_2 emissions are possible with the advanced technology.

Here BF = blast furnace; BOF = basic oxygen furnace; EAF = electric arc furnace. It is assumed for the advanced technology cases that the mix of primary iron ore and recycled steel inputs is the same as for OECD countries in 1990. For the advanced technology cases the energy requirements for "fossil electricity" are primary energy inputs for power plants that are 40 percent efficient; the energy requirements for "renewable electricity" (e.g. hydroelectric power) are counted at 100 percent efficiency.

Source: (Worrell, 1995)

cal, economic and environmental performance in basic industries would also be effective in improving energy efficiency.

3.2.4 Commercial and Residential Buildings

Energy for the buildings sector supports a wide variety of energy services such as cooking, water heating, space heating and cooling, lighting, food refrigeration and freezing, and office equipment.

At the global level, energy use in commercial and residential buildings was 104 EJ (commercial fuels only) or 36% of world primary energy in 1992, with buildings in industrialised countries accounting for 58% of the total, followed by 22% in developing countries and 20% in the economies in transition (WEC, 1995a). Energy use in residential buildings is about twice that of commercial buildings world-wide. However, energy demand in commercial buildings has grown

72

about 50% more rapidly than demand in residential buildings for the past two decades. Between 1971 and 1992, the growth rate for energy use for buildings averaged 2.7%/year, somewhat faster than total global energy use. The average annual energy growth rates for buildings between 1971 and 1992 was much slower in OECD countries (1.9%/year) than in the economies in transition (3.0%/year) and developing countries (6.2%/year). Average declines of 3.8%/year were experienced between 1988 and 1992 in the economies in transition (WEC, 1995a).

Studies estimate technical potential savings up to the year 2000 of 27-48% for residential buildings in various industrialised countries. For commercial buildings, estimates vary from 23-55% in industrial countries and up to 50-60% in economies in transition and developing countries (Worrell et al, 1997; IPCC, 1996a).

Various demonstration projects show that even larger reductions in energy use are feasible. For example, the Advanced Consumer Technology Test (ACT²) programme of the Pacific Gas and Electric Company in California is exploring creative combinations of energy-saving technologies for new and existing residential and commercial buildings (Brohard, 1992; Eberling, 1992) and is demonstrating very high savings that are fully cost-effective (e.g. savings of over 60% relative to present normal construction practices for new residential buildings (Eberling, 1994)). Similar projects in Scandinavia and Germany show comparable results in regions with colder climates.

3.2.5 Transportation

Energy use in the transport sector is linked to complex environmental and societal problems. These problems include air pollution, lost productivity due to traffic congestion, death and disabilities due to accidents, water pollution caused by spilled petroleum, and global warming (Sperling and Shaheen, 1995; WEC, 1995b; MacKenzie and Walsh, 1990).

Between 1971 and 1993, transportation energy use grew at a rate faster than total world primary energy use, from 37 EJ/year to 63 EJ/year. Road transport, both by passenger cars and commercial trucks, accounts for most (73%) of total energy use, followed by air (12%), rail (6%), and other modes.

The rate of growth in consumption for developing countries was much more rapid during this period (4.7%/year) than in the industrialised countries and economies in transition (2.1%/yr and 2.0%/year respectively) (WEC, 1995b). Energy use for transport in developing countries has increased from 6 EJ/year in 1971 to 14 EJ/year in 1992 (WEC, 1995b). Rapid economic growth has been accompanied by increased demand for personal mobility and increased truck-freight activity. Still, industrialised countries dominate transport energy use, accounting for nearly two-thirds (39 EJ) of total world consumption in 1992 (WEC, 1995b).

Transport energy use can be reduced by: *i*) shifting to less energy-intensive transport modes to achieve the same or similar transport service; *ii*) changing the mix of transportation fuels; *iii*) improving the transportation infrastructure (roads, railways); and *iv*) improving the efficiency of transportation technology (e.g., improving automobile fuel economy).

3.2.5.1 Shifting to less energy-intensive transport modes

Significant reductions in energy use can be achieved by encouraging shifts to less energy-intensive modes of transport, since strong variations in intensities exist for various modes. For example, shifting commuting from passenger cars to buses can reduce the energy intensity of travel (in MJ/pass-km) by 60% to 75%, depending on world region, although increasing the load factor of cars via carpooling would have a similar effect (Worrell et al., 1997).

3.2.5.2 Changing the mix of fuels

Shifting fuels can sometimes lead to energy savings. For example, shifting from gasoline to diesel fuel can save energy in two ways. Largely because of their higher compression ratios, compression-ignition engines that use diesel fuel are more energy-efficient than spark-ignited engines that use gasoline; the production of diesel fuel from petroleum requires less energy use at the refinery than does the production of gasoline from petroleum. Energy requirements for refining of both fuels are increasing, however, as a result of new air quality regulations in some regions that require a shift to reformulated gasoline and reduced sulphur content of diesel fuel (Schafer and van Basshuysen, 1995).

When fuel cell cars become available, fuel choice will have a large effect on automotive fuel economy. Initially, fuel cell cars probably will be fuelled by gasoline or diesel fuel-fuels that can be provided via the existing fuel infrastructure. These fuels would be converted onboard the vehicle into a hydrogen-rich gas that the fuel cell can utilise (see Section 3.2.5.4); however, fuel cell cars having the same performance would be about 50% more energy-efficient if operated on compressed hydrogen rather than gasoline or diesel fuel (Kreutz et al., 1996).

3.2.5.3 Improving the transportation infrastructure

Planners are beginning to examine methods to make better use of existing infrastructures or to improve infrastructures so as to reduce energy demand by transport vehicles. Actions such as restricting certain road lanes to high occupancy vehicles can be effective in reducing fuel consumption both by increasing load factors and by reducing "stop-and-go" energy losses as a result of reduced highway congestion. "Smart vehicle" technology (also known as Intelligent Highway Vehicle Systems) also make it possible for drivers to reach their destinations on the least congested routes. Policies that encourage large shifts to public transit systems in densely populated areas such as Singapore, Curitiba and Manila have been shown to reduce overall energy demand (Sathaye et al., 1994; Birk and Bleviss, 1991). In Curitiba, Brazil, the city's bus line accounts for 70% of total transport and, partly as a result, Curitiba's per capita energy use is 30% lower than in otherwise comparable Brazilian cities (Birk and Zegras, 1993; Rabinovitch, 1995). This example shows that land use planning can be an important tool for encouraging shifts to mass transit.

3.2.5.4 Improving the efficiency of transportation technology

Energy-efficient technologies for internal combustion engine vehicles include a variety of measures that improve engine efficiency (e.g., variable valve control, lean burn, increased compression ratio), improve transmission efficiency (e.g., five-speed transmission, continuously variable trans-

mission, torque converter lockup), and reduce loads (e.g., streamlined designed to reduce aerodynamic drag, tires with lower rolling resistance, and use of lightweight materials to reduce vehicle weight).

The collective application of such measures to gasoline internal combustion engine cars in the United States could cost-effectively increase the energy efficiency of new US cars 64% by 2005, relative to the efficiency of new cars in 1994 (Decicco and Ross, 1994). A WEC study projects a "Green Drivers Scenario" (with policies that encourage fuel economy improvements) in which the number of cars increases from 470 million in 1992 to 752 million in 2020 worldwide and from 59 to 204 million in developing countries. Under this scenario, the average efficiency of all automobiles would be increased 77% relative to the average efficiency of all cars in 1992 and amount of fuel used by automobiles in 2020 world-wide would be nearly 30% less than in 1992 (WEC, 1995b). Large potential energy savings are also possible for trucks (WEC, 1995b; ASE, ACEEE, NRDC, UCS, 1992; Sachs et al., 1992).

There are also major opportunities for simultaneously improving the efficiency of fuel conversion and reducing air pollution problems by introducing electric-drive vehicles (Sperling, 1996). A common characteristic of these technologies is that they employ electric motors to drive the wheels and extract energy from the car's motion via "regenerative braking" when the car slows down.

To date, most of the effort has focused on battery-powered electric cars. These cars' high costs, relatively short ranges, and long recharging times limit their market potential (De Neufville et al., 1996). However, consumer surveys in the United States indicate that about half of all households owning more than one car could adapt their driving patterns to make use of a battery-powered electric car for a second car, whose environmental benefits and the convenience of home recharging might compensate for its limited range (Sperling, 1995; Sperling, 1996).

Battery-powered electric vehicles also represent an important option for dealing with urban air pollution in the developing world. For example, battery-powered electric buses and battery-assisted bicycles are being introduced in Beijing. In Bangkok, prototype battery-powered electric buses will be introduced by 1998 (Ski Electric, 1996), and prototypes of battery-powered "tuk-tuks" (three-wheeled vehicles used as taxis and for urban cargo hauling) are being tested as prospective alternatives to conventional LPG-fuelled tuk-tuks (Walker and Kishan, 1996).

An electric-drive option offering much wider market potential is a hybrid electric drive vehicle that couples a small internal combustion engine plus electric generator (Ross and Wu, 1995; Ross et al., 1996; Colombo and Farinelli, 1994) as a "baseload electric power" device to a small battery, ultracapacitor, or flywheel, as a "peaking power" device. In automotive applications, at least a two-fold gain in energy efficiency is feasible via the use of such hybrids. In late 1996, a Japanese auto maker announced that it would soon begin manufacturing such hybrid vehicles. These vehicles would realise a gasoline consumption rate of 3.4 liters/100 km (70 miles per gallon).

Fuel cells are also attractive options for electric drive vehicles. Current interest is focused on the proton exchange membrane fuel cell (PEMFC) (Williams, 1993; Williams, 1994; Mark et al., 1994). In mass production, cars powered by PEMFCs would have much lower costs and much longer ranges between refuelling than battery-powered electric cars (Kircher et al., 1994; Ogden et al., 1994). The PEMFC can potentially compete with the petroleum-fuelled internal combustion engine in automotive applications, while providing transport services at a two-to-three-fold higher energy efficiency and emitting zero or near-zero local air pollution without the use of emission control technology. Fuel cell cars can be fuelled with hydrogen that might be stored onboard as a compressed gas or with a liquid fuel (e.g., gasoline, diesel fuel, methanol, ethanol) that would be converted onboard the car into a hydrogen-rich gas that the fuel cell can use as fuel.

The technology for PEMFC motor vehicles is advancing rapidly. Since the autumn of 1995, the cities of Chicago and Vancouver each purchased three hydrogen PEMFC buses. The Canadian PEMFC developer plans to offer hydrogen fuel cell buses commercially in 1998 (Prater, 1994). This fuel cell developer is in a joint venture with a major German car manufacturer to develop PEMFCs

for cars. The car manufacturer introduced a proof-of-concept hydrogen PEMFC van in 1994 (the NECAR I). In 1996 this company introduced a prototype passenger van (the NECAR II) and announced that it could start selling fuel cell-equipped cars as early as 2006. The fuel cell used in the NECAR II meets or exceeds the power density targets specified for fuel cell cars by United States auto makers. In late 1996, a Japanese auto maker also unveiled a prototype hydrogen fuel cell car. In early 1997, a major US auto maker announced that it is developing fuel cell cars that would initially be fuelled via the existing liquid hydrocarbon fuel infrastructure (e.g., with gasoline). The company hopes to have a proof-of-concept vehicle within two years, to have commercial prototypes by 2005, and to have full commercialisation of the technology by 2015.

3.2.6 Agriculture

In agriculture, energy is used directly (on-farm) and indirectly (for fertilisers, pesticides). Direct agricultural energy use accounted for 2.8% of total world energy consumption in 1990 (Worrell et al., 1997), but the percentage was much higher in the developing countries (4.9%) than in the industrialised countries (1.5%), with an intermediate share (3.5%) for the economies in transition. The declining share of energy used in agriculture with development level is compensated for, at least in part, by additional energy consumed in post-farm food processing. Pimentel and Hall (1984) estimate that only 35% of the total commercial energy consumed in the US food production system is consumed at the farm level; the rest is for food processing, packaging, storage, transport and preparation.

Growth in energy use, 1980-1992, was slower in industrialised countries (averaging 2.1%/year) than in developing countries (4.5%/year). Energy consumption in economies in transition decreased 7.0%/year between 1990 and 1992 as a result of a sharply decreasing agricultural production (Worrell et al., 1997).

Tractors are by far the greatest consumers of fuel in field operations, accounting for 90-95% of the fuel used (Bowers, 1992). On a global basis, approximately 15% of cropland is irrigated and produces about 30% of the world's food (Sloggett, 1992). Energy requirements for irrigation are especially high in rice production. Other direct on-farm commercial energy inputs include direct energy for drying, animal production, and horticulture (e.g., heating, cooling, ventilation and lighting).

Potential energy savings can be found through changes in the design and use of tractors, reduced tillage, and improvements in irrigation, drying, livestock production and horticulture. Renewable energy sources can also contribute to savings in fossil energy used in agriculture. Examples are solar and wind energy and energy from biomass residues or products from energy cropping for heat and power production, wind as a direct source for irrigation and solar energy as a direct source for drying.

3.2.7 Materials Efficiency Improvement

Historically, industrial production has been an open system, transforming primary resources into products that are eventually discarded after use by society. This system is unsustainable because it consumes non-regenerative resources and produces large quantities of waste. The environmental problems that occur at each step in industrial production and consumption processes have led to a re-examination of the way the economy works via the new field of "industrial ecology" (Socolow et al., 1994; Ayres and Simonis, 1994). Industrial ecology seeks to identify practices and policies that will steer the economic system in sustainable directions (Frosch, 1994). Important concerns of industrial ecology are to understand better the opportunities for increasing the efficiency of materials use and for reducing practices that involve major dissipative (non-recoverable) uses of materials.

Material efficiency improvement is defined as reducing the amount of (primary) material needed to fulfil a specific function or service. Improving material efficiency will reduce energy use, because it reduces the need for (primary) materials in manufacturing products or performing services. Particular emphasis should be given to the relatively small number of basic materials, the production of which accounts for over 50% of total industrial energy use.

Reducing material inputs into production can be achieved through more efficient use of materials and closing material chains. Strategies that can be used to improve material efficiency include: *i*) good housekeeping (e.g., reduction in material losses in existing production processes); *ii*) material-efficient product design (e.g., redesign to reduce the amount of material needed to manufacture a functional unit of the product, to increase its lifetime, or to improve its reparability); *iii*) material substitution (e.g., use of a material with a higher material efficiency); *iv*) product reuse (i.e., via redesign of a product to permit renewed use without changing the physical appearance of the product); *v*) material recycling (i.e., material reuse through the production of secondary materials by mechanical, chemical, or other means); and *vi)* quality cascading (i.e., the use of secondary materials for functions that have lower quality demands). Reducing material intensity may also have effects on other aspects of the material chain (e.g., via reduced energy requirements in transport because less materials have to be moved).

Examples using nitrogen fertiliser, cement, steel, and paper illustrate what has been accomplished in production as well as prospective future gains. Nitrogen fertiliser is an energy-intensive product whose use is inherently dissipative, so that closing of the material lifecycle chain is impossible. Yet there are a wide variety of opportunities for improving the material efficiency (Worrell et al., 1995b; Helsel, 1992). A study for The Netherlands has shown that in the short-term nitrogen fertiliser use could be reduced cost-effectively (e.g. by reducing losses due to leaching and evaporation) nearly 40% without yield losses (Worrell et al., 1995c). Over the longer term, fertiliser requirements could be reduced even more via the development of more nitrogen-efficient crops (WRR, 1992).

More effective management of the cement production cycle would include measures aimed at improving cement properties (e.g., high-strength cements), developing less material-intensive construction techniques, and increasing use of blended cements (e.g., use of alternative pozzolanic materials such as blast furnace slags and fly-ash) (Worrell et al., 1995a). Reducing clinker requirements for cement production would also decrease the emission of mineral CO_2 from burning limestone for cement manufacture, which accounts for over 1% of global CO_2 emissions.

Recycling of scrap is an integral part of steel production. Currently 40% of global crude steel is produced from scrap (IISA, 1992). The development of new high-strength steels has led to reduction of the amount of steel required for a function. The average iron content of cars in the United States decreased by 31% and the total car weight by 16% between 1975 and 1985 (Williams et al., 1987). This trend is expected to continue (Worrell et al., 1997).

Produced in over 80 countries, paper is a commodity used for various purposes in many different qualities and grades. The waste paper recovery rate has been increasing world-wide; it was estimated at 38% in 1992, with the highest rates in Austria (71%) and The Netherlands (63%) (Byström and Lönnstedt, 1995). In The Netherlands the so-called *Packaging Covenant* aims at reducing the amount of packaging materials (not only paper) used in 2000 to a level 10% below use in 1986. One German study (Greenpeace, 1991) estimated a possible reduction of paper consumption up to 50% for various paper products in Germany. Examples from industry (IIED, 1995) show that reductions of 20-50% of packaging materials are feasible within short periods. Improved office practice (like double-sided copying) at AT&T in the United States led to a 10-15% reduction in paper consumption and considerable cost savings (IIED, 1995).

Recycling reduces energy requirements for materials production. For example, in Japan in 1973, the energy required to make a tonne of crude steel from scrap in an electric arc furnace was 62% less than the energy required to make iron and steel from ore using a blast furnace and a basic oxygen furnace, when electricity is counted as the fossil fuel required to produce it; for hydroelectricity counted instead as the energy content of the electricity, the energy requirements using scrap would instead be 79% less (Eketorp, 1987). In industrialised countries, where steel is typically made with about a 50/50 mix of scrap and ore, the percentage savings associated with increased use of scrap would be less relative to average energy inputs for iron- and steel-making. The percentage savings would be even less if the energy requirements for making finished steel products rather than raw steel are taken into account. For an iron- and steel-making system in the United States

in 1983, making a tonne of finished steel from scrap in an electric arc furnace would have required 32% less energy than that required to make an average tonne of steel in that year through conventional techniques (Ross, 1987). For developing countries, where demand for steel is growing rapidly and much less scrap is available, the percentage savings from recycling could be considerably higher. Energy savings associated with recycling of other materials range from 33% for paper to 95% for aluminium (Elliott, 1994).

Ideally, industrial practices should be oriented toward ensuring management of full material chains, that takes into account environmental, energy, and other concerns at each point in the product cycle (Christiansen et al, 1995; OTA, 1992; van Weenen, 1995). Currently, policies in most countries are *not* designed to do this. Instead, to the extent that materials management policies have been enacted, they are typically limited to single aspects of the product lifecycle (e.g., mining or waste management). Providing consumers with information to encourage demand for environmentally benign products (e.g., via eco-labelling) is a step towards more sustainable production that has been taken in some countries. Some governmental and corporate procurement programs have also established "market-pull" instruments, although these are not yet used widely. There are, however, legislative proposals in several countries aimed at increasing the producer's responsibility for managing the total lifecycle of the product—proposals requiring involvement of producers in waste management and recycling activities and encourage design and development of products compatible with sustainable development objectives.

3.3 Supply Side: Renewables and Clean Fossil Fuel Technologies

Energy supply technologies that improve energy efficiency, reduce pollutant emissions, and reduce emissions of greenhouse gases can make significant contributions to sustainable development. To illustrate the possibilities, brief descriptions are provided of the significance of the growing role of natural gas in the global energy economy as well as some promising advances in fossil and renewable energy technologies for electric power generation, alternative electric-drive technologies for motor vehicles, and use of alternative fuels for transportation. Also addressed is the potential for expanding roles for fossil fuels in a greenhouse-constrained world via fuel decarbonization and storage of the separated CO_2. The technologies discussed are illustrative of the possibilities; no attempt is made to provide a comprehensive review.

3.3.1 The Growing Role of Natural Gas in the Global Energy Economy

Between 1983 and 1992 the contribution of natural gas to the global energy economy increased from 19% to 22%, while the share of oil declined from 43% to 40%, and that for coal fell from 27% to 25% (EIA, 1994). Moreover, all major projections of future global energy envision continuing greater roles for natural gas in the decades immediately ahead (IPCC, 1992; IPCC, 1996b; Kassler, 1994; WEC, 1993; WEC/IIASA, 1995).

A global shift to natural gas in the oil/natural gas mix will take place because ultimately recoverable conventional natural gas resources are probably at least as large as conventional oil resources (Masters et al., 1994), and presently natural gas is consumed at only about half the rate for oil. The low cost of natural gas in many parts of the world will help drive this shift. However, difficulties in raising capital for the large infrastructure investments needed for natural gas energy systems (e.g. long-distance transmission lines and local distribution networks) could slow a shift to natural gas in the developing world.

To the extent that the expanding role of natural gas is at the expense of coal and oil, the environment will benefit, since natural gas is the cleanest of the fossil fuels. The ongoing shift to natural gas also will lead to reduced greenhouse gas emissions, since natural gas has the lowest specific CO_2 emission rate of all fossil fuels at ~14 kg C/GJ, compared to ~20 kg C/GJ for oil and ~25 kg C/GJ for coal. Moreover, natural gas can, in general, be used more efficiently than coal. While methane is a strong greenhouse gas and there are significant methane emissions from coal mining and natural gas venting, as well as leakage from pipelines and distribution systems, approaches exist to reduce these emissions (IPCC, 1996b).

3.3.2 Technologies for Electric Power Generation and Combined Heat and Power

In fuel-based electric power generation, there are good prospects for routinely achieving efficiencies of 60-70% or more in the longer term, compared to the present 30% world average. Large efficiency gains can also be achieved by replacing the separate production of heat and power with combined heat and power (CHP) technologies. Moreover, rapid progress is being made in the use of renewable energy in power generation.

3.3.2.1 Gas turbine/steam turbine combined cycles

The natural gas-fired gas turbine/steam turbine combined cycle has become the thermal power technology of choice in regions having ready access to natural gas, because of its low unit capital cost, high thermodynamic efficiency, and low pollutant emissions. Because of increasingly competitive conditions in the electric power industry, turnkey combined cycle plant costs have fallen sharply (see Section 4.2.6.1) (Stoll and Todd, 1996).

Top efficiencies (HHV basis) of new units are in the range 50-52% (Farmer, 1995), up from about 46% in 1988 (Farmer, 1989). Under the United States Department of Energy's Advanced Turbine Systems Programme, combined cycles with efficiencies on natural gas are expected to reach 56% (62% on a LHV basis) by 2000 (Williams and Zeh, 1995). These advanced systems will involve combustors that premix fuel and air and thereby achieve low NO_x emission levels (< 10 ppmvd at 15% O_2) without the need for stack-gas emission controls (Corman, 1996). Moreover, their CO_2 emission rate (in grams of carbon per kWh) would be 36% of the rate for today's 35%-efficient coal steam-electric plants.

3.3.2.2 Coal integrated gasifier/combined cycles

Since the feasibility of firing combined cycle power plants with coal via the use of closely coupled coal gasifiers was demonstrated in the 94 MW$_e$ Coolwater Project in Southern California in 1984-1989, there has been much progress in commercializing the coal integrated gasifier/combined cycle (CIG/CC).

Local air pollutant emission levels for

CIG/CC plants can cost effectively be made as low as those from natural gas combined cycle plants—far lower than for conventional steam-electric plants equipped with stack gas emission controls. Solid waste disposal advantages are also significant. Most direct coal combustion processes recover sulphur from flue gases as a nonmarketable wet scrubber sludge or as a dry spent sulphur sorbent (the by-product gypsum can be marketed); for such systems the solid waste disposal volumes are more difficult to handle, market, and dispose of, and the volumes that must be managed are 2 to 3 times as large as for CIG/CC systems, which recover elemental sulphur as a marketable by product (SFA Pacific, 1993).

In 1994 a 41%-efficient 250 MW$_e$ CIG/CC plant began operation in The Netherlands and in late 1995, a 262 MW$_e$ CIG/CC plant began operating in the United States in Indiana. Several other CIG/CC plants are expected to be operational soon in various parts of the world (Stambler, 1996). With advanced gas turbines, it is expected that CIG/CC efficiencies will be able to reach 50% (Stambler, 1996; Lamarre, 1994).

The CO_2 emission rate for 50%-efficient CIG/CC power plant would be about 70% of that for a 35%-efficient coal steam-electric plant but about twice the rate for a natural gas combined cycle power plant using essentially the same gas turbine technology.

While present-day CIG/CC plants are not yet competitive in strictly economic terms with conventional coal steam-electric plants with flue gas desulphurization, improvements in gas turbine technology expected by the year 2000 are projected to make CIG/CC plants fully competitive in many circumstances (Stoll and Todd, 1996).

3.3.2.3 Fuel cells for stationary power and combined heat and power

The fuel cell is an "electrochemical device" that converts fuel directly into electricity without first burning it to produce heat. Fuel cells were first used for practical applications as a source of onboard electric power in spacecraft in the 1960s. They are now beginning to enter electric generation markets on earth, where they offer strong inherent advantages in electricity markets characterised by increasing competition and environmental regulations.

Fuel cells offer high thermodynamic efficiency, low maintenance, quiet operation, and zero or very low air pollutant emissions without exhaust-gas control technologies. Fuel cells could prove to be economically viable even in small-scale (100 kW$_e$ or less) CHP applications. Their properties make it possible to site fuel cell power systems in small, unobtrusive generating facilities close to end users. Such siting of fuel cells as "distributed power sources" makes CHP designs economically attractive and offers the potential of reducing capital outlays for electricity transmission and distribution equipment (Hoff et al., 1995).

Low-temperature phosphoric acid and proton exchange membrane fuel cells (PAFCs and PEMFCs) are well suited for CHP applications in commercial and residential buildings, providing domestic hot water and space heating and cooling (Little, 1995; Dunnison and Wilson, 1994). High-temperature direct carbonate and solid oxide fuel cells (DCFCs and SOFCs) are well suited for industrial CHP applications requiring high-quality process heat.

The PAFC, developed largely in the United States and Japan, is the only commercial fuel cell technology. Several hundred PAFC power plants (most of which are 200 kW$_e$ units supplied with natural gas) are operating around the world. The significant operating experience accumulated to date with the PAFC has demonstrated that fuel cell power plants can be made to operate very reliably. Costs are high for PAFC fuel cells, however, and whether costs can be reduced enough with volume production to make the PAFC widely competitive is uncertain.

The PEMFC, offering the potential for low cost and long life, has been demonstrated at a scale of 35 kW$_e$ in a stationary grid-connected power plant fuelled with by-product hydrogen from a nearby chlor-alkali plant in British Columbia, Canada. The manufacturer, in partnership with a major international electricity supplier, plans to offer commercial units supplied with natural gas at a scale of 250 kW$_e$ for CHP applications in 1998.

The DCFC is also approaching commercial status. A 2 MW$_e$, 45%-efficient (50%-efficient, LHV basis) demonstration plant supplied with natural gas began operation in the spring of 1996 in California. Air pollutant emissions are expected to be less than one-tenth of the most stringent allowable limits for a power plant. The DCFC improves on the PAFC in that the processor for converting the fuel to hydrogen is integrated into the fuel cell (it is a separate stage for the PAFC), thereby increasing efficiency, simplifying operation, and increasing reliability. If the demonstration is a success, it will be followed by commercial units at a scale of 3 MW$_e$ as early as 1999 (EPRI, 1995).

The SOFC is still another advanced fuel cell that offers the potential for low cost (Bakker et al., 1996); one version will be demonstrated, 1997-98, at a scale of 100 kW$_e$ at an auxiliary district heating plant at the Rivierweg in Westervoort, The Netherlands (Veyo and Lundberg, 1996).

Hybrid power systems in which high-temperature fuel cells (DCFCs and SOFCs) are combined with gas turbines offer the prospects of still further increases in energy efficiency relative to what can be achieved with either fuel cells or gas turbines deployed separately, along with reductions in unit capital cost relative to what can be realised with fuel cells alone. Modelling carried out at the Electric Power Research Institute indicates that a 56%-efficient (62% efficient, LHV basis), natural gas-fuelled SOFC combined with a regenerative gas turbine could lead to a system efficiency of 71% (79%, LHV basis) (Bakker et al., 1996).

3.3.2.4 Hydroelectric power

Hydroelectric power is a well established renewable electricity supply, providing 2,100 TWh, nearly 20% of the global electricity generation supply (11,300 TWh/year) in 1990. The theoretical potential, determined by annual water runoff (47,000 km^3), is 36,000 to 44,000 TWh/year world-wide. The estimated technically usable potential is 14,000 TWh/year, while the estimated long-term economic potential is 6,000 to 9,000 TWh/year (Moreira and Poole, 1993).

Because of growing environmental and social concerns, some of the economic potential for hydroelectric development might not be fully realised, but hydroelectric power will continue to be developed wherever these concerns can be dealt with effectively.

However, even in regions where there are no new hydroelectric projects, there can

be significant new roles for hydroelectric power in "firming up" electricity supplies from intermittent renewable supplies (wind, photovoltaic, and solar thermal-electric). Adding more turbine capacity at existing hydroelectric sites is a low-cost electricity storage option that would often make it possible for intermittent renewable supplies to meet large fractions of electric utilities' loads cost-effectively (Johansson et al., 1993).

3.3.2.5 Wind power

Largely as a result of government incentives provided to stimulate its development, a global wind power industry was launched in the early 1980s. The cost of electricity from new wind farms has fallen sharply since the mid-1980s; in areas of good wind resources in the United States it is now about the same as the cost of electricity from new coal plants (see Figure 3.7).

At the end of 1993, the global installed capacity of high-efficiency wind turbines was 3,100 MW$_e$, of which about 1,700 MW$_e$ was in the Americas and 1,200 MW$_e$ in Europe. Over 1,100 MW$_e$ of new capacity was added in 1995 (780 MW$_e$ in Europe, primarily in Germany and 380 MW$_e$ in Asia, concentrated in India). This brought total world-wide installed capacity at the end of 1995 to about 4,800 MW$_e$. Growth has been especially strong in India, where a modern wind energy programme was launched in 1989, and installed capacity reached 650 MW$_e$ by April 1996. China has especially good wind energy resources. While many of these resources are located in areas remote from electricity demand centres, electricity from large wind farms in these remote regions could be brought to the major electricity markets via the use of long-distance transmission lines—at costs potentially competitive with coal electricity in northern China (Lew et al., 1996).

The gross global wind-electric potential is 500,000 TWh/year. After subtracting from this gross potential the generation potential for cities, forests, and unreachable mountain areas, and taking into account a wide range of social, environmental, and land use constraints (including aesthetic concerns about visual impacts) Grubb and Meyer (1993) estimate that the practical global wind-electric potential is 53,000 TWh/year. The World Energy Council has estimated the practical potential to be 20,000 TWh/year (WEC, 1994).

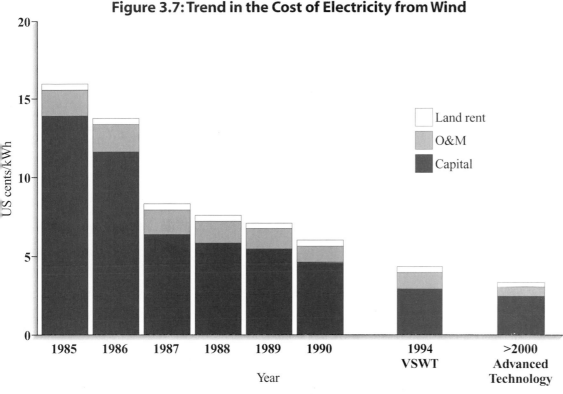

Figure 3.7: Trend in the Cost of Electricity from Wind

Wind power costs for the period 1985-1900 are based on the actual experience with wind farms in California. The cost shown for 1994 is for a new variable-speed wind turbine (VSWT) that went into commercial service in 1994; this cost is about the same as for electricity from a new coal steam-electric plant. For the period beyond 2000, the cost reflects expectations about improvements that could be realized over the next decade.

Source: (Johansson et al., 1993)

3.3.2.6 Biomass power

The electrical loads of rural villages of the developing world are typically in the range 5–200 kW_e. Producer gas-engine generator sets based on the use of biomass gasifiers coupled to small reciprocating engines are well-matched to these loads (Ravindranath, 1993; Ravindranath and Hall, 1995). Until recently, most biomass-producer gas-engine projects failed, largely because of excessive tar formation in the gasifier and maintenance problems posed by tars. However, these problems have been solved. Field demonstrations have been carried out successfully and the technology is ready for commercial applications (Mukunda et al., 1993; 1994). These generators often use diesel fuel, but biomass-derived producer gas could replace 75–95% of this diesel fuel. The technology makes it possible to serve small rural loads (such as water pumping) at costs that are lower than would be possible by providing such customers with electricity from

centralised power plants by extending to them distribution lines that would be used at only a modest fraction of their capacity most of the time.

In the United States, Scandinavia, and some European and developing countries, biomass also is used for steam turbine-based CHP in the forest-product and agricultural industries at scales of tens of megawatts. In these activities the biomass mainly consist of residues of the primary products of these industries. There is also a growing trend to co-firing coal-fired power plants with supplemental biomass inputs. In developing countries, there is a large scope for efficiency improvements in the use of biomass for energy in industry and growing interest in introducing modern steam-turbine CHP technology (e.g., in the cane sugar industry).

An advanced technology that could make it possible for electricity derived from plantation biomass (as well from less-costly biomass residues) to compete with coal in power generation is the biomass integrated gasifier/

81

Figure 3.8: Learning Curve for Biomass-Integrated Gasifier/ Combined Cycle Technology

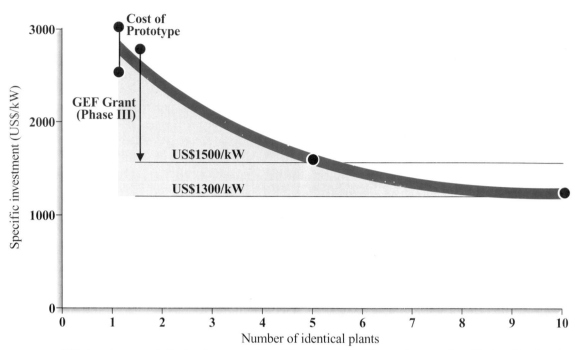

This learning curve indicates the expected trend in unit costs for biomass integrated gasifier/combined cycle (BIG/CC) technology based on a 25,000 kW_e demonstration plant that is scheduled to commence operation in the late 1990s in the northeast of Brazil. Shell researchers (Elliott and Booth, 1993) expect that the costs for the first 10 units will follow a learning curve characterized by an 80 percent progress ratio (*i.e.*, the installed cost is expected to decline 20 percent for each cumulative doubling of production), based on the expectations that: (*i*) most plant assembly would take place in the factory; (*ii*) there would be minimal site preparation and foundation requirements; (*iii*) onsite construction would consist mainly of integration of standard factory-built modules; and (*iv)* there would be short time lapses between ground breaking and plant start-up.

For modular technologies like this, the "cost of learning" is far less than for large-scale fossil or nuclear technologies. Note that:

Cost of BIG/CC learning = (shaded area)*(25,000 kW_e) = US$0.12 billion.

This can be compared to the cost of learning for large-scale technologies, e.g. for an advanced nuclear fission technology, such as a "passively safe" design for which the size target for commercial plants is 600,000 kW_e. If this technology were to follow exactly the same learning curve for unit capital cost, then:

Cost of learning at large scale = (shaded area)*(600,000 kW_e) = US$2.9 billion.

Also, it is much more difficult to obtain the benefits of "learning-by-doing" with large-scale technologies. Fisher (1974) pointed out that in building a large power plant instead of a small one, much of the construction that would have been carried out in the factory is shifted to the field, where labor costs are much higher. Moreover, the construction of a large plant takes many years, so that it is usually not possible to cut costs via the replication of a large number of identical units by the same construction team (learning-by-doing).

combined cycle (BIG/CC). Though BIG/CC technology is not as advanced as CIG/CC technology, catch-up might not take long, because: *i*) much of what has been learned in developing the CIG/CC is readily transferable to BIG/CC technology; *ii*) biomass is in some ways a more promising feedstock than coal for gasification (e.g., it contains very little sulphur and is much more reactive than coal); and *iii*) BIG/CC would facilitate rural elec-

trification and rural industrialisation and thereby promote rural development (a potentially powerful market driver). Moreover, the modest scales of BIG/CC power plants relative to conventional fossil fuel and nuclear plants facilitate cost-cutting as a result of "learning-by-doing" (see Figure 3.8). BIG/CC demonstration projects are underway in Brazil, Denmark, Finland, Italy, The Netherlands, Sweden, the United Kingdom, and the United

States (Williams and Larson, 1996). The largest is a 30 MW$_e$ unit in Brazil that will be fuelled by wood chips from an existing eucalyptus plantation; this project is being supported by the Global Environment Facility (Elliott and Booth, 1993).

Biomass-integrated gasifier/fuel cell (BIG/FC) systems involving DCFCs or SOFCs prospectively would make the realisation of high efficiencies practical at very modest scales (Kartha et al., 1997). These technologies would be especially well-suited for industrial CHP applications requiring high-temperature process heat. For power- only applications, hybrid BIG/FC/GT systems [in which SOFCs (or DCFCs) are combined with regenerative gas turbine bottoming cycles in systems fuelled by simple, unpressurised air-blown biomass gasifiers (the same kinds of gasifiers currently used in producer gas-engine generator sets)] offer the potential for achieving biomass-to-electricity conversion efficiencies in excess of 40% (HHV basis)—more than twice the efficiency of producer gas-engine generator sets—and prospectively cost-competitive

power at power plant scales of hundreds of kilowatts (Kartha et al., 1997). Such technology would have wide applications in rural areas in support of rural income generation and rural industrialisation.

3.3.2.7 Photovoltaic power

Direct production of electricity from solar energy via photovoltaic (PV) conversion can be accomplished either with flat-plate or concentrating collectors. With flat-plate collectors, PV conversion can be carried out even in areas with frequent cloudiness, and generation can be carried out close to users; for example, on rooftops and building facades. The area required for collectors is modest—about 20 m^2 per capita is adequate to provide (where the insolation is the global average) electricity at the current average generation rate in Europe. PV conversion with concentrating collectors is practical only in areas of high insolation (low cloudiness), but the potential there is large, because land areas required for collectors are modest.

World-wide sales of PV modules have increased from 47 peak megawatts/year (47

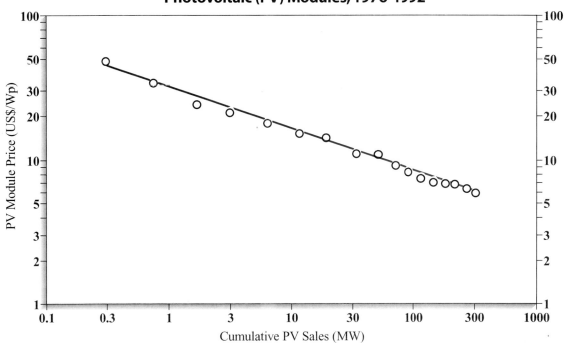

Figure 3.9: Log-Log Plot of the Selling Price of Photovoltaic (PV) Modules, 1976-1992

In the period 1976-1992, the world-average PV module selling price declined 18.4% for each cumulative doubling of PV module production.

Module sales data and prices are from Strategies Unlimited, Mountain View, CA, September 1993. Strategies Unlimited used the Consumer Price Index to convert current prices into 1992 prices.

Figure 3.10:
Stabilized Efficiencies of Small-Area Polycrystalline Thin-Film Photovoltaic (PV) Cells Made from Copper Indium Diselinide (CIS) and Cadmium Telluride (CdTe)

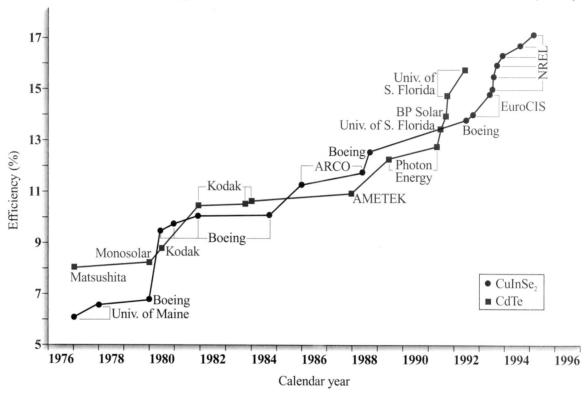

Thinfilm PV devices offer the potential for realizing very low unit capital costs at moderate efficiencies. (Conventional crystalline PV devices have the potential for realizing higher efficiencies but at higher unit capital costs.) The potential for low unit capital cost arises because the active layers of the cells are of the order of one micron thick and thus require very little material. (Note that a typical human hair is about 90-100 microns thick.) Thus, the materials cost is dominated by the costs for glass for encapsulation, wires, etc.

The efficiencies shown in this figure are for laboratory cells (areas ~ 1 cm^2). Further development is needed in order to realize the thin-film PV goal of 15% efficiency for large modules (~ 1 m^2 or more per module) and to engineer the processes for mass-producing such devices. It is expected that, with an aggressive R&D effort, this could be realized by 2010.

These data, from Ken Zweibel, Manager of the Thin-Film Project, National Renewable Energy Laboratory (NREL), are based on both NREL measurements and measurements reported in the literature.

MW$_p$/yr) in 1990 to 91 MW$_p$/year in 1996 (Curry, 1997). Between the mid-1970s and the present, the price of PV modules fell 10-fold, as the technology moved along its experience curve, with the cumulative volume of production increasing about 1000-fold (see Figure 3.9). Historically, most PV applications have been for a variety of consumer-electronic-product and other niche markets, but both stand-alone and grid-connected electric-power applications are becoming increasingly important aspects of PV technology.

There has been considerable experience over the last decade with PV technology deployed in small-scale, stand-alone power applications, remote from utility grids in many parts of the world—largely for provi-

sion of domestic lighting, refrigeration, and for educational purposes. Early experiences with PV technology in such applications yielded mixed results. Some projects were plagued by inadequate project design and installation procedures as well as by excessive costs. Moreover, some projects that were technically successful sometimes failed because of inadequate attention to local support structures (Cowan, 1990). However, a great deal has been learned from both the successes and failures of earlier projects. Today, well-designed PV systems and their infrastructures are able to provide electrical services cost-effectively to rural users while avoiding the economic inefficiencies associated with the alternative of bringing centralised power supplies to these customers by extending distribution lines that typically would be grossly under-utilised (Acker, 1996; Cabraal and Cosgrove-Davies; Schaeffer, 1996).

PV systems also are being installed in grid-connected applications sited at or near customers' premises. Electricity produced in such configurations is worth more to the utility than central-station power whenever the electrical output is highly correlated with the utility peak demand, largely because such siting makes it possible to defer transmission/distribution investments (Shugar, 1990; Hoff et al., 1995). In various industrialised, countries PV systems are being constructed as integral components of building skins. Integrating the systems into the building shells eliminates costs for structural elements or land; if the solar system serves as building skin as well as a collector, additional savings are possible.

Germany has already installed over 2,250 PV systems on homes, with a capacity totalling 6 MW_p (SEIA, 1996). The Netherlands has set a goal of installing 250 MW_p of building-integrated systems by 2010 and 1500 MW_p by 2020 (Horst, 1996). Japan's Ministry of International Trade and Industry is providing support for the implementation of 10,000 rooftop PV systems of unit capacity 3-4 kW_e in 1997. Japan has established an objective of installing 4,600 MW_p by 2010 (Cowley, 1996). And in the Sacramento Municipal Utility District in California, PV capacity is expected to increase from 1.8 MW_p in 1996 to about 12 MW_p over the next five years (Strong, 1996). The majority of this added capacity is expected to be in the form of building-integrated applications.

Present PV prices are still far too high for using PV in central-station power plants. This situation is changing rapidly, however, as the technology improves. Especially notable are the favourable economic prospects for various flat-plate thin-film PV technologies [such as amorphous silicon, which is commercially available, and for copper indium diselenide and cadmium teluride, which are not yet commercial but are improving rapidly (as illustrated in Figure 3.10)]. Various tracking, concentrating PV technologies, which are based on the use of the more energy-efficient, but more costly,

crystalline and polycrystalline solar cells, also have good prospects (IPCC, 1996b; STAP/GEF,1996).

An American company marketing amorphous silicon PV technology is building a 4 MW_e PV power plant in Hawaii, for an announced total installed cost of $2,000/$kW_e$ [for comparison, the previous least-costly electric utility grid-connected PV installation in the United States cost $7,800/$kW_e$ (Curry, 1996a)]. That company also has negotiated a power purchase contract at a low PV electricity price with the Rajasthan State Electricity Board in India for the output of a 50 MW_e PV plant that will be built at Jaisalmer. Construction will begin in 1997. It is expected that all the capacity will be installed by 2001. This same company has proposed to build a 100 MW_e PV power plant in Nevada, subject to the availability of tax-free industrial development bonds for financing the project and a government guarantee of an electricity price of 5.5 cents/kWh for the first year of operation, inflated 3% per year over the life of the facility. The proposal has been accepted, although the details of the power purchase agreement are yet to be worked out (Curry, 1996b).

3.3.2.8 Solar thermal-electric power

High-temperature solar thermal-electric technologies use mirrors or lenses to concentrate the sun's rays onto a receiver, where the solar heat is transferred to a working fluid that drives a conventional electric power-conversion system. Three major solar collector/receiver designs have been developed (see Figure 3.11): *i*) the parabolic trough system, which concentrates solar energy onto a receiver pipe located along the line focus of a parabolic mirror trough collector; *ii*) a central-receiver system, which uses sun-tracking mirrors called heliostats to reflect solar energy onto a receiver located on top of a tower; and *iii*) a parabolic-dish system, which uses a tracking parabolic dish reflector to concentrate sunlight onto a receiver mounted at the focal point of the dish. Applications for solar thermal-electric systems range from central-station power plants to modular, remote power systems.

Between 1984 and 1991 nine parabolic trough solar thermal-electric plants with a total installed capacity of 354 MW_e were built in southern California. Although it was able to

Figure 3.11:
Alternative High-Temperature
Solar Thermal Technologies

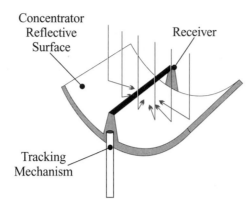

Concentrator Reflective Surface

Receiver

Tracking Mechanism

a) Parabolic trough

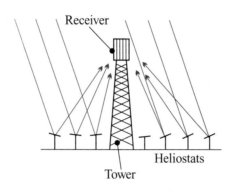

Receiver

Heliostats

Tower

b) Central receiver

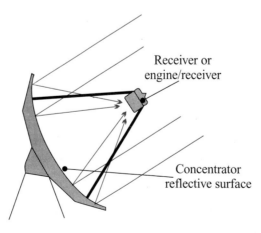

Receiver or engine/receiver

Concentrator reflective surface

c) Parabolic dish

Receiver temperatures up to 400° C are feasible with the parabolic trough concept. With the heliostat/ central receiver concept, receiver temperatures up to 1500° C can be realized. Parabolic dish receivers can achieve temperatures in excess of 1500° C.

Source: (STAP/GEF, 1996)

reduce the installed cost for its technology from US\$6,000/kW$_e$ to US\$3,000/kW$_e$ over this period, the company that built these plants went bankrupt in 1991, when government incentives for renewable energy technologies suddenly were withdrawn. Today the plants are operating reliably under new management.

An improved version of this technology currently is being developed, and projects are being planned in several developing countries, potentially resulting in several hundred megawatts of new solar thermal-electric capacity by the year 2000. A recent review of solar thermal-electric technology carried out under the sponsorship of the German Federal Ministry for Education, Science, Research, and Technology estimated that for advanced versions of parabolic trough solar thermal-electric units with steam-turbine-based natural gas backup, costs could be reduced roughly in half, via learning-by-doing, exploiting scale economies, and making modest technological improvements (PSI, 1996).

The more advanced heliostat/central receiver and parabolic dish technologies make it possible to recover solar heat at much higher temperatures. These advanced technologies are expected to lead to lower electricity generation costs and also to make thermal energy storage much more economically attractive (DeLaquil, 1993; IPCC, 1996; STAP/GEF, 1996; PSI, 1996).

Hybrid systems integrating solar thermal and fossil fuel-fired gas turbine and gas turbine/steam turbine combined cycle technologies, which are being developed for both parabolic-trough and heliostat/central receiver solar thermal technologies, promise to lower costs significantly for early commercial solar thermal plants. The annual solar fraction (the share of demand covered by solar) for these integrated, combined-cycle configurations typically is 20% or lower. Because of their potential to reduce both market-entry costs and risk hurdles, such hybrids may lead to earlier introduction of commercial plants. Higher-solar fraction plants can be built as the cost of solar-based electricity approaches the cost of fossil fuel-based electricity (PSI, 1996).

3.3.2.9 Managing renewable energy technologies in electric power generation

Large-scale adoption of renewable electric technologies will require that they be

Figure 3.12: Comparing Investment Portfolios for a Hypothetical Electric Utility

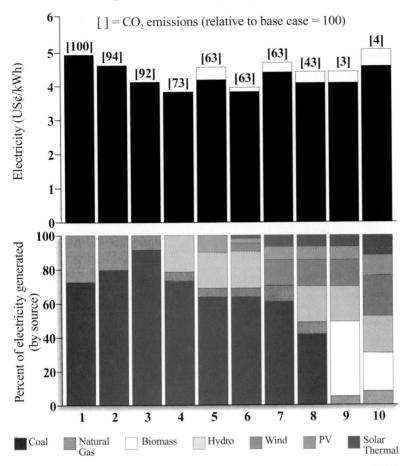

[ ] = CO₂ emissions (relative to base case = 100)

1 *conventional fossil*

2 *best new fossil*

3 *advanced fossil*

4 *advanced fossil with 21% hydro*

5 *advanced fossil with 10% PV and 21% hydro*

6 *advanced fossil with 10% intermittents and 21% hydro*

7 *advanced fossil with 30% mixed intermittents (three wind sites)*

8 *advanced fossil with 30% mixed intermittents (three wind sites) and 21% hydro*

9 *advanced biomass and gas with 30% mixed intermittents (three wind sites) and 21% hydro*

10 *advanced biomass and gas with 50% mixed intermittents (three wind sites) and 21% hydro*

The average lifecycle cost and relative CO₂ emissions for meeting the annual electricity needs (top) and the fraction of electricity generated by each energy source (bottom) are displayed for alternative configurations of a hypothetical utility. The lifecycle costs were calculated for a 6% discount rate using the SUTIL model (Kelly and Weinberg, 1993). The calculations involved a simulation of the utility that considered the variability of electricity demand and the output of intermittent renewable equipment, the loadleveling capabilities of hydroelectric facilities, and the dispatching of natural gas, coal, and biomass thermal electric plants. The electricity demand profile (that for an actual large utility in northern California) was specified on an hour-by-hour basis throughout the year. The assumed insulation values are for northern California. For the given demand profile, alternative electricity supply portfolios having the same degree of system reliability were constructed. Each portfolio involves specified levels of penetration by intermittent renewable electric and hydroelectric sources, and the model determines the least costly mix of thermal-electric equipment and fuels that would meet the remaining load, assuming alternative levels of technology for the thermal generating equipment and specified 30-year levelized life-cycle fuel prices. For all advanced fossil and renewable energy technologies highlighted in these constructions, it was assumed that R&D is successful in meeting performance and cost goals for the period near 2010. Thirty-year levelized coal, natural gas, and biomass prices were assumed to be US$2.0/GJ, US$4.4/GJ, and US$2.4/GJ respectively. Assumptions about capital and operation and maintenance costs and about performance characteristics of alternative technologies are presented elsewhere (Johansson et al., 1993). For the six cases displayed on the right, the photovoltaic (PV) systems are sited in distributed configurations; the clear segments at the tops of the bars represent the value of distributed PV power to the utility; the net cost is given by the level at the tops of the shaded bars—the gross cost less the distributed PV benefit.

Source: (Johansson et al., 1993)

connected to electric utility grids. Managing grid-connected renewable electric technologies poses new challenges for utilities.

Electricity from renewable energy sources often will be produced by plants that are much smaller than those in today's power systems, as the costs per unit of capacity are relatively insensitive to scale. Scales range from 1 kW_e for some photovoltaic systems to 25-300 MW_e for BIG/GT systems. Many of the smaller-scale technologies will be sited at or near customers' premises rather than in central-station plants. Some photovoltaic and fuel-cell systems can be operated unattended and even installed at individual houses. Electricity produced from such "distributed power systems" is worth more to the utility than central-station power whenever the electrical output is highly correlated with the utility peak demand, largely because such siting makes it possible to defer transmission/distribution investments (Shugar, 1990; Hoff et al., 1995).

Intermittent supplies can be managed by a combination of: load-management techniques (e.g., using a time-varying electricity price to induce load shifting); backing up the intermittents with an appropriate mix of dispatchable generating capacity; using interconnecting grid systems for transferring electricity over large distances to cope with

some of the daily variations of wind and solar energy; and energy storage (mechanical,
electrochemical, thermal, or other)
(Sørensen, 1984).

Hydropower plants allow prompt regulation and can back up intermittent generators,
as can some types of thermal power plants.
The ideal thermal complements to intermittent renewable energy plants on grid systems
are plants characterised by low-unit capital cost
(so they can be operated cost-effectively at low
capacity factor) and fast response times (so they
can adjust to rapid changes in intermittent output). Natural gas-fired gas turbines and combined cycles satisfy these criteria, but
supercritical fossil and nuclear steam-electric
plants do not. Thus natural gas and renewable
electric systems are complementary supply
strategies, while nuclear and intermittent
renewables are competitive strategies at high
grid-penetration levels.

The economics of long-distance transmission of intermittent renewable electricity can often be improved substantially with
energy storage technology. For example, it
has been shown that with commercially-
ready, compressed-air energy storage technology, intermittent wind electricity can be
converted into baseload electricity that can
be transmitted cost-effectively via long-distance transmission lines from large, remotely
located wind resources to electricity demand
centres (Cavallo, 1995; Lew et al., 1996).

New analytical tools are being developed to assist utilities in valuing renewable
electricity supplies and managing power
systems that involve combinations of intermittent and dispatchable power supplies.
One such tool, the SUTIL (Sustainable
UTILity) simulation model (Kelly and
Weinberg, 1993), calculates the average cost
of electric generation as the result of an
hour-by-hour simulation that takes into account demand, the variable output of intermittent renewable equipment, the load-lev-
elling capabilities of hydroelectric plants,
and the dispatching characteristics of alternative thermal-electric plants. The model
can identify the optimal mix of dispatchable
generating capacity for backing up a specified contribution from intermittent
renewables. Results of a SUTIL simulation
of 10 alternative portfolios for a hypothetical utility and a consistent set of assumptions regarding relative fuel and technology
costs are shown in Figure 3.12. For this set
of alternative utility investment portfolios:

- All configurations involving advanced
  technology (cases 3-10) are less costly
  than the conventional fossil fuel technologies base case (case 1).
- There is little variation in cost among
  advanced technology options, although
  the advanced fossil fuel options (cases
  3 and 4) are the least costly.
- Advanced fossil fuel options offer relatively modest reductions in CO_2 emissions.
- Without new electrical storage technology the fraction of electric energy provided by intermittents can rise to about
  30% before costs start rising significantly.
- At high levels of penetration of intermittent renewables, baseload power becomes
  less important and load-following and
  peaking power become more important.
- The option offering the greatest reduction in CO_2 emissions (case 9), involving biomass for baseload power and a
  30% contribution from intermittent
  renewables, has CO_2 emissions that are
  only 4% of those for the least costly case
  (case 4) and an average generation cost
  that is only 7% higher.

While the results of such modelling exercises might differ in detail from region to region and over time, the major findings relating to the potential for integrating intermittent
renewables into utility grids are supported by
other studies. Specifically, typical percentages
of wind or solar in systems without storage
are about 20% for grid systems and up to 50%
for large systems with reservoir-based hydro
or time-zone variations of loads (Sørensen,
1981, 1987; Grubb and Meyer, 1993). Short-
term storage will ease regulation and possibly
improve power quality, but only intermediate
and long-term storage will allow large systems
to have shares of variable renewable-energy
sources that significantly exceed 50% (Jensen
and Sørensen, 1984).

The costs for technologies that are not
yet commercially available cannot be estimated precisely. Moreover, relative costs for
different technologies will vary by region.
Nevertheless, on the basis of what is presently known about the prospective costs of
advanced renewable and fossil fuel electric-
generating technologies, it is plausible that
in the early decades of the next century utility planners will be able to assemble electric

power systems (involving substantial contributions from renewable energy sources) that generate very low local pollution and CO_2 emissions, at costs that are not much different from costs for electricity generated with conventional technologies. At the same time, it probably will be difficult to provide electricity at lower direct costs than with fossil fuels. For instance, both coal and biomass will be able to exploit the same basic advances in gas turbine and fuel-cell conversion technologies. This judgement is based on the assumption that various promising renewable-energy technologies will be targeted for research and development and commercialisation programs, and that these programs will meet their objectives.

3.3.3 Solar Heating, Cooling and Lighting for Buildings

Solar technologies can be utilised to provide heating, cooling, and lighting for buildings. One approach involves passive techniques that employ architectural designs for integrating the solar resource into building operations to meet building space heating and/or cooling needs. These strategies use the building itself—walls, windows, overhangs, thermal mass—to capture, store, and distribute solar energy. The most cost-effective applications are those which employ dual-functional building components that optimise the design to site conditions. During the last decade in the United States, hundreds of thousands of passive solar homes were constructed.

Passive cooling is a natural means of providing comfort in the warmer months which utilises elements of the building design to block unwanted solar gain, to reduce heat transfer through the building shell, and to passively ventilate and cool interior spaces. For example, appropriately placed trees can provide shading which considerably reduces cooling loads over summer months, while still allowing for desirable winter solar gain in locations with severe winters.

Architectural daylighting techniques can be employed along with passive solar heating and cooling. This approach requires careful design but uses little or no materials beyond what is needed for building construction and thus is frequently cost-effective (OTA, 1995). Alternatively, discrete or active collectors on building roofs or near buildings can be used to capture sunlight as heat and pipe the energy to where it is needed in buildings for space heating or cooling (e.g., via the use of heat-driven absorption chillers) and for domestic hot water production.

Solar water heaters (SWHs) are commonplace in several parts of the world. There are 4.5 million SWHs in Japan and 600,000 in Israel. In Cyprus, over 90% of residences have SWHs. In developing countries, SWHs are not widely used as yet but the economic prospects for their use are more favourable than for most industrialised countries. This potential is partly due to the generally higher insolation levels and higher ambient temperatures in tropical regions compared to temperate regions. Moreover, natural gas is not available for domestic use in many regions, so that the "reference" technology is typically an electric water heater, which can contribute significantly to the electric utility's peak load.[2] Therefore, emphasis on SWHs would help slow electricity demand growth, since otherwise the demand for electric water heaters can be expected to rise quickly as incomes grow.

Furthermore, SWH costs are likely to be much lower if manufactured in developing countries, once an industry is well established, owing to the labour-intensive nature of the manufacturing and marketing of SWHs, and to the relatively low labour costs prevailing in those areas (STAP/GEF, 1996). An estimated 22 manufacturers and distributors of SWHs are operating in 10 countries of Southern Africa (Peters et al., 1992). In many instances, domestic SWHs in these countries have demonstrated paybacks of 3 to 5 years (Karekezi and Karottki, 1989). Where electricity prices properly reflect long-run marginal costs, the economics of SWHs in developing countries can be very attractive at present costs, especially where a local manufacturing capability is well established. Moreover, SWH economics likely could be improved upon, via both technological advances and the realisation of economies of scale, if

---

2   Electrical loads for water heating account for 20% to 25% of domestic electricity demand in Brazil, Colombia, Ecuador, and Guatemala; in Sao Paulo SWHs used for showers draw as much as 7 kilowatts and account for perhaps half of the residential peak electrical demand (OTA, 1992b).

SWHs were to become routinely available. The challenge for energy planners then is to find effective ways to speed up the dissemination of this technology.[3]

3.3.4 Biogas

Simple anaerobic digesters are used in rural areas of some developing countries to produce biogas from manure and crop residues at scales ranging from household to village. They provide fuel for cooking and power (Rajabapaiah et al., 1993), by-products in the form of fertiliser and feed for pigs and fish farms, and substantial environmental and human health benefits (DEPE, 1992). The potential for biogas may be considerable, particularly if organisational issues are satisfactorily resolved; for instance, if local operations and maintenance expertise can be ensured and if users assume responsibility for collecting biomass for the biogas plant (Rajabapaiah et al., 1993).

Projects involving small-scale biogas systems designed for use by rural households have not been successful in Africa, due largely to two factors: *i)* the unexpectedly complex management and maintenance back-up they require, and *ii)* the absence of operational experience at the household level. On the other hand, small-scale biogas projects targeting rural institutional applications have demonstrated very encouraging results. Available field evidence indicates that combined septic tank/biogas units run by institutions such as rural hospitals and schools represent an attractive option for introducing biomass technology in rural areas of Africa (Katihabwa, 1993; Karekezi, 1994).

In India, experience has also been mixed. Some projects have fallen far short of expectations (Comptroller and Auditor General of India, 1994). However, cattle-dung biogas plants at the village scale have been demonstrated to be economically viable for providing biogas-generated electricity (~5 kW$_e$) for lighting and pumping water in projects that involve a high level of community participation. Plans are underway to replicate the technology in many villages (Reddy et al., 1994).

3.3.5 Clean Fuels for Transportation

World-wide, there is growing interest in alternative clean fuels for transportation. This attention has arisen in response to: *i)* the increasing demand for liquid fuels, especially in the developing countries;[4] *ii)* the longer-term need for alternatives to oil in transportation;[5] *iii)* the need for ever tighter regulations to improve air quality; and *iv)* the shortcomings of strategies for meeting air quality goals which rely solely on requiring the installation of emission control devices.[6] Alternative fuels are likely to be important in developing countries as well as industrialised countries,

---

[3] That interventions can be effective is indicated by a comparison of the situations in Cyprus, where SWHs have been promoted by the government, via the provision of a testing facility, advisory services, and financing incentives, and in Malta, where there has been no government intervention. The countries have about the same climate, similar costs for solar water heaters, and similar electricity prices. Yet in Cyprus, the total installed SWH capacity is 0.9 m^2 per capita—360 times the value for Malta (STAP/GEF, 1996).

[4] The United States Department of Energy projects that in developing countries the demand for oil will increase 55%, 1990—2000, from one-fourth to more than one-third of the world total (EIA, 1995).

[5] If all remaining recoverable resources of conventional oil (reserves plus estimated undiscovered resources), as estimated by the United States Geological Survey (Masters et al., 1994), were consumed by the year 2100, the average rate of global consumption in this period would be only 90, 74, or 62% of the rate of oil consumption in 1990, for the high, midrange, and low estimates of remaining undiscovered resources, respectively. In the face of rapidly growing demand for fluid fuels for transportation, this prospect highlights the need for supplements to conventional oil in the decades ahead.

[6] In the United States, lifecycle emissions of carbon monoxide, hydrocarbons, and oxides of nitrogen from new model year 1993 cars are expected to be 5.0, 4.1, and 1.8 times the tailpipe emission standards for these pollutants (Ross et al., 1995). Over the lifetime of a motor vehicle the actual emissions of criteria pollutants are so much higher than the tailpipe emissions standards because: *i)* pollution control devices are designed to meet the performance levels specified in a test which does faithfully reflect real-world operating conditions; *ii)* pollution control equipment sometimes malfunctions; and *iii)* some emissions come from sources other than the tailpipe (evaporative emissions from the fuel tank, and emissions from the fuel production and delivery system upstream of the motor vehicle).

in light of the rapidly growing demand for road transport services in the developing world,[7] the high population densities of urban centres, the increasing air pollution in the world's megacities (see Figure 2.7 in Section 2.2.1), and the difficulties many developing countries will have in reaching air quality goals with end-of-pipe emission control technologies.

3.3.5.1 Reformulated gasoline

In the United States, the focus of clean fuel initiatives is on gasolines reformulated to reduce ozone-producing emissions, carbon monoxide emissions, and benzene. The Clean Air Act Amendments of 1990 require the use of "reformulated gasoline" in the nine cities that most often exceed ozone air quality standards. In California, all gasoline sold must be reformulated. The introduction of reformulated gasoline represents a relatively unobtrusive approach to improving air quality; however, it is not an inexpensive option. United States oil companies are in the process of investing an estimated $10 billion over the 1990s in order to upgrade refineries to produce reformulated gasoline (Sperling, 1996).

3.3.5.2 Compressed natural gas

The use of compressed natural gas (CNG) in motor vehicles would lead to significantly reduced emissions, but would not eliminate them entirely. In the near-term, the use of CNG vehicles is inhibited by the lack of the needed gaseous transport fuel infrastructure. Over the longer-term, CNG in internal combustion engine vehicles is likely to compete with hydrogen in fuel cell vehicles.

3.3.5.3 Synthetic middle distillates and dimethyl ether

Synthetic middle distillates (SMD) and dimethyl ether (DME) are clean fuels that are likely to gain increased attention as alternative fuels for coping with the air pollution challenges posed by diesel engines. They are likely to be especially important for both European and developing countries, where diesel engine vehicles continue to be used widely. Both fuels offer outstanding performance in diesel engines (high cetane numbers), with considerably reduced air pollutant emissions, compared to ordinary diesel fuel. Both products have essentially zero sulphur[8] and zero aromatic content, which are key to their outstanding emissions characteristics.

A demonstration SMD plant, with a 12,500 barrels/day output capacity and based on the use of a natural gas feedstock, began operating in Malaysia in 1993. One market served by this plant, in a blend with ordinary diesel fuels, is in California, where the blend is able to meet the severe state regulatory requirements for diesel-powered vehicles (Tijm et al., 1995). In addition, in late 1996 it was announced that a major multinational oil company will build a large (50,000 to 100,000 barrels/day) natural gas-based synthetic middle distillates plant in Qatar.

Diesel engine tests without tailpipe emission controls show that use of DME fuel would make it possible to meet California's ultra-low emission vehicle regulations for medium-duty vehicles, such as commercial trucks and buses, as well as to meet all but the carbon monoxide limit in the proposed European limits for heavy-duty trucks. Use of DME fuel would exceed the carbon monoxide limit by only 10% (Fleisch et al., 1995). If necessary, catalytic converters could be used to reduce emissions further, in light of the absence of sulphur in the fuel.

Both SMD and DME fuels can be made from various carbonaceous feedstocks—including natural gas, residual fuel oil, heavy crude oils, coal, municipal solid waste, and biomass, via processes that begin with the

---

[7] According to the Motor Vehicle Manufacturers Association (MVMA, 1982; 1992), the number of cars and commercial vehicles world-wide increased between 1980 and 1990 from 411 million to 583 million, while the number in developing countries increased from 49 million (12% of the total) to 92 million (16% of the total). Growth was especially rapid in the developing countries of Asia in this period—from 14 million to 39 million.

[8] The high sulphur content of diesel fuels (for example, averaging 2000 ppmv for diesel oil in Great Britain, compared to a 1990 California average level of 150 ppmv for gasoline, and a requirement of 40 ppmv for reformulated gasolines in California beginning in 1996) contributes significantly to the formation of particulates. Moreover, elimination of sulphur facilitates the reduction of hydrocarbon and carbon monoxide emissions via catalytic converters in exhaust gases, since sulphur, even in very small quantities, tends to occupy active sites of the catalysts.

production of synthesis gas, a gaseous mixture consisting mainly of carbon monoxide and hydrogen. As long as low-cost natural gas is readily available somewhere in the world, it will be the preferred feedstock for making either fuel. However, in countries where natural gas is scarce and alternative carbonaceous feedstocks are abundant, the latter feedstocks might be given serious attention in the near term.[9]

3.3.5.4 Alcohol fuels

Alcohols (methanol and ethanol) have attracted considerable interest as alternative automotive fuels, especially in the United States and Brazil. While the use of alcohol fuels in internal combustion engines can lead to reduced oil dependence, it is now generally believed that alcohol fuels—especially when blended with gasoline and used in flexible-fuel internal-combustion engine vehicles (ICEVs)—offer little or no air-quality advantages, other than reduction in carbon monoxide (CO) emissions (Calvert et al., 1993). Moreover, reformulated gasolines can meet or surpass the air-pollution reductions of alcohol-gasoline blends (CTOFM, 1991). With methanol, CO emissions would be reduced, and emissions of volatile organic compounds would be less problematic than for gasoline, but NO_x emissions probably would not be reduced. Ethanol offers fewer air-quality benefits than methanol and may produce more ozone per carbon atom (Calvert et al., 1993).

However, emissions from the use of alcohol fuels in fuel cell vehicles would be a tiny fraction of the emissions from gasoline internal-combustion-engine vehicles, and their use in fuel cell vehicles would lead to marked improvements in fuel economy compared to their use in internal combustion engine vehicles (Kreutz et al., 1996).

3.3.5.5 Traditional biofuels

Efforts to produce biofuels for transport have focused on ethanol from maize, wheat, and sugar cane and on vegetable oils such as rapeseed. The most substantial commercial programs are in Brazil and the United States.

In 1989, Brazil produced 12 billion litres of fuel ethanol from sugar cane, which was used to power 4.2 million cars running on hydrated ethanol and 5 million cars on gasohol, a gasoline-ethanol blend (Goldemberg et al., 1993). In 1993, the United States produced 4 billion litres of ethanol from maize for gasohol applications.

All traditional biomass-derived transport fuels are uneconomic at present. However, substantial cost reductions are being made for sugar cane-derived ethanol (Goldemberg et al., 1993). Additionally, there are good prospects for making cane-derived ethanol competitive at the present low world oil price if electricity is cogenerated from cane residues using BIG/GT technology (see Section 3.3.2.6) along with ethanol from cane juice (Williams and Larson, 1993). In contrast, the prospects are poor for economically making ethanol from grain (Wyman et al., 1993).

Most traditional biofuels are inefficient users of land, with low yields of transport services (vehicle-km/ha/year) compared with what is achievable with advanced technologies using woody biomass feedstocks (see Table 3.1). Many of these fuels have marginal energy balances, and greenhouse performance also tends to be marginal (IPCC, 1996b; STAP/GEF, 1996).

3.3.5.6 Advanced biofuels

Advanced biofuels derived from low-cost woody biomass could offer higher energy yields at lower cost and with lower environmental impacts than most traditional biofuels (IEA, 1994). The advanced biofuel that has received the most attention is ethanol derived from wood via enzymatic hydrolysis (Wyman et al., 1993). For a woody feedstock yield of 15 dry t/ha/year—which is generally believed to be achievable in large-scale production—the ethanol yield could be more than twice that from grain, as shown in Table 3.1. If the United States Department of Energy's year-2000 goals for performance and cost are met, energy balances would be favourable; lifecycle emissions of CO_2 for

---

[9] A key needed technology is the gasifier for making synthesis gas. In the case of coal, what is needed is an oxygen-blown gasifier. In China, where coal is used intensively, this coal gasification technology is becoming well established in the chemical process industry. China already has many modern oxygen-blown coal gasification plants, mainly used for making ammonia for fertilisers.

Table 3.1: Energy Yield for Alternative Feedstock/Conversion Technologies

Option	Feedstock (dry tonnes/ha/yr)	Yield Transport Fuel (GJ/ha/yr)	Transport Services[h] (10³ v-km/ha/yr)
Rape Methyl Ester (Netherlands)[a]	3.7 of Rapeseed	47	21 (ICEV)
EthOH from Maize (US)[b]	7.2 of Maize	76	27 (ICEV)
EthOH from Wheat (Netherlands)[c]	6.6 of Wheat	72	26 (ICEV)
EthOH from Sugar Beets (Netherlands)[d]	15.1 of Sugar Beets	132	48 (ICEV)
EthOH from Sugar Cane (Brazil)[e]	38.5 of Cane Stems	111	40 (ICEV)
EthOH, Enzymatic Hydrolysis of Wood (present technology)[f]	15 of Wood	122	44 (ICEV)
EthOH, Enzymatic Hydrolysis of Wood (improved technology)[f]	15 of Wood	179	64 (ICEV)
MeOH, Thermochemical Gasification of Wood[g]	15 of Wood	177	64/133 (ICEV/FCV)
H₂, Thermochemical Gasification of Wood[g]	15 of Wood	213	84/189 (ICEV/FCV)

a Per tonne of seed: 370 liters of rape methyl ester plus (not listed) 1.4 tonnes of straw (Lysen et al., 1992).

b For wet milling, assuming the U.S. average maize yield, 1989-1992; per tonne of grain: 440 liters of ethanol plus (not listed) 0.35 tonne of stover (out of 1 tonne of total stover, assuming the rest must be left at the site for soil maintenance, 275 kg of corn gluten cattle feed, and 330 kg of CO_2 (Wyman et al., 1993).

c Per tonne of seed: 455 liters of ethanol plus (not listed) 0.6 tonnes of straw (Lysen et al., 1992).

d Per tonne of sugar beet: 364 liters of ethanol (Lysen et al., 1992).

e For the average sugar cane yield in Brazil in 1987 (63.3 tonnes of harvested cane stems, wet weight); per tonne of wet cane stems : 73 liters of ethanol (Goldemberg et al., 1993). In addition, (not listed) the dry weight of the attached tops and leaves amounts to 0.092 tonnes and that for the detached leaves amounts to 0.188 tonnes per tonne of wet stems—altogether some 18 dry tonnes per hectare per year (Alexander, 1985).

f Per tonne of feedstock: 338 liters of ethanol plus (not listed) 183 kWh (0.658 GJ) of electricity, present technology; 497 liters of ethanol plus (not listed) 101 kWh (0.365 GJ) of electricity, improved technology (Wyman et al., 1993).

g For the indirectly heated Battelle Columbus Laboratory biomass gasifier; per tonne of feedstock: 11.8 GJ of methanol or 14.2 GJ of hydrogen; per tonne of feedstock, external electricity requirements are 107 kWh (0.38 GJ) for methanol or 309 kWh (1.11 GJ) for hydrogen (Williams et al., 1995a).

h The fuel economy of the vehicles (in liters of gasoline-equivalent per 100 km) is assumed to be: 6.30 for rapeseed oil (the same as for diesel), 7.97 for ethanol, 7.90 for methanol, and 7.31 for hydrogen used in internal combustion engine vehicles (ICEVs); and 3.81 for methanol and 3.24 for hydrogen used in fuel cell vehicles (FCVs) (DeLuchi, 1991). Note that 1 liter of gasoline equivalent = 0.0348 GJ, HHV.

ethanol production and use in ICEVs (in gC/km) would be only about 2% of those from such vehicles operated on reformulated gasoline (Wyman et al., 1993). Furthermore, ethanol would be competitive with gasoline, given oil prices greater than $25/bbl (Wyman et al., 1993).

Other advanced biofuels include methanol and hydrogen derived via thermochemical gasification of biomass. These fuels are well suited for use in fuel cell vehicles, where they offer good prospects for dealing with the multiple challenges of transportation. Hydrogen or methanol fuel probably would be produced initially by steam-reforming natural gas. This is the least-costly route for which the required technology is commercially available. Where natural gas is readily available, biomass-derived transport fuels

likely would be introduced only after natural gas supplies had become tight and natural gas prices had risen, making it possible for biomass-derived fuels to compete. On the basis of projected prices for natural gas, coal, and biomass, production costs might be comparable for these three feedstocks before 2025 (Williams, 1996; Williams, 1997).

The useful energy yield (GJ/ha/year) for methanol or hydrogen produced from woody biomass would be 2 to 3 times that for ethanol derived from grain and would be comparable to that for ethanol derived from wood via enzymatic hydrolysis (see Table 3.1). However, the potential for displacing gasoline used in ICEVs with biomass-derived methanol or hydrogen used in FCVs could be more than twice that for wood-derived ethanol used in ICEV applications, because FCVs can be more than twice as energy-efficient as ICEVs (see Section 3.2.5.4). The potential role of ethanol in providing transportation services could be increased perhaps 50% by shifting from ICEVs to FCVs (Kreutz et al., 1996). However, a hydrogen FCV would typically be 50% more energy-efficient than an ethanol FCV, so that for fuel cell applications, the transportation services obtainable from a given amount of biomass would be about 75% more for biomass-derived hydrogen than for biomass-derived ethanol.

The FCV thus offers the potential for substantially increasing the role of biomass in transportation, supporting 5 to 7 times as many vehicle-km of transport services per hectare as ethanol derived from grain used in ICEVs (see Table 3.1). This high energy service yield is reflected in lifecycle CO_2 emissions for fuel cell vehicles operated on methanol or hydrogen derived from biomass that are only 5 to 10 percent as large as for gasoline internal combustion engine vehicles (Williams et al., 1995a; 1995b).

3.3.5.7 Transition fuel strategies for fuel cell vehicles

While hydrogen is the natural fuel for fuel cell vehicles, a hydrogen fuel infrastructure does not yet exist. Because of the difficulties of simultaneously introducing both a new vehicle technology such as a fuel cell and a new fuel infrastructure, fuel cell cars likely will be fuelled initially by gasoline or diesel fuel that is processed onboard the vehicle into a hydrogen-rich gas that the fuel cell vehicle can utilise effectively. The fuelling of fuel cell vehicles with gasoline is the focus of a considerable development effort in the United States (Mitchell et al., 1995). In January 1997, an American automaker announced its plan to develop gasoline fuel cell cars, selecting this process as the most rapid path to commercializing fuel cell cars (Borroni-Bird, 1996). Such fuelling strategies for fuel cell vehicles offer dramatic reductions in air pollutant emissions compared to internal combustion engines during routine operation, although emission characteristics during engine start-up and transient operating modes are not yet well-understood (Borroni-Bird, 1996).

Subsequently, nonpetroleum-derived liquid fuels such as ethanol (derived from biomass), or methanol, SMD or DME (all of which can be derived from natural gas, coal, other fossil fuels, or biomass) might also be used for fuel cell vehicles with onboard fuel processing. Hydrogen fuel cell vehicles would be more fuel-efficient, simpler, and probably less costly to buy and operate as well. These potential benefits to the consumer plus the various societal benefits offered by hydrogen provide a strong rationale for planning an eventual shift to hydrogen as a major energy carrier in transportation.

3.3.5.8 Hydrogen: its importance as an energy carrier for transportation in the long term

Hydrogen offers good prospects for simultaneously dealing with the multiple challenges facing the energy system in the 21st century (Marchetti, 1989; Rogner and Britton, 1991; Leydon and Glocker, 1992). It is a versatile, easy-to-use energy carrier. Local pollutant emissions from hydrogen fuel cell vehicles are zero. Hydrogen can be used safely, if systems are designed to respect its unique physical and chemical properties (see Box 3.3), as is necessary for any fuel. Hydrogen can be derived from a variety of primary energy sources. Even when it is derived from fossil fuels, hydrogen can help address climate change concerns by reducing lifecycle CO_2 emissions (see Section 3.3.6). Thus there are strong reasons for evolving the global energy system so as to facilitate the eventual widespread use of hydrogen as an energy carrier.

Hydrogen can be produced via thermochemical processes from any carbonaceous material. It can be produced from natural gas with commercial technology and from heavy fuel oil or coal with technology already developed (Williams et al., 1995a; 1995b). Hydrogen could also be made from municipal solid waste (Larson et al., 1996a; 1996b) or biomass (Williams et al., 1995a; 1995b), at about the same estimated cost as hydrogen from coal (see Figure 3.13), and with technologies that could be commercialised over the next decade. It can also be made by electrolysis of water with zero lifecycle CO_2 emissions from carbon-free sources such as nuclear, wind, and photovoltaic energy.

Hydrogen generally will cost more to produce than conventional hydrocarbon fuels. Moreover, hydrogen derived via electrolysis of water will typically be much more costly than hydrogen derived thermo-chemically from carbonaceous feedstocks (see Figure 3.13). Despite the fuel cost penalty, thermochemically-derived hydrogen could be competitive if it could provide the desired energy service (e.g. vehicle-km of driving) at a similar cost.

Figure 3.14 shows estimates of the costs of owning and operating fuel cell cars powered by hydrogen derived from alternative sources at the costs to consumers shown in Figure 3.13. Because of the much higher fuel economy of fuel cell vehicles, the fuel cost per km for a fuel-cell car powered by thermochemically derived hydrogen is likely to be less than 65% of that for a gasoline-fired internal combustion engine car of comparable performance, and the total lifecycle cost of owning and operating a fuel-cell car might be slightly less.

3.3.6 Decarbonization of Fuels and CO_2 Storage

Fossil fuels can play much greater roles in a greenhouse-constrained global energy economy if satisfactory ways can be found to restrict CO_2 emissions from their use. Removal of CO_2 from fossil fuel power station stack gases is feasible but reduces the conversion efficiency and increases substantially the cost of electricity. A less costly approach in power generation, entailing much lower efficiency penalties, is to remove the CO_2 before the fuel is burned. In a CIG/CC system, for example, a hydrogen-rich fuel gas can be made by converting the carbon monoxide in the gasifier output via $CO + H_2O_{(g)} \rightarrow CO_2 + H_2$. The CO_2 can be separated from these product gases, and the remaining hydrogen-rich fuel gas can be burned in the combined cycle (Hendriks et al., 1993; Hendriks, 1994). But even in this case, the cost of electricity would be perhaps 30-40% higher than without CO_2 separation and storage (IPCC, 1996b).

If low-temperature fuel cells (e.g. PEMFCs) came to be widely used in transport and distributed CHP applications, the costs of decarbonization could be reduced considerably more because this technology prefers centrally produced hydrogen as fuel. The centralised production of hydrogen from a carbonaceous feedstock involves generating a stream of relatively pure CO_2 as a "free" by-product; that is, the cost of separating the CO_2 from the hydrogen is part of the hydro-

Box 3.3: Hydrogen Safety

Hydrogen can be used safely, if its unique properties—sometimes better, sometimes worse, and sometimes just different from other fuels—are respected (Ringland, 1994). An advantage to hydrogen is that in the event of a fuel tank leak, hydrogen will disappear quickly (because of its buoyancy), in contrast to gasoline, which will "puddle." Major concerns about hydrogen are its wide flammability and detonability limits in mixtures with air and its low ignition energy. However, these concerns should be considered in the context of how hydrogen would actually be used in transport applications. While hydrogen has a wider range of flammability and detonability in mixtures with air than any other fuel, at low concentration levels, which are applicable in open-air settings: *i*) the lower flammability limit for hydrogen is four times as high as for gasoline and is only slightly less than for methane; and *ii*) the lower detonability limit for hydrogen is 18 times as high as for gasoline and three times as high as for methane. Also, for a stoichiometric mixture of fuel and air (i.e., exactly the amount of air needed to oxidise the fuel), hydrogen has a very low ignition energy—about a factor of ten lower than for gasoline or methane. However, the ignition energy also is small relative to real sources (e.g., the discharge from an electrostatic charge on a person) for gasoline and methane; moreover, at low fuel concentrations (i.e., for mixtures with considerable excess air), the ignition energy for hydrogen is about the same as for methane.

gen production cost, not an added expense (Blok et al., 1997; Williams, 1996).

A major challenge is to store the separated CO_2 permanently so that it does not escape to the atmosphere. The most-frequently discussed option has been deep ocean disposal, but much more research is needed to better understand the security of various ocean disposal schemes and their environmental impacts (Turkenburg,

Figure 3.13: Estimated Lifecycle Costs to Consumers and CO₂ Emissions, per GJ of Hydrogen (H₂) from Alternative Sources for Transport Applications, with a Comparison to Gasoline Derived from Crude Oil

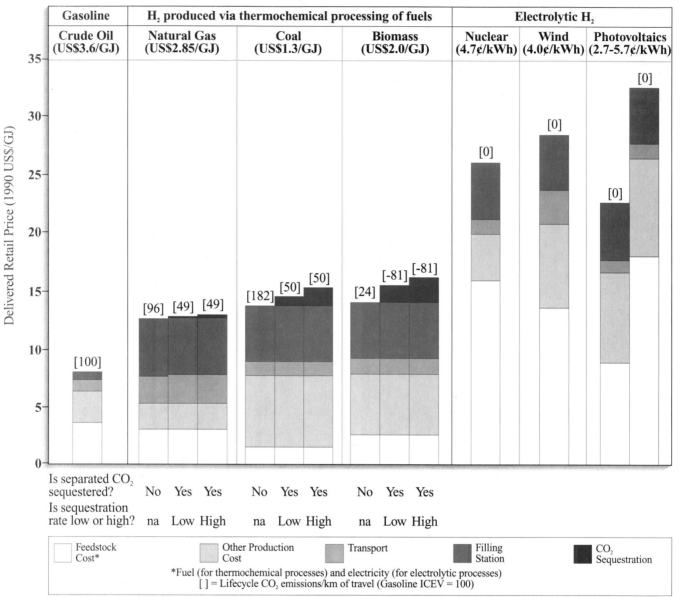

This figure and Figure 3.14 present alternative measures of cost and lifecycle CO₂ emissions characteristics for systems that provide H₂ derived from natural gas (via steam reforming), coal and biomass (via thermochemical gasification), and from electrolytic sources, with comparisons to gasoline (Williams, 1996). Costs were calculated assuming a 10% discount rate. Fuel taxes are excluded.

The assumed crude oil, natural gas, and coal prices are, respectively, the world oil price, the US average wellhead price, and the average US electric utility price projected for 2010 by the US Department of Energy. The consumer gasoline price is for reformulated gasoline derived from US$22/barrel crude oil. Plantation biomass prices that are comparable to or lower than the assumed price could be realized in large-scale applications in Brazil today and in the United States by 2020 if yield and cost goals for 2020 are realized as a result of successful R&D. The assumed electricity costs are for: a 600 MWₑ advanced passively safe nuclear plant having an installed cost of US$1680/kW; post-2000 wind technology with an installed cost of US$780/kWₑ; installed costs of US$550 to US$1125 per kWₑ for photovoltaic (PV) electricity—targets that could plausibly be met in areas of high insolation using advanced thin-film PV technologies in the long term.

Thermochemical production of H₂ generates a byproduct stream of CO₂, that can be released to the atmosphere or compressed and piped to a site where it might be sequestered. The first bar for natural gas, coal, and biomass is the cost with venting. The second and third bars are for when the separated CO₂ is sequestered, assuming low and high estimates of the sequestering cost. In the natural gas cases it is assumed that the H₂ plant is located near a natural gas field and that the separated CO₂ is sequestered in depleted gas wells. For the coal and biomass cases, it is assumed that the separated CO₂ is sequestered in saline aquifers located 250 km from the plant. [Alternatively these feedstocks might be transported from where they are produced to hydrogen production plants sited near depleted natural gas fields, in which the separated CO₂ might be stored. The cost of transporting coal halfway around the world would add only about US$0.5/GJ to the cost of H₂ (about 4% of the total cost).]

Source: (IPCC, 1996b)

Figure 3.14: Estimated Lifecycle Costs to Consumers for Owning and Operating Fuel Cell Vehicles (FCVs) and CO$_2$ Emissions, per km of Driving a FCV, for Hydrogen (H$_2$) from Alternative Sources for Transport Applications, with a Comparison to Gasoline Derived from Crude Oil and Used in Internal Combustion Engine Vehicles (ICEVs) and FCVs

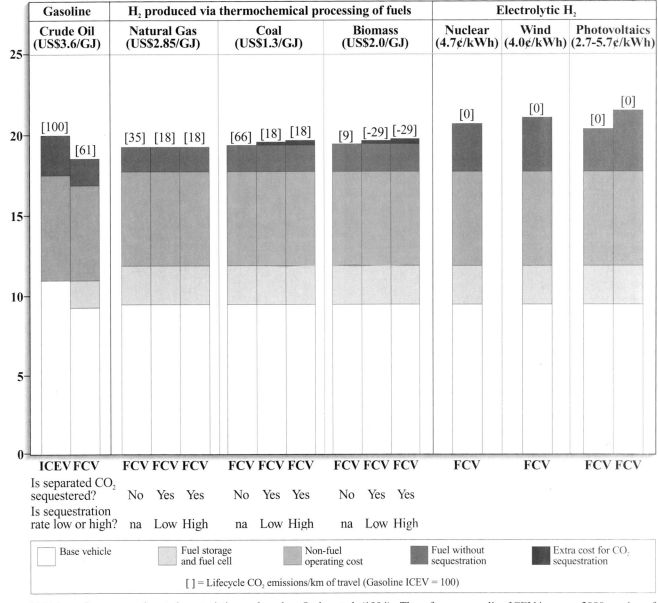

Vehicle performance and cost characteristics are based on Ogden et al. (1994). The reference gasoline ICEV is a year-2000 version of the Ford Taurus automobile with a fuel economy of 11.0 km/liter. The H$_2$ FCV has performance characteristics that are comparable to those for this ICEV and a gasoline-equivalent fuel economy of 30.4 km/l. The weight of the H$_2$ FCV is estimated to be 1.3 tonnes, compared to 1.4 tonnes for the ICEV. Initial costs are estimated to be US$17,800 for an ICEV and US$25,100 for a H$_2$ FCV (in mass production). Costs are also shown for a FCV operating on gasoline. (In this case, the gasoline is converted via partial oxidation onboard the vehicle to a gaseous mixture of H$_2$ and CO$_2$, which is a suitable fuel gas for operating the fuel cell.) The estimated fuel economy for the gasoline FCV is 18.0 km/l. The initial cost for a gasoline FCV is assumed to be US$21,700, the same as the estimated costs for a methanol FCV. An operating lifetime of 11 years is assumed for both ICEVs and FCVs; however, FCVs are assumed to be driven 23,000 km per year, compared to 17,800 km per year; this reflects the lower operating costs expected for FCVs operated on thermochemically derived fuels and the expectation that FCVs will have longer operating lifetimes. It is assumed that H$_2$ is stored onboard vehicles in carbon-fiber-wrapped aluminum tanks at high pressure (550 bar). Because of the bulkiness of gaseous H$_2$ storage, the H$_2$ FCV is designed for a range between refuelings of 400 km, compared to 640 km for a gasoline ICEV.

The costs for H$_2$ and gasoline delivered to consumers are from Figure 3.13. Retail fuel taxes are included under "other non-fuel operating costs" at the average US rate for gasoline used in ICEVs; to ensure that road tax revenues are the same for all options, it is assumed that retail taxes are 0.75 US¢ per km for all options (equivalent to 8.2 US¢ per liter or 31 US¢ per gallon for gasoline used in ICEVs).

Source: (IPCC, 1996b)

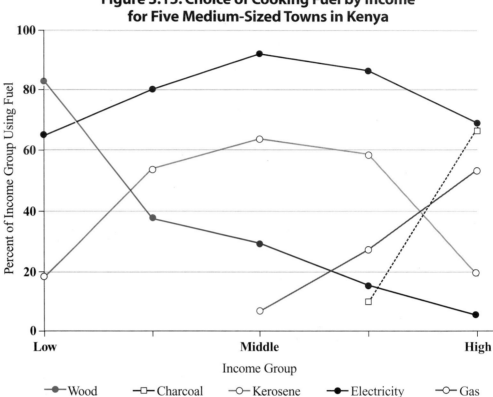

Figure 3.15: Choice of Cooking Fuel by Income for Five Medium-Sized Towns in Kenya

Many households use more than one fuel depending on the particular food cooked and the supply and cost of fuel. Note the shift in fuel choice from wood to charcoal and kerosene, and then from charcoal and kerosene to gas and electricity. This transition is very complex and not yet well understood. Factors that affect a household's shift to modern stoves and fuels include: household income and fuel producing assets (land, trees, animals, etc.); reliability of access to modern fuels; relative cost of traditional and modern fuels and stoves; level of education of the head of household; cooking habits; division of labor and control of finances within the household; and the relative performance of the stove/fuel.

Source: (Soussan, 1987)

1992). The most promising options for sequestration are in depleted oil and natural gas fields and in saline aquifers. Sequestration in depleted oil and gas fields is generally thought to be a secure option if the original reservoir pressure is not exceeded (van der Burgt et al., 1992; Summerfield et al., 1993). The prospective sequestering capacity associated with depleted and proven reserves plus estimated undiscovered conventional resources (most of which will be used up during the next century) is estimated to be about 100 GtC for oil fields and about 400 GtC for natural gas fields (Hendriks, 1994). CO_2 injection for enhanced oil recovery, which is established technology, might become the focus of initial efforts to sequester CO_2 recovered in hydrogen production in a profitable way. Saline aquifers are much more widely available than oil or gas fields, but more research is needed to better determine their overall potential capacity, their security of storage, and the environmental impacts of aquifer disposal (Hendriks, 1994).

A major study carried out under the Joule II Non-Nuclear Energy Research Programme of the European Commission (Holloway, 1996) concluded that underground storage in depleted oil and gas fields and deep aquifers is a feasible method of disposing of large quantities of CO_2 and that all the necessary technological steps are proven. The study estimated that storage reservoirs accessible to the European Union and Norway would be adequate to store more than 200 GtC. This storage capacity is equivalent to 250 years of CO_2 emissions from all of OECD Europe at the current emissions rate.

Figures 3.13 and 3.14 also show that lifecycle emissions of CO_2 associated with providing hydrogen for fuel cell vehicles could be greatly reduced if the CO_2 separated at hydrogen production plants were sequestered in depleted natural gas fields or saline aquifers, and that so doing would add only modestly to the cost of hydrogen to consumers and to the total cost of driving—for high as well as low estimates of the sequestration cost (Williams, 1997). The sequestration cost would be especially low for natural gas-derived hydrogen if the hydrogen production facility were sited near a depleted natural gas field in which the separated CO_2 is sequestered. In this case, the net cost of sequestration would be near zero, because enhanced natural gas production from reservoir repressurization would nearly pay for the sequestration cost (Blok et al., 1997). These figures also show that thermochemically derived hydrogen will be much less costly than electrolytic hydrogen for many decades to come, even with costs for sequestering the separated CO_2 taken into account (Williams, 1997).

Experience with aquifer disposal will be provided by two projects involving injection into nearby aquifers of CO_2 separated from natural gas recovered from CO_2-rich gas reservoirs. One is a project begun in 1996 to recover 1 million tonnes of CO_2/year from the Sleipner Vest offshore natural gas field in Norway (Kaarstad, 1992). The second, which will commence in about a decade, will involve the recovery of over 100 million tonnes/year from the Natuna natural gas field in the South China Sea (71% of the reservoir gas is CO_2) (IEA, 1996). It has been recommended that governments collaborate scientifically with the oil companies involved in these CO_2 disposal projects to improve understanding of aquifer disposal (Holloway, 1996).

3.4 Fuels and Stoves for Cooking

The most important energy service in many developing countries today is cooking food. In rural areas of developing countries, traditional fuels—wood, crop residues, and dung—remain the primary cooking fuels, while in many urban areas, charcoal is used also. About 2 billion people depend on these crude polluting biomass fuels for their cooking and other energy needs (see Section 2.1.1).[10] Higher incomes and reliable access to fuel supplies enable people to switch to more modern stoves and cleaner fuels such as kerosene,[11] LPG, electricity, and, potentially, to modern biomass[12]—a transition that is widely observed around the world largely irrespective of cultural traditions (see Figure 3.15).[13] These technologies are preferred for their convenience, comfort, cleanliness, ease of operation, speed, efficiency, and other attributes.[14] The efficiency, cost, and performance of stoves generally increase as consumers shift progressively from wood stoves to charcoal, kerosene, LPG or gas, and electric stoves (see Figure 3.16).[15]

---

[10] Useful recent reviews of cooking technologies and issues include: (Dutt and Ravindranath, 1993), (Barnes et al., 1994), and (Baldwin, 1986).

[11] For example, kerosene is the predominant household cooking fuel in parts of Asia—35%, 42%, and 30% of urban households in India, Pakistan, and Sri Lanka, respectively (Floor and van der Plas, 1991).

[12] With modern technologies biomass can be converted into liquid or gaseous fuels (see Sections 3.3.5.5 and 3.3.5.6) or into electricity (see Section 3.3.2.6) that can provide cooking services with low emissions.

[13] Cultural factors frequently have been cited as a barrier to the adoption of improved wood, charcoal, or other stoves/fuels. However, a wide variety of stoves and fuels have been adopted across the full range of class, cultural, and income groups in developing countries, and a strong preference is displayed for superior stoves/fuels such as kerosene, LPG, or electricity. More typically, the reason why various improved biomass stoves have not been adopted by the targeted developing country group is that the proposed technology did not work well or did not meet the multiple needs of the user (see Appendix A).

[14] These issues, particularly the problems of smoke pollution and other environmental impacts from traditional biomass stoves/fuels, the effort required to forage for biomass, and the role of women are discussed in (OTA, 1991) and in Chapter 2 of this volume.

[15] Even among high efficiency stoves, such as those using LPG or gas, there can be further improvements in efficiency. In practice, the high efficiency of gas stoves can be largely negated when pilot lights are used. Gas stoves that are lit by electric ignition systems (or simply matches) typically use just half the energy that stoves with pilot lights consume. Higher efficiency natural gas stoves under

Figure 3.16: Representative Efficiencies and Capital Costs for Various Stoves

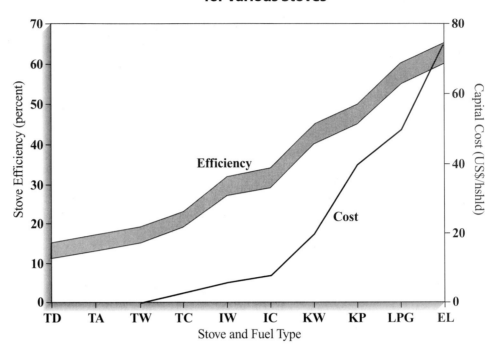

Stoves listed are: (TD), (TA), (TW), (TC)—traditional stoves using dried animal dung, agricultural residues, wood, and charcoal, respectively; (IW), (IC)— improved wood and charcoal stoves; (KW), (KP)—kerosene wick and kerosene pressure stoves; (LPG)—LPG or natural gas stoves; and (EL)—electric resistance stove. Efficiencies and capital costs are for the stove alone and do not include up-stream capital costs for producing and delivering fuel. The range of performance both in the laboratory and in the field is much larger than that suggested by this figure and is affected by such factors as the size of the stove and pot, the climate (wind), the quality of the fuel used, the care with which the stove is operated, the type of cooking done, and many other factors. The type of material that the pot is made of is also a significant factor: aluminum pots are almost twice as efficient as traditional clay pots due to their better conduction of heat.

Source: (OTA, 1992b)

At the same time, efficiencies and costs tell a much different story when examined from a system, rather than the individual purchaser's, perspective. When the energy losses of converting wood to charcoal and fuel to electricity, refining petroleum products, and transporting these fuels to consumers are included, the system efficiency of delivering cooking energy by charcoal and electric stoves drops precipitously (see Figure 3.17).[16] These are important attributes to consider when evaluating the environmental impacts and financial feasibility of different cooking systems.

As for the efficiency estimates, there are substantial variations between the capital costs for individual stoves and for the entire

development combine advanced ceramic materials and new designs to augment both infrared and convective heating in a burner with very low emissions. There are similarly many potential efficiency improvements in ovens (such as convection ovens), pots used to cook with (such as pressure cookers), and other cooking devices. See (Geller, 1988), (Norgard, 1989), and (Shukla et al., 1985).

[16] Actual capital and operating costs will vary widely from these nominal values according to local fuel and stove costs, taxes, and other factors. Actual stove and system efficiencies and other performance factors will vary widely according to household size, diet, income, fuel availability, cooking habits, activity level, season, and many other factors. Some of these factors also tend to change at the same time stove type is changed. Migrants to urban areas may simultaneously change their stove and fuel type, family size, or diet. Financial savings gained by moving up to more efficient stoves may also

cooking system. This is particularly notable in the case of electricity where the upstream costs of generation, transmission and distribution, and other facilities are much larger than the capital cost that the consumer confronts for the stove itself (see Figure 3.18).[17]

Depending on relative fuel and stove prices, substantial reductions in both operating costs and energy use can be obtained from switching from traditional stoves using commercially purchased fuelwood to improved biomass, gas, or kerosene stoves (see Figure 3.19). There may be opportunities to substitute high performance biomass[18] stoves for traditional ones or to substitute liquid or gas (fossil- or biomass-based[19]) stoves for biomass stoves.[20] Local variations in stove and fuel costs[21] and availability, and in consumer perceptions of stove performance, convenience, and other attributes will then determine consumer choice. Regardless, there are substantial differences in systemwide capital and operating costs for different stoves, many of which are not directly observed by the consumer.

Within a given country, public policy can help shift consumers toward the more economically and environmentally promising cooking technologies. In particular, while improved biomass stoves may be the most cost effective option for the near- to mid-term, they require significant additional work to improve their performance (see Appendices A and B). In rural areas, biomass is likely to be the fuel of necessity for cooking for many years to come. Alternatively, liquid or gas fuelled stoves may offer the consumer greater convenience and performance[22] at reasonable costs, especially in urban areas. However, in order to make improved stove purchases economically feasible to most households, foreign exchange considerations will require that stove and system efficiencies be maximised and that as much as possible of the stove and other system equipment be manufactured in-country.

Finally, although early efforts in solar cooking were often disappointing (Pinon, 1983), recent work suggests that solar box ovens may yet offer an opportunity to meet

---

induce greater energy consumption as diet is changed, cooking habits relax, or more food is consumed. For example, estimates are that 15-25% of the savings with improved charcoal stoves will be offset through subsequent, income-induced consumption. The system-wide fuel savings achieved by going from traditional wood stoves to kerosene or LPG stoves also tend to be less than that expected from simply comparing the efficiency of different stoves as measured in the laboratory. See Jones (1988), and Fitzgerald et al. (1990).

[17]   The impact of electric cooking on the grid can be substantial. For example, more than one-third of electricity consumption in Costa Rica and Guatemala is for cooking, where about half of all electrified households have electric stoves. Annual electricity consumption for cooking in Guatemala is roughly 2,500 kilowatt hour (kWh)/year per household compared to 700 kWh/y in the United States, perhaps due to less use of prepared foods or differences in cuisine. In parts of Asia, electric rice cookers are becoming a substantial electric load. These demands can cause significant local problems for the power grid where loads are low and there is little diversified demand. With larger, more diversified grids, however, such demands pose fewer difficulties. Further, in some cases such as the use of microwave ovens for some baking, electric cooking may lower total energy use compared to, for example, baking in a conventional gas oven. Costa Rican and Guatemalan data from Ketoff and Masera, (1990).

[18]   Unless otherwise noted, biomass stoves is used here to denote stoves burning solid biomass; biomass derived liquids or gases are indicated separately.

[19]   Liquids or gases derived from biomass for use in stoves might include ethanol, plant oils, thermochemically derived, or other liquids; as well as methane from anaerobic digestion or thermochemically derived gases from thermal gasification systems.

[20]   Some argue that the biomass not used in cooking could instead be diverted to high efficiency electricity generation or process heat applications. Backing biomass out of the household sector in this manner poses significant difficulties in the collection and transport of the biomass to a central facility.

[21]   The values shown are for residential stoves. Commercial stoves exhibit similar trends, with a general shift upwards in efficiency and down in cost per quantity of food cooked due to scale effects. Further, this analysis does not separately consider foreign exchange costs.

[22]   Key factors in performance include efficiency, turn-down ratio, peak power, and emissions.

Figure 3.17: Stove and System Efficiences

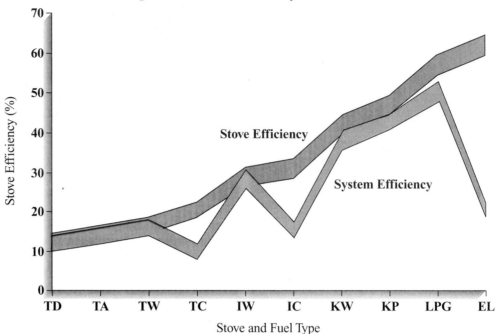

Stove and Fuel Type

Stove efficiencies are nominal values for the stove alone; system efficiencies include the energy losses in producing, converting, and delivering fuel to the consumer. (See the caption for Figure 3.16 for the identification of alternative stoves). Note, particularly, the low system efficiencies for charcoal (TC and IC) and electric (EL) stoves due to the large energy losses in converting wood to charcoal, and fuel to electricity.

Source: (OTA, 1992b)

Figure 3.18: Stove and System Capital Costs

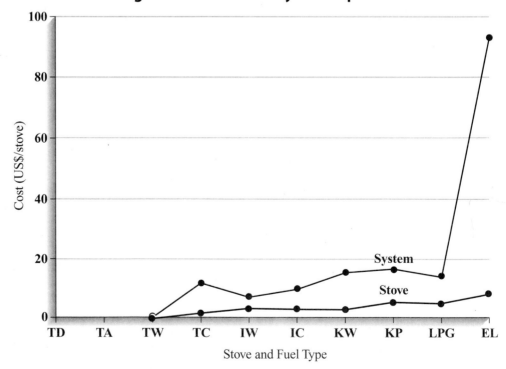

Stove and Fuel Type

When system costs are included, electric stoves can be seen to be particularly expensive. There is a wide range of costs around these nominal values. See the caption for Figure 3.16 for the identification of alternative stoves.

Source: (OTA, 1992b)

Figure 3.19: Annual Cost of Cooking for Different Stoves

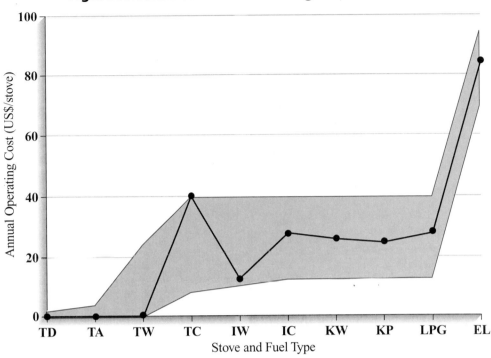

Data points show the cost as estimated from the nominal values. The gray band suggests the wide variation in costs using any particular stove depending on local stove and fuel costs, diet, and a host of other factors.
Source: (OTA, 1992b)

a portion of cooking needs in areas with high levels of sunshine and cuisine that is adaptable to that style of cooking (i.e., boiling or baking, not frying) (Kammen and Lankford, 1990). The potential of solar cookers nevertheless remains uncertain due to past difficulties. Solar cookers are expensive, bulky, and fragile; they may require changes in cooking practice; and materials to repair them may be difficult to obtain. More extensive analysis of field experience and further field trials are needed to independently characterise the performance of the current generation of solar cookers and determine their potential. If practical on a large scale, such an option has obvious attractions.

In the long-term (assuming income growth and the ability to finance imports), the transition to high quality liquid and gas fuels for cooking is inevitable.[23] With this transition, substantial amounts of labour now expended to gather biomass fuels in rural areas may be freed. The time and attention

needed to cook when using crude biomass fuels may be reduced substantially. Furthermore, household, local, and regional air pollution from smoky biomass (or coal) fires may be largely eliminated. On the other hand, high quality fuels will increase monetary costs to the individual consumer. Moreover, if fuels or stove equipment are imported, this situation could have significant impacts on national trade balances and foreign exchange holdings. The use of commercial liquid fuels from biomass, advanced gasification designs for stoves, and other options may be particularly important here. To realise any of these advanced biomass based systems, however, will require a substantial further research and development effort.

The transition to modern stoves and fuels thus offers users many benefits—including reduced time and labour as well as a potential reduction in cooking fuel inputs and in local air pollution levels.[24] Nevertheless, this transition can be constrained

---

[23] It may be possible, however, to use biomass in a domestic gasifying stove or to generate producer gas in a central gasification plant from which the gas is then piped to households for cooking.

[24] It might, however, increase global carbon dioxide emissions

sharply by the frequently higher capital and operating costs of modern stoves and uncertain fuel supplies. Means of lowering both capital and operating costs and ensuring the reliability of supply are needed if the poor are to gain access to these clean, high-efficiency technologies. Further, this transition could impose a substantial financial burden on poor nations.

A large-scale transition to LPG, for example, would require a significant investment in both capital equipment and ongoing fuel costs. Optimistically assuming that the capital cost of LPG systems would average $50 per household (including bottling, storage, and transport), the investment would be roughly 3.5 percent of current Gross National Product and 20 percent of the annual value-added in manufacturing for the three billion people in the lowest income countries [see Tables 1 and 6 in (World Bank, 1989a)]. The LPG used[25] would be equivalent to one-fourth total commercial energy consumption today by these countries and would be a significant fraction of their export earnings.[26] Significant economic growth and a gradual phase-in of these technologies are needed if these costs are to be absorbed. Given these costs and impacts, advanced biomass fuels—liquids or gases—could be highly beneficial in meeting cooking requirements for efficiency, cleanliness, and convenience, while minimising greenhouse gas emissions and trade balance impacts, and increasing domestic rural employment. A significant effort in advanced biomass fuels and cooking technologies is highly desirable.

---

[25] Assuming a per-capita power rate for cooking with LPG systems of 100 Watts. This is comparable to that seen in the United States and about twice that seen in European countries. It is likely that people in developing countries would continue to eat less processed foods, less restaurant food, and probably more grains and so would continue to use somewhat more fuel than that seen in households in the industrialised countries. Energy use rates for household cooking in different countries are given in (Prasad, 1982).

[26] From Table 5 in (World Bank, 1989a), converting kilogram oil equivalent to energy at 42 megajoules (MJ) per kg.

Appendix A: Improved Stoves in Developing Countries[27]

Traditional stoves, with their high levels of smoke and heat, awkward use, and heavy demand for fuel (and its attendant laborious collection), have long been a central focus of efforts to improve the lives of women in developing countries. Gandhian organizations developed stoves with chimneys to reduce indoor smoke pollution as early as the 1930s. S.P. Raju, who worked on stove design at the Hyderabad Engineering Research Laboratory, published a pamphlet, "Smokeless Kitchens for the Millions" in 1953 in which he promised women five freedoms—from smoke, from soot, from heat, from waste, and from fire risk. Following its own energy crisis in 1973, the Western World began to perceive corresponding energy problems in developing countries, particularly that of fuelwood use in traditional stoves and a possible connection between fuelwood use in cooking and deforestation.[28]

Following the path pioneered in India and elsewhere, a variety of improved stove programs were begun by western donors and host countries in the mid- to late-1970s. Program design and technology choice were strongly influenced by the "appropriate technology" movement: local materials were used, designs were kept simple (and supposedly low-cost), and low-skill labour intensive construction was emphasized.

The first generation of woodstoves that resulted from these considerations were typically thick blocks of a sand and clay mixture. Chambers and holes were carved in the block for the fire, for the pots to sit on, and for the smoke to exit to the chimney. A fire was built under the first pot; the second and subsequent pots were heated by the hot gases flowing toward the chimney. These were known as "massive multi-pot" stoves.

In many cases, little or no testing was done of these first generation designs before dissemination programs began. Numerous competing projects were launched—for example, some countries in West Africa had a dozen or more largely independent stove programs supported by different international non-governmental organizations, bilateral and multilateral aid agencies, and domestic organizations. These countries never individually had a critical mass of technical manpower to do proper design work, perform detailed field evaluations or follow-up, or conduct careful economic or social analysis. Operating independently and with little inter-program communication, the same mistakes often were repeated.

When field evaluations of these massive stoves began, serious problems surfaced. Field surveys found that most users quickly had returned to traditional stoves use. Laboratory and field studies alike showed that the massive stoves often used more fuel and emitted as much smoke as did traditional stoves. The stoves not only cost users a significant amount of time and effort (and sometimes money) to build, they also were hard to maintain, cracking and crumbling easily in the heat of the fire.

Contrary to then accepted wisdom, it appeared that traditional stoves were actually well optimised for local materials, pots, and other conditions as the result of many years of trial and error. Further improvements therefore called for sustained technical input in design, quality control in production, careful field testing and follow-up, and extensive input at every stage from women users. Considerations such as use of heat resistant materials (e.g., metals or ceramics) also proved important. These factors were missing from nearly all the programs.

In response to the numerous independent stove programs, their lack of success, and the need for firm technological under-

---

27 Appendix A is based on (Raju, 1953, reprinted 1961; Baldwin, 1986; Smith, 1989; Gill, 1987; Crouch, 1989; Jones, 1989; World Bank, 1989b; Kammen, 1995; Barnes et al., 1994).

28 It is now generally acknowledged that use of wood for fuel is not usually a strong contributor to deforestation. There are a few exceptions, particularly arid regions where biomass growth is low, or around urban or industrial areas with unusually high levels of fuel demand. See (OTA, 1991).

Table 3A.1: Dissemination of Improved Cookstoves

Country	Improved Cookstoves Disseminated (millions as of 1991)
China	120
India	8.0
Bangladesh	1.2
Kenya	0.55
Burkina Faso	0.33
Niger	0.20
Tanzania	0.05

Sources: (Karakezi, 1992; Barnes et al., 1994)

pinnings, efforts were launched in the early 1980s to co-ordinate the various stove programs and develop the technological foundations necessary for improved stove production and use. The technical effort showed that, at least under West African conditions, massive stoves typically used substantially more wood than traditional stoves. Using principles of engineering combustion and heat transfer, a "second generation" of simple lightweight stoves made of metal or ceramic was developed which achieved fuel savings in the field of about one-third compared with traditional stoves.

Realisation of these savings required that critical stove dimensions be adhered to, within a fraction of an inch. This requirement indicated that the stoves be "mass-produced" to match standard pot sizes. Thus, production would be best undertaken at central sites where strict quality control measures could be assured. In comparison the on-site handcrafting of massive stoves, centralised production also entailed the advantages of more rapid production, lower stove and program costs, and ready commercialisation. For the user, the new generation of lightweight stoves had the advantage of somewhat more rapid cooking, protection from burns that are

likely when cooking over an open fire, and portability e.g., a stove could be moved across a courtyard to take advantage of afternoon shade or across town if the household moved).

Massive stove programs made related changes, in careful dimensioning, quality control, and monitoring and evaluation, and consequently also realised much broader success. These stoves have proven popular in the field, as indicated by the levels of dissemination recently observed (see Table 3A.1).

Ironically, the widespread failure of the first generation "massive" stoves discredited stove programmes generally and caused many aid organizations to cut back financial support—just as significant improvements in stove performance finally were being realised through second generation lightweight and massive stoves.

In some cases, centralised mass production and commercial sale of lightweight stoves has shifted the programmatic focus of stove efforts from traditional rural areas largely outside the cash economy to poor urban areas. Effective means of addressing rural areas require additional efforts. Moreover, considerable work remains to further refine biomass stove designs so as to improve efficiencies and reduce noxious emissions.

Appendix B: Research Needs for Improved Biomass Stoves in Developing Countries[29]

The use of biomass resources for fuel contributes to several important problems. First, biomass fuels generate air pollution—particularly in village households—and possibly greenhouse gases. Second, supplying biomass fuels requires large amounts of time and labour. Third, in some areas, use of these fuels can contribute to deforestation. Nevertheless, biomass will continue to be the primary cooking fuel for rural and poor urban areas in developing countries for many years to come. Higher quality liquid or gas fuels are simply too expensive and too irregular in supply to supplant biomass anytime soon.

Although biomass will continue to be a primary fuel over the mid-term, it may be possible to improve the performance of biomass stoves significantly. Some successes have already been realised (see Appendix A) but much more could be done. Significant technical challenges remain to be overcome in order for clean-burning, fuel-efficient biomass stoves to be developed.

The performance of a biomass stove is the product of several difficult technical trade-offs. Fuel efficiency is improved by narrowing the gap between the pot wall and the stove to increase convective heat transfer; by limiting the flow of air into the stove to increase the average temperature of the combustion gases; by lowering the pot closer to the fire to increase the fraction of radiant heat from the fire that is intercepted by the pot; and by other means. But too narrow a gap can choke the fire and greatly increase cooking times; too little airflow into and through the stove can increase emissions of carbon monoxide and hazardous smoke; and lowering the pot closer to the fire can prevent complete combustion and greatly increase smoke emissions (as can easily be seen by putting an object into the flame of a candle). Further, unlike commercial fuels such as kerosene or LPG, biomass fuels vary markedly in density and form (from grass to logs), in composition, by moisture content,

and with respect to a host of other factors important in determining combustion characteristics. Combustion of biomass is also extremely complex, involving many thousands of interacting chemical species. Achieving both high fuel efficiency and low smoke emissions in a cook stove thus remains a substantial technical challenge.

The technical complexity of this task has several important implications. First, the technical complexity requires a high level of technical expertise that is difficult to assemble given the often small size of existing improved stove projects and funding in both developing and industrial countries. Some communications to address this "subcritical mass" problem, by pulling together researchers from around the world, have developed in recent years through internet listserves, but is not sufficient by itself. Additionally, it would be helpful to form regional centres of excellence in developing countries where a relatively large number of researchers can be brought together to form the critical mass of skilled manpower that is needed. Such a centre would draw the best manpower and concentrate the research effort, but base selection and continued participation on peer-reviewed performance. After the technology has been developed, these researchers could then return to their respective regions to direct further development and dissemination efforts.

Such regional centres of excellence could themselves have several important benefits. They would provide an opportunity to further develop institutional capacity through goal-oriented research focused on technologies of particular interest in developing countries.

Regional centres of excellence might also offer a means of enhancing the training of scientists and engineers. In some cases, young researchers returning with Masters or Doctoral degrees in science or engineering are expected to play important roles imme-

29   Appendix B is based on (Baldwin et al., 1985; Baldwin, 1986; Ahuja, 1990; Smith, 1987; Prasad et al., 1985).

diately in national research organizations. To be fully effective, however, scientists and engineers often require several years—even after receipt of their doctorate—working under the tutelage of a more experienced researcher, both as a postdoctoral fellow and as a member of a research team. Such experience is important. Much of what is required to select a viable approach to solving a research problem, to direct the research, and to manage the research budget and related administrative matters is not taught in school; it is instead learned through the modern equivalent of an apprenticeship. A regional centre of excellence would provide budding scientists and engineers more opportunity to learn such skills from mentors, rather than being expected to learn it all by trial and error on their own.

Regional centres of excellence in developing countries have been successfully developed for agricultural research, development, and field trials. An example is the International Rice Research Institute. The experience of these institutions may hold useful lessons for the development of energy technologies beyond what can be achieved through simple information exchange via the internet as it becomes more widely available.

Second, appropriate technologists often have suggested that technologies must be adapted as well as possible to the locality in which they are used and that failure to make such adaptations is a principal cause of failure. In this context it is important to recognize that a number of different factors might be "adapted," including the underlying technology, product design, manufacturing process, or means of product dissemination.

The basic technology of a stove or of most other related devices will remain largely the same across regions. Indeed, the technical complexity of biomass combustion and the similarities of wood in Latin America, Africa, or Asia suggests that much of the basic research might be best undertaken at the global level, as long as it is closely coupled with nearby field trials.

Variations in the practical use of stoves between regions may require some adaptation of the product design—such as the means of holding pots down when vigorously stirring, modified shapes to hold different types of pots, etc. Nevertheless, gas and kerosene stoves have been used equally well in the United States, Africa, and Asia, with little or no adaptation of their design.

The choice of fabrication method is more commonly an aspect that might be adapted to local conditions. Although the maintenance of precise dimensions in stoves will generally require mass production and quality control techniques, these requirements can be implemented in ways as varied as field outreach using forms, village metalsmith artisanal production using standardised templates or automated metal stamping facilities. Similarly, the choice of materials can also be varied somewhat depending on local conditions, from clay forms, to low quality scrap metal recovered from barrels or wrecked cars, to new high quality steel alloys or ceramics. Finally, product dissemination methods must be adapted to local conditions if they are to be successful.

Third, past failures in improved stove programs indicate the need to link laboratory research activities with practical field experience. It is important to avoid the creation of laboratory curiosities with no practical field application. Means of rewarding researchers that successfully see their work through to full-scale commercialisation need to be explored.

Fourth, the complexity of biomass combustion and heat transfer requires close attention to design and quality control. This is particularly significant because of the importance of the informal artisanal sector in disseminating such technologies as biomass stoves. Greater effort needs to be made to work with this important sector in terms of upgrading their production technologies, improving their access to adequate finance, developing better means of technology transfer, providing training, and other issues.

Finally, the experience with improved biomass stoves has shown the market mechanism to be a particularly valuable tool in urban areas for weeding out poor technology designs or weighing alternatives through competition. The market mechanism is not as effective, however, in rural areas largely outside the cash economy. Methods of adequately meeting the needs in these areas should be developed.

4 Sustainable Strategies

While conventional energy strategies pose severe social, economic, environmental, and insecurity problems that jeopardise realisation of the goal of a sustainable world, as discussed in Chapter 2, there are many promising energy options that are supportive of sustainable development objectives, as explored in Chapter 3. Global energy scenarios can facilitate understanding the prospects for alternative combinations of such technologies in addressing these objectives.

4.1 Global Energy Scenarios

Several scenarios developed by international organisations are reviewed here with regard to the relative roles each ascribes to energy efficiency, fossil fuels, nuclear energy, and various combinations of renewable energy sources in meeting sustainable development objectives.[1]

4.1.1 Introduction

The six IS92 scenarios generated by the Intergovernmental Panel on Climate Change (IPCC) describe how global energy might evolve over the next century *if society were to take no actions to deal with climate change*

risks (IPCC, 1992). One of these, IS92a, the Reference Scenario in Table 4.1, is reviewed in this chapter. In this scenario, global population and primary energy use increase more than 2-fold and 4-fold, respectively, over the period 1990-2100.

In the private sector, the Group Planning Division at the Shell International Petroleum Company in 1994 introduced two long-term global energy scenarios in its biennial global scenarios analysis: a Sustained Growth Scenario (Kassler, 1994) and a Dematerialisation Scenario (Shell International Petroleum Company,1995), both of which are addressed in this chapter and summarised in Table 4.1. Primary energy demand grows more than 7-fold and 3-fold, 1990-2100, under Sustained Growth and Dematerialisation conditions, respectively. Sustained Growth represents a world where abundant energy supply is continually provided at competitive costs, as energy supply productivity increases to compensate for resource constraints. Dematerialisation represents a world where human needs for energy services are provided via the use of technologies and systems that require much lower

---

[1] Other notable global energy scenario exercises that have been carried out in recent years that are not closely reviewed here include: *i)* a Renewables Intensive Global Energy Scenario (RIGES), prepared as an input to the 1992 United Nations Conference on Environment and Development (Johansson et al., 1993a); *ii)* the scenarios generated in a major 1993 study of world energy by the WEC Commission (WEC, 1993); and *iii)* a recent French study (Dessus, 1996) that advances a New Options for Energy Scenario (NOES).

The RIGES describes contributions renewables might plausibly make to global energy by the year 2050, on the basis of a detailed international assessment of the prospects for making electricity and fuels from renewable energy sources (Johansson et al., 1993b). The RIGES, modified and extended to the year 2100, provided the basis for the Biomass-Intensive Variant of the IPCC-LESS Constructions.

The 1993 WEC Commission scenarios focused on the year 2020 but extended in outline to 2100 were the point of departure for the more recent and elaborated WEC/IIASA scenarios that look to the long-term future in much more detail.

The NOES is similar in spirit to the energy-efficient, low-nuclear variants of the IPCC-LESS Constructions and the low-nuclear variant (C1) of the WEC/IIASA Ecologically-Driven Scenario, in that it emphasises the efficient use of energy and renewable energy and de-emphasises nuclear energy. The NOES sets far more ambitious targets for energy efficiency improvement in the industrialised countries than either of these other scenarios (e.g., per capita energy use in industrialised countries in 2100 in the NOES is just 2/5 of the level at that time in the energy-efficient LESS Constructions). Fuel decarbonisation with CO_2 sequestration, an option explored in some detail in the alternative LESS Constructions, is not considered in the NOES. The CO_2 emission rate from fossil fuel burning in 2100 is about 50% higher for the NOES than for the LESS Constructions and the Ecologically-Driven Scenarios.

Table 4.1: Alternative Scenarios for Global Energy Use in 2050[a] (EJ per year)

Primary Energy Source	Actual 1990	IS92a, the IPCC's Reference Scenario[b]	WEC/IIASA[c] B (Reference)	WEC/IIASA[c] C₁ (Ecologically Driven)	Shell International Petroleum Corporation Sustained Growth[d]	Shell International Petroleum Corporation Dematerialization[e]	Biomass-Intensive Variant of the the IPCCs less Constructions[f]
Coal	96.9	356	179	66	184	150	56
Oil	142.9	153	179	121	148	121	75
Natural Gas	76.0	143	210	182	140	182	120
Fossil Fuel Subtotal	**315.8**	**652**	**568**	**369**	**472**	**453**	**251**
Nuclear	22.8	87	121	22	94	62	11
Renewables[g]	31.9 (+41.6)	252	141 (+56)	195 (+55)	619 (+61)	207 (+61)	312
Total[g]	**370.5** (+41.6)	**991**	**830** (+56)	**586** (+55)	**1185** (+61)	**722** (+61)	**574**

a. *Fuel values are higher heating values (HHVs). In the original references, HHVs were used only in the IPCC's LESS constructions. The lower heating values (LHVs) in the other scenarios were converted to HHVs by dividing by 0.96, 0.94, 0.90 and 0.94, for coal, oil, natural gas, and biomass respectively. Primary fuel input equivalents for hydropower, nuclear powere and intermittent renewables were converted to HHVs by dividing by 0.94.*
b. *Source: (IPCC, 1992)*
c. *Source: (WEC/IIASA, 1995)*
d. *Source: (Kassler, 1994)*
e. *Source: (Shell International Petroleum Company, 1995)*
f. *Source: (IPCC, 1996a)*
g. *The numbers in parentheses are noncommercial biomass energy use.*

energy inputs than under Sustained Growth conditions.

A study (WEC/IIASA, 1995) by the World Energy Council (WEC) and the International Institute for Advanced Study (IIASA) analysed three High-Growth scenarios (A1, A2, and A3), one Reference Scenario (B), and two Ecologically-Driven Scenarios (C1 and C2). Here the focus is on the Reference and Ecologically-Driven Scenarios. Primary commercial energy demand grows 4.2-fold and 2.4-fold, 1990-2100, for the Reference and Ecologically-Driven Scenarios, respectively. In the Ecologically-Driven Scenario high levels of energy efficiency improvement are realised. The two Ecologically-Driven Scenarios differ largely in the role of nuclear power. In C1, nuclear power is phased out by 2100; while in C2, the nuclear power industry is revived and nuclear generation increases approximately 10-fold, 1990-2100.

The Energy Supply Mitigation Subgroup of the IPCC's Working Group II developed alternative Low CO₂-Emitting Energy Supply Systems for the world (alternative LESS Constructions) for the IPCC's Second Assessment Report (IPCC, 1996a; Johansson et al., 1996) to provide an integrated assessment of the prospects for

achieving deep reductions in CO₂ emissions from the energy supply system over the course of the next century. This effort included alternative combinations of energy supply technologies and strategies that the subgroup had assessed—including more energy-efficient conversion technologies, renewable energy technologies, fuel decarbonisation/CO₂ sequestration technologies, and nuclear energy. LESS variants were constructed both from the "bottom up" (Williams, 1995a) and the "top down" (Edmonds, Wise, and McCracken, 1994).

Five alternative LESS variants were constructed from the bottom up: Biomass-Intensive, Natural Gas-Intensive, Coal-Intensive, and Nuclear-Intensive Variants, all of which emphasised the efficient use of energy (constructed in the same spirit as the WEC/IIASA Ecologically-Driven Scenario), with primary commercial energy use increasing 1.9-fold, 1990-2100, and a High-Demand Variant, in which primary commercial energy use increases 3.7-fold, 1990-2100 (see Figure 4.1). For the two LESS variants constructed from the top down that lead to deep reductions in emissions by the end of the next century at about the same level as in the bottom-up LESS Constructions, primary commercial energy use levels in 2100 are

Figure 4.1: Global Primary Energy Use for Alternative IPCC-LESS Constructions

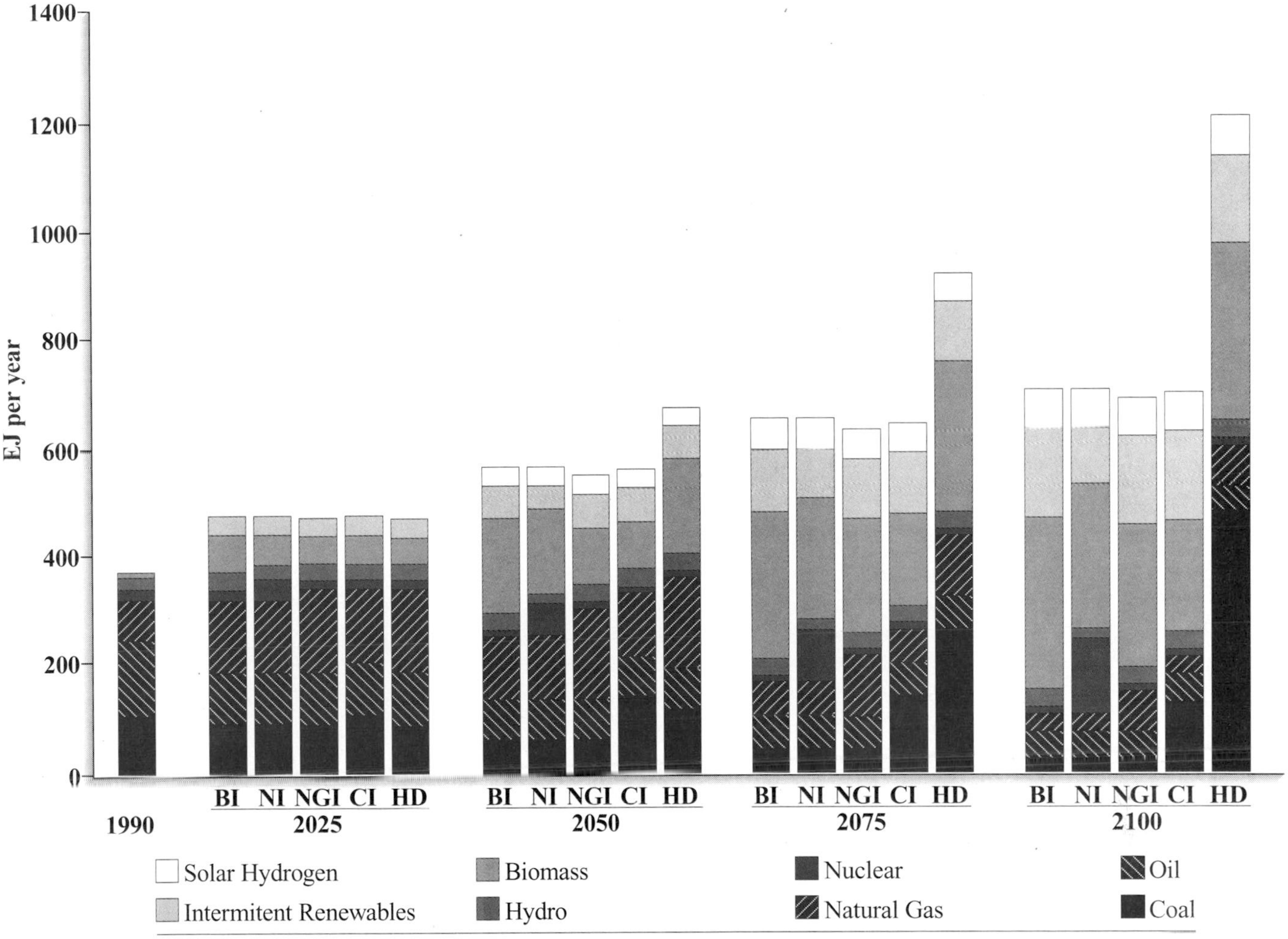

BI – Biomass Intensive Variant, NI = Nuclear Intensive Variant, NGI = Natural Gas Intensive Variant, CI = Coal Intensive Variant, HD – High Demand Variant

Source: (IPCC, 1996a).

1.6 and 2.8 times primary commercial energy use in 1990.

While the starkly different levels of energy use as well as the different mixes of energy sources among these different scenarios during the period 2050 to 2100 arise partly as a result of different economic growth rates, they primarily result from differing views of how energy technology might evolve over the period. Significant technological differences among scenarios are to be expected over the long term. By 2100 the entire global energy system will "turn over" at least twice, offering much opportunity for

change as new investments are made. Many technologies which now are unavailable commercially will then be widely used. However, there is no way to predict which advanced technologies will be chosen over the long-term.

Although this chapter addresses each of the scenarios, attention is focused on two subsets of them—the WEC/IIASA Ecologically-Driven Scenarios[2] and the energy-efficient variants of the IPCC-LESS Constructions. These scenarios emphasise energy options that are generally supportive of sustainable development objectives, including options for mak-

---

[2]   The WEC/IIASA A3 Scenario also has some attributes consistent with sustainable development, including emphasis on natural gas (the cleanest fossil fuel) and large contributions from renewable energy sources (equivalent by 2050 to total fossil plus nuclear energy in 1990 and three times this amount by 2100). The large projected role for renewables at the expense of coal (phased out by 2100)

ing more efficient use of energy, for reducing environmental impacts of fossil fuel use, and for using renewable energy sources. Both sets of scenarios include nuclear-intensive variants, in which the nuclear power industry is revived and nuclear capacity expands approximately 10-fold, 1990-2100, as well as variants in which nuclear power does not grow or is phased out during the next century.

These "sustainable development" scenarios were constructed under the assumption that public policies would be implemented to promote the efficient use of energy, environmental values in the energy system, and energy innovation. Both also emphasise international cooperation and a high rate of technology transfer to, and energy innovation in, developing countries.

The WEC/IIASA Ecologically Driven Scenarios reflect aggressive efforts to advance international economic equity and environmental protection. The assumed measures include large direct transfers from North to South plus stringent environmental taxes or other levies and grants that are paid principally by OECD countries and transferred to the developing world. As a result of these transfers, GDP in OECD countries grows slightly more slowly (- 0.2%/year, 1990-2050) than in the WEC/IIASA Reference Scenario, which does not involve such transfers, but at the global level the result is slightly faster global GDP growth (+ 0.05%/year, 1990-2050) as compared to the Reference Scenario, because growth is more rapid (+ 0.4%/year, 1990-2050) in developing countries.

For the energy-efficient IPCC-LESS

Constructions, it was assumed that policies with the same objectives are enacted. However, the set of measures identified for meeting these objectives in the WEC/IIASA Ecologically Driven Scenarios were not specified in the LESS Constructions, since there are other possible instruments that could bring about similar results. One plausible set of alternative policies for reaching essentially the same ends would be expanded public-sector support for research and development and for commercialisation incentives to help launch new technologies in the market, and adoption of economic reforms in the energy sector. The latter could include elimination of permanent subsidies to producers and consumers and the pricing of energy to reflect actual costs, including environmental costs not reflected in market prices. Such a combination of policies plausibly could lead to similar outcomes without large direct income transfers from OECD to developing countries, because of a natural convergence of interests between developing and industrialised countries with regard to the energy technologies needed for these scenarios, and an energy market dynamic that might develop in the pursuit of these mutual interests (see Chapter 5).

4.1.2 The Efficient Use of Energy

In 1987 the World Commission on Environment and Development (WCED, 1987) concluded that, "a low energy path is the best way towards a sustainable future...it will buy time to mount major programmes on sustainable forms of renewable energy, to so

---

arises from an assumed rapid rate of technological innovation brought about by free market forces. The C (Ecologically-Driven) Scenarios rather than the A3 Scenario are given more attention in the present review because at the lower level of energy demand in the C scenarios made possible by emphasis on efficient use of energy, it is technologically less challenging to realise sustainability objectives and society is given more choice to reduce dependence on options that become problematic, especially at high levels of development.

Commercial energy use grows so much (2.8-fold by 2050 and 5.3-fold by 2100 relative to 1990) that the A3 Scenario can be realised only if optimistic outcomes can be realised for *all* the emphasised energy supplies. Cumulative natural gas consumption, 1990-2100, is approximately the sum of the *high estimate* of remaining conventional natural gas resources (Masters et al., 1994) plus estimated ultimately recoverable non-conventional resources (WEC/IIASA, 1995), a plausible but optimistic outlook for the natural gas resource base. The biomass production level by 2100 exceeds that of the Biomass-Intensive Variant of the LESS Constructions (IPCC, 1996a)—again a conceivable but optimistic outcome in light of land-use competition issues that must be resolved to reach such high levels of biomass development (WEC/IIASA, 1995). Finally, nuclear power generation increases 20-fold by 2100 relative to 1990, which requires that the major constraints now facing nuclear power are overcome (see Section 4.1.4). Moreover, despite the assumed high rate of innovation for low CO_2-emitting energy technologies, CO_2 emissions from energy in this scenario rise to a peak level near 10 GtC per year in the second half of the next century before declining somewhat by the year 2100.

begin the transition to a safer, more sustainable energy era." The more efficient use of energy is often far more cost-effective than investment in energy supply expansion.

While large gains in energy efficiency are possible with commercially available technologies, continuing gains are feasible with advanced technologies for a long time to come (i.e., "energy efficiency resources" are not likely to be soon depleted). An important additional benefit of a low-energy future is the flexibility it offers in addressing the multiple challenges posed by the energy system in the pursuit of sustainable development. By keeping demand levels low via the exploitation of technological opportunities for improving the efficiency of energy use, such as those discussed in Chapter 3, society could gain greater flexibility in choosing energy supply options to meet its needs for energy services. This course also could help minimise, or avoid entirely, dependence on the more troubling sources.

The potential aggregate impacts on energy demand of opportunities for improving the efficiency of energy use change continually as technology evolves. A recent study carried out for the United Nations Division for Policy Co ordination and Sustainable Development (Worrell et al., 1997) provides an up-to-date quantitative assessment of these opportunities for the period to the year 2020. This analysis examines energy futures for four alternative scenarios relating to energy-efficient technology, each offering the same levels of energy services: *i*) business-as-usual; *ii*) state-of-the-art technology for efficient use of energy; *iii*) advanced technology for efficient use of energy; and *iv*) advanced technology for efficient use of both energy and materials. According to this assessment, per capita primary energy consumption levels in 2020 relative to 1990 levels are 1.9 (business-as-usual), 1.5 (state-of-the-art technology for efficient use of energy), 1.15 (advanced technology for efficient use of energy), and 1.0 (advanced technology for efficient use of energy/materials) for developing countries. The corresponding values are 1.3, 1.1, 0.9, and 0.85 for industrialised countries plus economies

in transition, and 1.25, 1.0, 0.8, and 0.75 at the global level. Although the appropriate policies needed for realising the more ambitious energy efficiency gains identified as achievable in this analysis are imperfectly known, this exercise is useful as a yardstick for understanding better the extent to which energy efficiency improvement opportunities are being exploited in the alternative global energy scenarios reviewed here.

For IS92a, per capita primary commercial energy consumption rates in 2020 relative to 1990 are 1.8 for developing countries and 1.3 for industrialised countries plus economies in transition—clearly identifying this scenario as a business-as-usual future with regard to exploitation of opportunities for making more efficient use of energy.

The use of advanced technologies for using energy more efficiently, including emphasis on materials that are lighter and stronger and the reduced need for materials (the production of which tends to be especially energy-intensive) via such innovations, is a key feature that distinguishes Shell's Dematerialisation Scenario from its Sustained Growth Scenario. With a global average per capita commercial energy use rate in 2020 of about 1.25 times the 1990 rate, Sustained Growth also represents business-as-usual. The corresponding ratio for Dematerialisation is about 1.15, a modest improvement over business-as-usual.

The scenarios reviewed here that involve the most aggressive pursuit of opportunities for making more efficient use of energy are WEC/IIASA's Ecologically-Driven Scenarios and the energy-efficient variants of the IPCC-LESS Constructions. In the former, primary global commercial energy consumption increases, relative to 1990 levels, 1.3-fold by 2020, 1.6-fold by 2050, and 2.5-fold by 2100. In the latter, primary global commercial energy consumption increases 1.3-fold by 2025, 1.6-fold by 2050, and 1.9-fold by 2100.[3] By the period 2020-2025 these scenarios are characterised by per capita commercial energy use rates for developing countries that are 1.4 to 1.5 times the use rates in 1990 and the corresponding ratio for industrialised countries and econo-

---

3   In the energy-efficient LESS Constructions, primary commercial energy use per capita in 2100 is 0.85 times the 1990 level in industrialised countries plus economies in transition and 2.0 times the 1990 level in developing countries.

Table 4.2a: WEC/IIASA Projections of Cumulative Global Oil and Natural Gas Consumption, 1990-2050[a] (10³ EJ)

WEC/IIASA Global Energy Scenario	Cumulative Oil Consumption	Cumulative Natural Gas Consumption
A1 (High-growth)	15.8	11.3
A2 (High-growth)	13.4	12.2
A3 (High-growth)	12.3	14.0
B (Reference)	11.5	10.7
C (Ecologically Driven)	9.3	9.5

Table 4.2b: U.S Geological Survey Estimates of Remaining Recoverable Conventional Oil and Natural Gas Resources[b] (10³ EJ)

Estimate	Conventional Oil	Conventional Natural Gas
High	13.7	16.5
Mean	11.1	11.9
Low	9.4	8.7

a   *Source: (WEC/IIASA, 1995)*
b   *Identified reserves + estimated undiscovered resources. Source: (Masters et al., 1994)*

mies in transition is 0.8. These scenarios are thus consistent with exploiting advanced technologies as they become available in industrialised countries and economies in transition, and state-of-the art energy efficiency technologies in developing countries. Thus the energy efficiency levels established for the Ecologically-Driven Scenarios and the LESS Constructions in the period to the end of the first quarter of the 21st century are consistent with what is known about the potential for energy efficiency improvement.

4.1.3 Fossil Fuels

Fossil fuel resource exhaustion is not a concern for the 21st century. However, because of the rising global demand for fluid fuels and constraints on conventional oil and natural gas resources, new sources of fluid fuels will be needed during the next century. These could be non-conventional oil and natural gas resources, synthetic fuels derived from coal or biomass, or some combination of these options. Choices among alternative options will be determined largely by considerations of local, regional, and global environmental impacts and energy security concerns, as well as by the relative levels of technology development and direct economic costs.

4.1.3.1 Oil and natural gas

In the Shell scenarios, oil plus natural gas production peak at 1.6 to 1.8 times the 1990 rate in the period 2030-2035 and decline slowly thereafter. This peaking is envisioned *not as a response to fossil fuel supply exhaustion* but rather as *a reflection of expected limits on fluid fuel productive capacity*, as conventional oil and natural gas resources are drawn down and less concentrated resources are developed.

The WEC/IIASA scenarios and the IPCC-LESS Constructions are distinguished by different assumptions regarding the provision of fluid fuels. In the WEC/IIASA scenarios, conventional oil and natural gas resources are used up to a large degree by the middle of the next century (see Tables 4.2a and 4.2b), and both non-conventional oil and natural gas resources and synthetic fuels play major roles in meeting fluid fuel needs during the course of the next century. For the LESS Constructions it is assumed that oil and natural gas exploitation in the 21st century is limited to conventional resources, 80% of which are consumed by the year 2100. For the LESS Constructions it is assumed that fluid fuel requirements which are not met by conventional oil and natural gas instead are provided by synthetic fuels derived from biomass and from coal, with some sequestering of the CO_2 recovered at the synthetic fuel conversion facilities. The main trade-offs among these different approaches are likely to be the environmental risks associated with developing various non-conventional oil and natural gas sources, environmental risks of coal recovery, concerns about CO_2 sequestration, and concerns about land use requirements for growing biomass for energy when biomass is a major contributor to energy supplies.

4.1.3.2 Coal

In the Shell scenarios, global coal production increases until the middle of the next century and declines slowly thereafter. Peak coal production levels differ markedly in the two scenarios, however; peak production reaches 2.5 times the 1990 level in the Sustained Growth Scenario, but only 1.4 times the 1990 level in the Dematerialisation Scenario.

In the WEC/IIASA Reference Scenario, coal production grows throughout the next century, increasing to 1.5, 1.9, and 3.5 times the 1990 level by 2020, 2050, and 2100, respectively. In contrast, for the Ecologically Driven Scenarios, global coal production rises about 5% by 2020 and then declines to two thirds of the 1990 level by 2050 and to one third that level by 2100.

In the Biomass-Intensive, Nuclear-Intensive, and Natural Gas-Intensive variants of the IPCC-LESS Constructions, global coal production declines monotonically, reaching about one quarter of the 1990 level by 2100, although coal production first increases 70% in developing countries (84% in China) by 2025 before beginning a long-term decline. However, in the Coal-Intensive Variant of the LESS Constructions, coal production increases until it reaches an average rate during the second half of the next century that is 1.4 times the 1990 rate.

In those LESS Constructions for which coal use declines in the next century, it is assumed that if renewable energy sources were to be available at approximately the same cost, the renewables would be favoured in the market. It would be very difficult for renewables to compete with coal in the absence of significant environmental constraints on coal use. However, in the LESS Constructions it is assumed that air-pollution standards similar to the most stringent in the industrialised world are in place and enforced world-wide. Without these conditions being effectively applied, the WEC/IIASA (1995) study indicated that even by 2020 ambient air quality in South and East Asia would deteriorate chronically in a high-coal scenario (A2), and acid deposition would greatly exceed what their ecosystems could sustain (see Section 2.2.2.3). Under stringent air-pollution standards, there are good prospects that over the course of the next couple of decades, electricity and fluid fuels produced from renewables would be able to provide energy services at about the same costs as for coal, if adequate R&D support and commercialisation incentives are provided for these alternatives (IPCC, 1996a; Johansson et al., 1996).

4.1.4 Nuclear Power

While annual nuclear power plant construction starts world-wide have fallen from a peak value of about 30 GW$_e$ per year in the mid-1970s to an average rate of just 3 GW$_e$ per year in the 1990s (IPCC, 1996a), nuclear energy could replace baseload fossil fuel electricity generation in many parts of the world if generally acceptable responses can be found to concerns such as reactor safety, radioactive-waste transport and disposal, and nuclear proliferation (IPCC, 1996b).

The various scenarios listed in Table 4.1 represent quite different future courses for nuclear energy. Some assume that a nuclear revival takes place. The WEC/IIASA Reference Scenario (B) envisages a 20-fold increase in annual nuclear power generation, 1990-2100, and the IS92a Scenario and the nuclear-intensive variants of both the WEC/IIASA Ecologically-Driven Scenario (C2) and the IPCC-LESS Constructions envisage a 10-fold increase within this time frame. For the nuclear-constrained variant of the WEC/IIASA Ecologically-Driven Scenario (C1) and for the other variants of the IPCC-LESS Constructions it is assumed that a nuclear revival does not take place.

A key consideration is the cost to society of reviving the nuclear option. One estimate of the investment needed to rebuild public confidence in nuclear fission is US$30 to US$50 billion—largely for developing and demonstrating two or three advanced, safe reactors; for developing technologies and strategies for the disposal of high-level radioactive wastes; and for developing internationally-controlled nuclear fuel services (Fulkerson and Anderson, 1996). The last of these measures would significantly reduce (but not eliminate) nuclear proliferation risks.

In a world where installed nuclear capacity reaches 3,000 GW$_e$ by 2100 (the projection for IS92a and the nuclear-intensive variants of the Ecologically-Driven Scenarios and the LESS Constructions), annual plutonium flows in spent fuel discharged from reactors would be about 600,000 kg/year in 2100 if only once-through nuclear fuel cycles were deployed. If instead plutonium recycle and breeder reactors were then the norm, about 3,000,000 kg/year of plutonium would be recovered from spent fuel via reprocessing for use as fresh fuel.[4] In either case, securing all this material against occasional diversions to nuclear weapons purposes

---

[4] Using only once through fuel cycles would involve cumulative consumption of about 20 million tonnes of uranium, 1990-2100. Because this level of cumulative uranium requirements approaches the

would be a daunting challenge (see Section 2.4.2). (Less than 10 kg of plutonium is required for a nuclear explosive.)

4.1.5 Renewable Energy

Apart from emphasis on improving the efficiency of energy use, which is often more cost-effective in providing a given level of energy services than any energy-supply strategy, widespread application of renewable energy technologies offers some of the best prospects for providing needed energy services in ways that are consistent with addressing the multiple challenges to sustainable development posed by conventional energy, including local, regional, and global environmental problems.

In the near term, the penetration of the energy economy with renewables will be inhibited by low fossil fuel prices. For example, it will be difficult for renewables to compete on standard economic terms with natural gas, currently the energy source of choice for many applications in those parts of the world where natural gas is readily available.[5] Despite low fossil fuel prices there are substantial near-term opportunities to grow renewable energy industries.

Today, renewables make it possible to bring modern energy technologies more quickly and at lower cost than with conventional energy sources to many in the large fraction of the population that does not yet enjoy their benefits. About 63% of the population of the developing world live in rural areas (WRI, 1994), 67% of which do not have grid connection (Clement-Jones and Mercier, 1995). Where the population density is less than two people per km^2, the cost of the electricity cable will be more than US$5,000 per hook-up. In such remote areas, there are often good opportunities for using renewables at competitive costs in meeting small-scale mechanical or electric power needs at levels of the individual household, farm, or village.

Also, there are many regions of the world where electric grid connections are in place but where natural gas is not readily available, either because of the relatively poor prospects for substantial domestic production (e.g., China, India, and Brazil), or because of the high capital investment levels and long lead times required to put natural gas infrastructure in place. In such regions there are good prospects for introducing renewables under competitive conditions over the next couple of decades if the use of coal is held to high local environmental standards (see Section 4.1.3.2) and if adequate incentives are provided for R&D on and commercialisation of a wide range of renewable energy technologies.

Even where low-cost natural gas is available but energy demand is growing rapidly, the growing of competitive renewable energy industries could probably be accomplished relatively quickly at relatively low cost, because many of the promising renewable energy technologies require relatively modest investments in R&D and commercialisation incentives. The need for only relatively modest investments is a reflection largely of the small scale and modularity of these technologies and the fact that they are generally clean and safe (Williams, 1995b). After the research phase, the high costs of "scaling up" in the development process can be avoided with small-scale technologies. Many renewable and other related energy technologies (e.g. fuel cells) offer the potential for major cost reductions as a result of both technological improvement and organisational learning (i.e., learning-by-doing). Many are good candidates for cost-cutting via organisational learning because they are modular and readily amenable to the economies of producing large numbers of identical units. Also, the time from initial product design to operation for these technologies is short, so that needed improvements can be

---

limit of estimated conventional uranium resources, there would be pressures at least in the second half of the next century either to exploit unconventional uranium resources (e.g. to begin to extract uranium from sea water, a dilute but vast resource) or to shift to plutonium breeder reactors.

[5] However, emphasis on natural gas in the near term is likely to be helpful to renewables in the long term. In power generation, for example, natural gas-fired combustion turbine and combined cycle power plants are good complements for intermittent renewable electric systems (see Section 3.3.2.9) and advanced technologies (e.g., advanced gas-turbine and fuel-cell technologies) that are now being developed for natural gas applications in stationary power and transport systems can be used later with renewable energy sources (see Sections 3.3.2.6, 3.3.2.8 and 3.3.5.6).

determined in field testing and quickly incorporated into modified designs—making possible many generations of marginally improved products in relatively short periods of time. For technologies such as renewables that are also characterised by high degrees of inherent safety and cleanliness, R&D resource requirements for improving safety and environmental performance are small. Thus, it should be feasible, even with relatively limited resources for R&D and for new technology commercialisation incentives to support diversified portfolios of renewable energy technology options.

The World Energy Council has estimated that the R&D expenditures needed world-wide to advance a range of solar energy technologies is in the order of US$8 billion (WEC, 1994). R&D programmes are necessary but not sufficient to establish new technologies in the marketplace. Commercial demonstration projects and programmes to stimulate markets for new technologies also are needed. The World Energy Council estimates that subsidies in the order of US$ 7-US$12 billion will be needed to support initial deployment of various solar energy technologies until manufacturing economies of scale are achieved, in order to compete with conventional options (WEC, 1994). Thus, the total investment needed for research and development on and support for initial deployment of renewable energy technologies is estimated to be US$15-US$20 billion. This cost would amount to only 0.1% of the annual global gross national product at the turn of the century if the entire expenditure were made in one year; in practice the expenditures as a percentage of global gross national product would be much less, since this support would be spread out over a couple of decades. These costs are also much less than the estimated cost of US$30-US$50 billion for new technology needed to rebuild public confidence in nuclear energy (Fulkerson and Anderson, 1996).

Because of such considerations, the contribution of renewables to global commercial energy in all the scenarios listed in Table 4.1 is expected to increase over time from the 9% contribution (mostly hydroelectric power) made in 1990. The average contribution for the six scenarios shown is 17 % in 2020-2025 and 35% in 2050, with more than a 50% contribution from renewables by 2050 in the Shell

Sustained Growth scenario and the Biomass-Intensive Variant of the IPCC-LESS Constructions.

The Shell scenarios envisage a rapidly growing role for renewable energy at the expense of fossil fuels after about 2030-2040, as a reflection of both perceived limits on fossil fuel productive capacity (see Section 4.1.3.1) and a projected market dynamic in which the rate of innovation in the mature fossil-fuel industries would not be able to keep up with that for renewables, once the latter gained footholds in the energy market.

Most of the scenarios listed in Table 4.1 project that renewables could contribute some 200 EJ per year or more by 2050. If low energy demand scenarios (e.g. the WEC/IIASA Ecologically-Driven Scenario or the IPCC's energy-efficient LESS Constructions) could be realised and if renewable energy industries were producing at a level of about 200 EJ per year by the middle of the next century, these industries would then be sufficiently well-established that they plausibly could meet all energy requirements not met by fossil fuels throughout the rest of the next century, even if fossil fuel use were thereafter to decline to the extent needed to stabilise the concentration of CO_2 in the atmosphere at about 400 ppmv (see Section 4.1.6).

While there has been remarkable progress to date toward commercialisation of renewable energy technologies, and some renewables are ready for commercial applications in significant niche markets, many of these technologies are not yet ready for widespread adoption in the energy economy. Renewables-intensive energy futures such as those described in the Shell Scenarios and LESS Constructions cannot be realised without a high rate of innovation in the energy sector in both the industrialised and the developing worlds. Such futures can come about only if society takes actions that include providing needed support for research and development on renewable energy technologies and incentives to help launch new industries based on technologies that are successfully developed.

4.1.6 Energy and Climate Change in the Scenarios

One of the major purposes of constructing global energy scenarios with time horizons extending as far as the year 2100 is to understand better the prospects for dealing with the challenge of climate change, which requires a considerably longer-term perspective than other issues.

Carbon cycle analyses that relate alternative ceilings on atmospheric CO_2 concentrations to CO_2 emission profiles over time (IPCC, 1994) are helpful in understanding the implications for climate change of alternative global energy scenarios. These studies indicate that a stable level of CO_2 concentration up to 750 ppmv can be achieved only if the CO_2 emission rate eventually drops below the 1990 rate, and that, to a good approximation, the stabilised concentration of CO_2 in the atmosphere depends primarily on the cumulative CO_2 emissions between now and the time of stabilisation and less on the exact path taken to realise stabilisation. Results of these studies for atmospheric stabilisation levels ranging from 350 ppmv to 750 ppmv along with the associated cumulative anthropogenic CO_2 emissions are shown in Table 2.9 of Chapter 2 for the period 1990-2100. Cumulative emissions associated with the IPCC's IS92 scenarios are shown for comparison. For IS92a, the IPCC Reference Scenario, CO_2 emissions from fossil fuel burning increase from 6 GtC/year to 20 GtC/year, 1990-2100; moreover, cumulative CO_2 emissions, 1990-2100, reach 1500 GtC, which is consistent with stabilisation at a CO_2 concentration in excess of 750 ppmv.

In the Shell scenarios, as non-fossil fuel technologies come to play ever greater roles in the global energy economy, CO_2 emissions peak at 10 GtC/year near 2030 and then decline slowly to 4 GtC/year by 2100. The cumulative emissions envisioned in these scenarios are consistent with stabilisation at a CO_2 concentration of 550-600 ppmv, about double the pre-industrial level.

For the WEC/IIASA Reference Scenario, CO_2 emissions increase throughout the next century, reaching 13 GtC by 2100; cumulative emissions, 1990-2100, are 1200 GtC, consistent with stabilisation near 650 ppmv. For the WEC/IIASA Ecologically-Driven Scenarios emissions fall by 2100 to 2 GtC/year by 2100, and cumulative emissions are less than 600 GtC, consistent with stabilisation at about 430 ppmv.

Annual CO_2 emissions for the IPCC-LESS Constructions are indicated in Figure 4.2, along with emissions from the IPCC's

IS92 scenarios, for reference. As in the case of the WEC/IIASA Ecologically-Driven Scenario, global CO_2 emissions from fossil fuel burning fall to about 2 GtC/year by 2100; cumulative emissions from burning fossil fuels, 1990-2100, are 450 to 475 GtC, consistent with stabilisation of the atmosphere at a CO_2 level near 400 ppmv.

Deep reductions in CO_2 emissions are facilitated in the LESS Constructions by emphasis on centralised production of methanol and hydrogen from carbonaceous feedstocks (fossil fuels and biomass) for use in fuel cells for transportation and for distributed combined heat and power applications, with underground sequestration of the CO_2 recovered in pure streams at the fuel conversion plants. For the Biomass-Intensive and Nuclear-Intensive variants, cumulative sequestration requirements, 1990-2100, are low (20 GtC), but by mid-century biomass requirements for meeting fluid fuel demand are high (118 EJ/year), while for the Natural-Gas Intensive and Coal-Intensive Variants, sequestration requirements are much higher, (40 GtC and 140 GtC, respectively), and biomass requirements for fluid fuels production much lower (34 to 49 EJ/year). For the High-Demand Variant, cumulative sequestration requirements are high (some 320 GtC), as are biomass requirements for fluid fuels production (118 EJ/year). For all the energy-efficient LESS Constructions, and perhaps for the High Demand variant as well, cumulative sequestration requirements are likely to be less than estimated secure sequestering capacity that would be available in the time frame of interest (Johansson et al., 1996).

An important distinguishing feature of the energy-efficient LESS Constructions is that, with the exception of the sequestration technologies, all the important technologies that make it possible to achieve low CO_2 emissions (e.g. more-efficient energy conversion and end-use technologies and various renewable energy technologies) would be highly desirable technologies to pursue, even if there were no climate change issue to worry about. And even in the case of CO_2 sequestration associated with hydrogen production from carbonaceous feedstocks, the sequestration cost penalties would often be negative initially when sequestration is likely to be associated mainly with enhanced oil recovery (Chakma, 1992), near zero for the much larger potential sequestration volumes

Figure 4.2: Annual CO$_2$ Emissions from Fossil Fuels for Alternative IPCC-LESS Constructions, with Comparison to Emissions for the IPCC's IS92a-f Scenarios

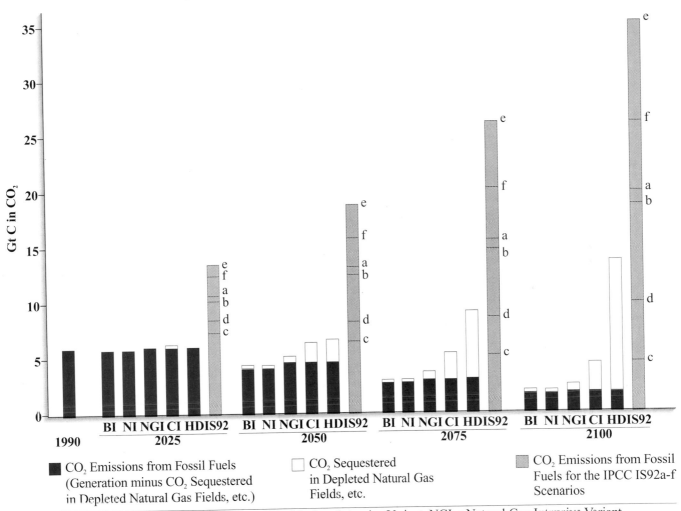

BI = Biomass-Intensive Variant, NI = Nuclear-Intensive Variant, NGI = Natural Gas-Intensive Variant,
CI = Coal-Intensive Variant, HD = High Demand Variant

Source: (IPCC, 1996a)

available in depleted natural gas fields, for which small quantities of enhanced natural gas recovery become possible as a result of reservoir repressurization (Blok et al., 1997), and relatively modest for the even larger potential sequestration volumes involved in aquifer disposal (Williams, 1996), if low-temperature fuel cells that place a high market value on hydrogen and hydrogen-rich energy carriers are successfully developed (see, for example, Figures 3.13 and 3.14).

The realisation of a stabilised CO$_2$ concentration in the range 400 to 450 ppmv, as would be achieved in the Ecologically-Driven Scenarios and the LESS Constructions, depends critically on being able to bring about a rapid pace of technological change in the energy sector. By the middle of the next century low CO$_2$-emitting energy supply technologies must become so well-established in global energy markets that their increased use could then plausibly make up the difference between total energy demand and what can be supplied with conventional fossil fuels, under the constraint that the atmospheric CO$_2$ concentration stabilises at a low level.

Assessment of the energy supply technologies (see Chapter 3) for the sustainable development scenarios provides a basis for optimism that there are various combinations of energy supply technologies that could plausibly be implemented in the time schedules needed to stabilise the CO$_2$ concentration in the atmosphere at low levels.

119

Moreover, with the degree of emphasis on efficient energy use that characterises these scenarios, human needs for energy services could plausibly be met with alternative clean energy sources that collectively could make it possible to reduce CO_2 emissions to about 2 GtC/year by the end of the next century, either with or without reviving the nuclear option.

4.2 Some General Implications of Energy Strategies for Sustainable Development

4.2.1 Energy and Poverty

For people living in poverty, the most pressing priority is the satisfaction of basic human needs such as shelter, availability of potable water, sanitation, and access to health services and education. While low energy consumption is not a cause of poverty, the lack of available energy services correlates closely with many poverty indicators. Addressing the problems of poverty requires addressing its many dimensions—for example, inadequate or unavailable educational opportunities, health care, and accessible and functional sanitation facilities. Addressing these issues involves increasing the level of *energy services.*

While the pursuit of any energy strategy cannot, by itself, guarantee that basic human needs will be satisfied, energy strategies for sustainable development goals would help increase the levels of energy services provided to people in poverty. These goals would be accomplished in part through targeting the introduction of specific technologies in ways which would increase energy services for the poor (e.g., efficient lighting technologies, water pumping technologies, efficient cookstoves, modern energy carriers for cooking).

At least as important, energy strategies for sustainable development would help deal with the roots of poverty by promoting employment generation (e.g., in rural areas where large fractions of the world's people in poverty live—see Section 4.2.2).

And finally, the emphasis given to promoting the wide availability of modern energy carriers and inherently clean energy technologies would help people living in poverty, who are often the most vulnerable to the negative environmental effects of current energy development.

4.2.2 Creating Jobs

Globally, an estimated 1 billion people are unemployed or under-employed, according to the International Labour Organisation (ILO). Energy strategies supportive of sustainable development would help create income-earning opportunities for these people.

For example, biomass energy offers significant possibilities for job creation. The programme to produce ethanol from sugar cane in Brazil created 700,000 jobs. Advanced biomass power technologies now under commercial development that could use sugar cane residues as fuel to produce by-product electricity offer the potential for making cane-derived alcohol fully competitive at present oil prices and thus greatly expand the potential for job creation in the sugar industry (Williams and Larson, 1993), by expanding the market opportunities for cane-derived alcohol and electricity. This technology also would make it possible to produce electricity competitively in rural areas with biomass feedstocks grown on dedicated biomass energy plantations, which could attract industries to rural areas. While biomass production for such activities would generate employment, the number of jobs created by industries attracted to rural areas by competitive biomass electricity probably would dwarf the number of jobs created simply by growing and processing biomass for energy. These jobs could help to reduce rural-to-urban migration. Assuming that appropriate national and subnational revenue collection policies and procedures are in place, the resulting increased rural tax base could help support investments in new rural schools, hospitals, and other infrastructure needed to provide basic public services in rural areas and provide resources for maintaining and improving such infrastructure.

4.2.3 Energy and Women

A shift to a sustainable energy development path would have a significant, positive impact for women in terms of labour, health, income generation and quality of life. Although energy is only one of the many factors determining gender equality, scenarios emphasising the introduction of modern energy carriers, energy efficiency improvement, and renewable energy sources do open new opportunities for women.

In the very near term the pursuit of sustainable development strategies would involve the wide dissemination of commercially available technologies such as: *i*) energy-efficient stoves that would reduce the amount of time needed for fuelwood gathering; *ii*) village-scale energy systems (biogas- or producer-gas driven pumping systems) that would pump water to homes, thereby reducing the burdens of carrying water; and *iii*) village-scale (e.g., biogas- or producer-gas engine-generator sets) or household-scale (e.g., photovoltaic) energy systems that would provide electricity for lighting, thereby significantly improving the quality of life in rural areas that don't have access to centralised electricity grids.

Expansion of rural income-generating activities, such as those associated with biomass production for industrial applications and with the industries drawn to rural areas by the availability of low-cost biomass electricity could make it possible for rural households to use modern energy carriers for cooking and heating, thereby eliminating altogether the drudgery of fuelwood gathering by women and children and greatly reducing the smoke-related health problems, mainly in women, associated with traditional biomass stoves.

Decentralised approaches open up opportunities for women entrepreneurs both in improving energy efficiency and using renewable sources in the many fuel-intensive energy enterprises. The challenge now is to expand the track record of women and their organisations as effective entrepreneurs to include their potential roles as effective energy entrepreneurs. The role of the public sector is to create support systems that promote entrepreneur response and ensure access to technology and resources. There is a need to ensure that women's concerns and needs are properly reflected in energy policy-making.

4.2.4 Rural Development

Opportunities for introducing more energy-efficient end-use technologies and technological developments relating to biomass energy, wind power, small-scale hydropower, and photovoltaic power have created new possibilities for rural development.

Under sustainable development strategies, decentralised energy demand and supply technologies contribute significantly to improving the living conditions of rural populations *in the near term* by increasing the levels of energy services provided (e.g.

via the introduction and diffusion of energy-efficient fluorescent lighting technologies, energy-efficient cookstoves, PV systems that can provide electricity for households and medical and educational facilities, biogas or producer gas for cooking, biogas and producer gas engine-generator sets for small-scale mechanical power and electric power, mini-hydroelectric systems for electric power, and wind energy for water pumping). Such technologies are especially important for outlying areas that cannot be cost-effectively connected to electricity grids. For many such technologies, the barriers to their adoption are institutional, not technological. Particularly important will be new institutional mechanisms to make credit available for financing, since current capital markets discriminate against investments in energy efficiency improvements and small-scale energy supplies (WEC/IIASA, 1995).

In the medium- to long-term, renewable energy is also used under sustainable development strategies to promote rural employment generation and rural industrialisation. For example, modernised, energy-efficient biomass electric generation technologies based on the use of gas turbines and fuel cells coupled to biomass gasifiers (which could become commercially available in less than a decade) offer the potential for providing electricity at small scales at costs competitive with conventional large-scale, fossil fuel power generating technologies. Such energy-efficient conversion technologies provide opportunities not only to use residues of agricultural and forest-product industries (e.g. bagasse from cane sugar production and various pulp and paper industry residues) but also energy crops grown on dedicated plantations. When such technologies are first introduced, the produced electricity might be sold to urban centers. Biomass power plants could send baseload electricity cost-effectively via transmission lines to urban centres, thereby generating rural income from biomass production and electricity generation even before job-creating energy-intensive industries can be established in rural areas. Such technologies could justify extending power lines to rural areas, with electrons flowing from the rural areas to the cities, confounding the conventional wisdom about the economics of extending power lines to rural areas.

In the longer term, as supply constraints come to limit continued growth in the production of conventional oil and natural gas resources, synthetic fluid fuels produced from biomass could become major competitors to synthetic fluid fuels from coal and non-conventional oil and natural gas. Some studies indicate that in this time frame regions with adequate productive land resources (e.g., parts of South America and Sub-Saharan Africa) could become major producers and exporters of biomass-derived fluid fuels (Johansson et al., 1993a; Johansson et al., 1996; IPCC, 1996a).

4.2.5 Urban Development

The bulk of population growth in developing countries will be concentrated in cities. Thus the modes of urban development will be major factors impacting the growth of energy consumption, and technological choices for energy will strongly impact urban life. Energy strategies are closely linked with other aspects of urban development, such as land use planning and regulation, transport policy, and the management of buildings and facilities.

One important benefit offered by sustainable development strategies is that the promotion of rural industrialisation (especially with modernised biomass energy) would help reduce the exodus of large populations from rural areas, thereby relieving pressures on urban centres to provide these populations with jobs and services.

The energy technologies provided under sustainable development strategies would also facilitate sustainable urban development. Emphasis on clean, modern energy carriers and energy-efficient conversion and end-use technologies could lead to a greatly improved quality of life and to reduced urban management burdens. Introduction of grid-connected distributed electricity systems such as building rooftop- or facade-mounted photovoltaic systems, or fuel cell combined heat and power systems, would make it possible to provide electricity with zero or near-zero pollutant emissions without the need for either pollution control technology or the complicated regulatory infrastructures needed to enforce the need for such controls. Such systems would also reduce the capital investments needed for electricity transmission and distribution relative to costs associated with centralised electricity generation.

In transportation sustainable energy strategies simultaneously would promote improved mobility, reduced environmental impacts, and reduced infrastructure investment requirements by land-use planning measures such as those that have been so successfully demonstrated in Curitiba. Moreover, in transportation as in power generation, emphasis given to fuels and conversion technologies that are characterised by a high degree of *inherent* cleanliness (e.g., hydrogen and fuel cell vehicles) would simultaneously improve air quality, reduce the need for regulatory infrastructures for controlling pollution, and increase urban energy supply security by facilitating the adoption of domestic energy supplies as alternatives to oil imports in meeting transportation energy needs.

4.2.6 Energy and the Economy

A sustainable energy future is compatible with strong economic growth. Moreover, pursuit of a sustainable energy path facilitates the realisation of sustainable socio-economic growth over the longer-term.

Although the costs of energy services cannot be projected in any detail over long periods of time, the IPCC analysed the issue from both top-down and bottom-up perspectives, using projected costs based on engineering data. It concluded that one or more of the variants of the LESS Constructions for the global energy system would probably be able to deliver energy services at costs that are approximately the same as projected costs for conventional energy systems (IPCC, 1996a).

4.2.6.1 Investment requirements

Investment in the energy sector accounts for 15 to 20 % of all fixed capital investment in the world economy. Meeting energy-sector investment needs is particularly a problem in developing countries, where the capacity to finance investments is a major factor limiting growth.

While future capital requirements for energy are huge and are expected to continue to increase, the challenge of meeting capital needs for energy is not inherently so daunting as was thought to be the case just a few years ago (WEC/IIASA, 1995). Moreover, pursuing a sustainable development strategy would reduce the magnitude of the energy investment challenge. However, particular attention would have to be given to how capital resources are allocated, since the smaller-scale, clean, and innovative energy supply investments and the energy efficiency investments needed under a sustainable development strategy are discriminated against in existing capital markets (WEC/IIASA, 1995).

Under a sustainable development strategy, energy pricing reform would be given high priority. This would make energy-sector investments more attractive to prospective investors, easing the capital crisis conditions that now exist in many developing countries and giving developing countries considerable power in capital markets relating to energy. The capital challenge is not so much the unavailability of the needed capital as it is the risks perceived in energy market investments by would-be investors.

For a number of years capital markets have grown faster than total GDP, and this trend is unlikely to change (WEC/IIASA, 1995). The formation of domestic capital markets in developing countries would be encouraged under a sustainable development strategy, so as to expand capital availability by mobilising domestic savings for productive investments. At present the domestic savings rate averages about 24% of GDP in developing countries compared to 21% in OECD countries (WEC/IIASA, 1995).

Also, policies aimed at driving down capital costs would be pursued under sustainable development conditions. Already, increasingly competitive conditions in global energy markets have led to sharp declines in specific capital costs in recent years. For example, turnkey plant costs for 250 MW$_e$ coal steam-electric plants fell from US$1355-US$1720/kW in 1992 to US$985-US$1265/kW in 1995, while those for 250 MW$_e$ natural gas combined cycle plants fell from US$615-US$720/kW to US$480-US$535/kW in this period (Stoll and Todd, 1996). Reductions in capital costs over time would be characteristic of sustainable development scenarios because many of the technologies that are best-suited for meeting sustainable development objectives are small, modular, and very good candidates for cost-cutting via organisa-

tional learning after they are launched in the market.

Although a shift to renewables and other energy technologies suitable for use in the pursuit of sustainable development objectives sometimes will lead to higher specific capital costs for energy-producing equipment compared to conventional fossil energy supplies, this is not always the case. For example, grid-connected combined heat and power systems located near users typically lead to savings of capital as well as fuel. Also, providing electricity via stand-alone renewable energy systems for applications such as lighting to households remote from utility grids, is less costly than extending central grids to these low-demand users. Installing distributed grid-connected power sources (e.g., photovoltaic and fuel cell systems) reduces investment needs by reducing distribution capacity requirements to meet peak loads. Finally, the overall need for new energy supply capacity would be less for sustainable development than for business-as-usual development, because of the emphasis given to efficient use of energy. At present, less capital is often required in all countries to save a given amount of energy (by employing more energy-efficient technologies) than to expand the energy generating capacity by an equivalent amount.

Finally it should be noted that higher specific capital costs are not inherently problematic, since savings in fuel and other operating costs can offset higher up front costs. Properly functioning capital markets make it practically feasible to evaluate alternative energy technologies on a lifecycle-cost rather than a first-cost basis.

In aggregate the WEC/IIASA study[6] estimated that capital requirements for energy supply would be less under the C1 (low-nuclear) Ecologically-Driven Scenario than for all the other WEC/IIASA scenarios, throughout the entire periods 1990-2020 and 2020-2050. For example, capital requirements for energy world-wide and for developing countries average US$430 billion per year and US$200 billion per year, respectively, for this Ecologically-Driven Scenario, 1990-2020, com-

---

6   This study did not take into account needed investments in energy-efficiency improvement. However, an earlier WEC study (WEC, 1993) concluded that energy efficiency improvements were likely to represent about 25% of total energy investment requirements (i.e., about one-third of the figures given here).

pared to US$530 billion per year and US$230 billion per year, respectively, for the Reference Scenario.

4.2.6.2 Foreign exchange

In energy futures compatible with sustainable development objectives there would be a diversification of energy supplies to the extent that oil would compete with synthetic fluid fuels (derived from natural gas, biomass, and coal, sometimes in conjunction with fuel decarbonisation and sequestration of the separated CO_2). To the extent that these alternatives are based on the use of domestic feedstocks, they would not require as much foreign exchange as oil imports. This would be advantageous for the many countries with balance of payment problems, releasing foreign exchange for other developmental needs.

4.2.7 Local and Regional Environmental Problems

The adverse environmental impacts of rapid growth in the use of fossil fuels are offset in all scenarios to some degree by the ongoing shift to natural gas (see Table 4.1), the least polluting and most climate-friendly fossil fuel. Moreover, a general tightening of environmental regulations can be expected in all scenarios, as attempts are made to deal with increasingly severe environmental problems, including health impacts, posed by energy production and use. However, more restrictive environmental laws do not always lead to improved environmental quality. In the decades ahead, relying on regulations to meet environmental needs will be especially problematic for those countries that have largely undeveloped and weak regulatory infrastructures.

A key feature of the sustainable development scenarios in Table 4.1 (the WEC/IIASA Ecologically-Driven Scenarios and the IPCC-LESS Constructions) is emphasis on technological innovation as a generic strategy for meeting environmental objectives—innovation aimed at introducing inherently clean energy technologies for which environmental objectives can be met with little or no reliance on "end-of-pipe" controls installed on conversion equipment originally designed with no attention to environmental concerns.

In addition, all energy technologies, including various renewable energy technolo-

gies, would be held to high environmental standards in these scenarios with a holistic approach taken to evaluate concerns such as the impacts of inundation created by large hydroelectric projects, visual intrusion from wind energy schemes that are inappropriate in location or scale, and potential adverse impacts on biodiversity of biomass energy development (WEC, 1994).

As a result, the sustainable development scenarios lead to cleaner cities, reduced acidification, and generally lower adverse environmental impacts compared to conventional energy projections.

4.2.7.1 Local and regional air pollution

Clean, renewable energy technologies for power generation emphasised in the environmental scenarios include wind, photovoltaic, solar thermal electric, biomass-integrated gasifier/combined cycle, and biomass-integrated gasifier/fuel cell systems.

Low pollution levels in power generation also characterise the nuclear-intensive variants of the Ecologically-Driven Scenarios and the LESS Constructions. However, the pollutant emissions characteristics of these scenarios differ little from those in the low-nuclear variants of these scenarios, since nuclear power is substituted for renewable energy in the LESS Constructions and largely for renewables and natural gas in the Ecologically-Driven Scenarios.

The use of biomass is emphasised for the production of transport fuels in the Biomass-Intensive and Nuclear-Intensive LESS Constructions. In particular, biomass-derived methanol and hydrogen are emphasised, leading to zero air pollutant emissions when used in hydrogen fuel cell vehicles and near-zero pollutant emissions in methanol fuel cell vehicles.

The sustainable development scenarios also emphasise inherently low-polluting advanced fossil fuel technologies, including, for power generation, coal-integrated gasifier/combined cycle and coal-integrated gasifier/fuel cell power plants that can be as clean as natural gas combined cycle power plants, and, for transportation, the production of synthetic middle distillates, dimethyl ether, methanol, and hydrogen—clean transport fuels derived from any fossil fuel feedstock.

The poverty-reducing aspects of the Biomass-Intensive LESS Construction (e.g. the promotion of rural industrialisation and in-come-generation via the introduction of modern cost-competitive biomass-electric technologies) also make it possible to greatly reduce air pollution (including indoor pollution) arising from the use of biomass and coal for cooking, because this strategy could help the poor afford clean energy for cooking (e.g. LPG, natural gas, electricity, biogas, producer gas, ethanol).

4.2.7.2 Synthetic fluid fuels production and the environment

The leading contenders for meeting fluid fuel needs in the next century in excess of what can be provided by conventional oil and natural gas are: *i*) non-conventional oil (heavy crudes, tar sands, shale oil) and natural gas (gas in Devonian shale, coal seams, tight-sand formations, and geo-pressurised aquifers); *ii*) synthetic fluid fuels from coal; and *iii*) synthetic fluid fuels from biomass. All these routes to producing additional fluid fuels pose significant environmental challenges that must be dealt with effectively in order to meet sustainable development goals.

In order to achieve deep reductions in CO_2 emissions via the fossil fuel options, extensive fuel decarbonisation (e.g., to produce methanol and hydrogen) with sequestration of the separated CO_2 would be required. All the candidate feedstocks are suitable for such applications. Both the conversion plants and the end-use technologies could be very low polluting. But mining and recovery of low-grade non-conventional oil and gas resources would often be far more environmentally challenging than conventional oil and natural gas recovery. In the case of oil shale, resource recovery based on the use of high-temperature retorting techniques would also lead to the release of up to four times as much CO_2 per unit of recovered energy as coal combustion, as a result of decomposition of carbonate minerals in the shale (Sunquist and Miller, 1981), so that it would be very difficult to achieve low lifecycle CO_2 emissions if oil shale were developed this way. Moreover, environmental problems in mining would become increasingly problematic as coal production shifts to lower and lower grade resources. And, in producing hydrogen-rich energy carriers from any carbonaceous feedstock, it becomes more chal-

lenging to find adequate secure CO_2 storage capacity, as the levels of fuel decarbonisation/sequestration increase.

If fuel decarbonisation/sequestration strategies are to be pursued at large scale, a detailed understanding will be needed of lifecycle environmental and safety issues, from resource recovery through final disposal of the separated CO_2 in underground storage reservoirs, including a reservoir-by-reservoir assessment of the security of long-term storage. But there is adequate time to do the needed research, if such research is adequately supported; it is only after the first quarter of the next century that centralised production of hydrogen carriers is undertaken with sequestration of the separated CO_2 in the LESS Constructions, as this much time will be needed for low-temperature fuel cells to become well-enough established in the market to warrant building the large, centralised fuel production facilities that would make sequestration of the separated CO_2 practical.

Many prospective problems associated with fuel decarbonisation/sequestration strategies could be avoided if instead biomass were emphasised for the production of fluid fuels, as in the Biomass-Intensive and Nuclear-Intensive Variants of the LESS Constructions. Biomass was emphasised in these variants because of the substantial prospective rural development benefits offered by biomass, the prospect that biomass could compete with coal in producing fluid fuels, and the climate benefits offered by biomass energy. Yet large-scale use of biomass for energy has been challenged on various grounds—especially the potential for competition with food production and the setting aside of land areas for natural habitat preservation.

Because of the high land-use intensity of biomass production, it will be necessary to overcome potential obstacles associated with competing uses for land, if biomass is to become a major contributor to a modern energy economy. Preliminary scoping studies indicate that in many regions potential conflicts with food production could be minimised if agricultural production could be modernised with increased chemical and energy inputs (Marrison and Larson, 1996; Larson et al., 1997). In principle, low-cost biomass energy could attract to rural areas industry that could provide jobs to generate the incomes needed to pay for the intensification of agricultural production (Johansson et al. 1993a; Riedacker and Dessus, 1991). In practice agricultural expansion via intensification must be made more environmentally desirable than expansion from putting more marginal lands into production. The potential for conflict with land set-asides for preserving biological diversity has received less attention than the potential for conflict with agricultural production. The potential for land-use competition warrants more careful scrutiny on a region-by-region basis. Land-use issues associated with biomass energy farms, giving attention to issuesof scale, must be assessed (e.g., the appropriate mix of large-scale plantations and small-scale farm forestry), and highlighting the key socio-economic, cultural, and environmental issues.

Establishing biomass farms on deforested and otherwise degraded lands has been identified as a promising strategy for minimising potential land-use conflicts (Johansson et al., 1993a). Broad-brush assessments indicate that degraded land areas suitable for reforestation in developing regions are large in aggregate. But the potential for using such lands for energy plantations must be much better understood. Part of what is needed is a region-by-region assessment of degraded lands that might be considered for biomass energy farms—indicating total potential areas, prospective yields, distribution by subregion and size of typical land plots, socio-economic and cultural conditions, and key technical challenges that must be addressed. In addition to such assessments, field research is needed on a region-by-region basis to identify and develop technical strategies for restoring these lands to the point where they can be used productively and sustainably for biomass energy purposes.

On the basis of the large potential benefits relating to rural development, climate change, and local air pollution, together with the concerns that have been raised about large-scale development of modernised energy, a substantial research effort is called for to address these concerns. As in the case of the fossil-fuel based synfuels strategy, there is time to do the needed research, if adequate research support is available, because modernised biomass energy industries

will be launched largely via the use of residues over the course of the next decade or so, and because where natural gas is readily available, biomass energy will have difficulty competing until natural gas prices are much higher than at present. While in the LESS Constructions some 100 to 380 million hectares of land are targeted for biomass plantations by 2050, the land area in plantations is only 8 to 80 million hectares by 2025 (Williams, 1995a).

However, for both fossil fuel- and biomass-based synfuels strategies there is an urgency to get the needed research underway. The fruits of this research could provide a good basis for deciding the appropriate mix of fossil fuel-based and biomass-based synfuels that will be needed to supplement conventional oil and natural gas resources in an environmentally constrained world. There are good prospects that at least one combination of these supply options will be fully compatible with sustainable development criteria (Johansson et al., 1996).

4.2.8 Energy and Security

Concerns about energy supply security, energy demand security, and the risk of nuclear proliferation depend on both the energy supply mix and the overall level of energy demand. Energy supply security concerns are likely to diminish more rapidly under scenarios consistent with sustainable development. Moreover, energy demand security is not likely to be a serious problem for oil and gas producers in any global energy scenario. And finally, scenarios that stress the efficient use of energy and promote a high rate of technological innovation in energy offer the opportunity for minimising nuclear proliferation risks.

4.2.8.1 Energy supply security

The concentration of 65% of the world's proven oil reserves in the Middle East (British Petroleum, 1996) has led to concerns about the security of energy supplies from this region (see Section 2.4.1). However, the experiences of the oil crises of the 1970s demonstrate that if oil prices rise rapidly, alternative technologies can be brought into the market relatively quickly to help to stabilise prices. These experiences also showed that wide fluctuations in oil prices are detrimental to both consumers and producers. While it is likely that there will be growing dependence on conventional oil from the Middle East in the decades immediately ahead, prospective oil price increases are likely to be relatively modest, unless there are major disruptions in fuel supply, because of such prospective competition and the shared consumer/producer interest in relative oil price stability.

Dependence on Middle East oil will be tempered by a growing shift in the global oil/gas mix toward natural gas, as reflected in all major global energy projections (see, for example, Table 4.1). The shift to natural gas will be accompanied by some regional diversification of natural gas supply sources, and an increasing share of natural gas in world energy trade. The countries of the former Soviet Union, which account for about 35% of remaining recoverable conventional natural gas resources (Masters et al., 1994), will be especially important in such trade, providing natural gas not only for Europe, as at present, but probably also for various markets in Asia.

Natural gas will serve not only conventional gas markets (e.g. power generation and heating) but also markets now served by oil. The recent launching of natural gas-derived synthetic middle distillate fuel in the global liquid fuel market (see Section 3.3.5.3) will help bring stability to world oil prices and reduce the potential for conflict over threatened access to oil supplies in politically unstable regions.

In the longer-term, energy supply security risks will be reduced further in all scenarios, in part because mean estimates of the Middle East's shares of estimated ultimately recoverable conventional oil and natural gas resources, 44% and 25% respectively (Masters et al., 1994), are much less than the Middle East's share of proved oil reserves. Also the Middle East's share of the world's non-conventional oil resources is modest (Masters et al., 1987).

Still, natural gas resources tend to be concentrated in just a few parts of the world. Yet much of the global trade in natural gas will be via pipeline; pipelines can be politically stabilising because of the strong mutual dependence between suppliers and consumers.

Also, as both conventional oil and gas supplies are drawn down, energy security will be further increased as the supply of fluid fuels becomes more diversified, both in terms of energy carriers and regional sources. In some scenarios, this diversification will be achieved via exploitation of non-conventional oil or gas resources or synthetic fuels from coal. But in the biomass-intensive variant of the LESS Constructions, the need for additional fluid fuels is instead provided by biomass-derived synfuels; for example, by 2050, 28% of global exports of liquid fuels is accounted for by biomass-derived methanol, most of which is exported from Latin America and Sub-Saharan Africa (Williams, 1995a).

The most important contribution to enhanced energy supply security that would arise in the WEC/IIASA Ecologically-Driven Scenarios and the energy-efficient LESS Constructions is from the accelerated pace of introducing clean synthetic fluid fuels and associated vehicle technologies (e.g. hydrogen-rich energy carriers and fuel cells for transportation) and the competition in global fluid fuel markets that these innovations would foster.

4.2.8.2 Energy demand security

The uneven distribution of oil and natural gas resources in the world has led to major global trade in oil and natural gas which, in turn, has become a crucial component of the national economies of energy-exporting countries. Considerations of alternative world energy futures can cause anxiety in these countries about the continuing prospects for their energy exports.

The issue of energy demand security involves the concern of oil and natural gas exporters that markets for their products will shrink. This is not likely to be a concern under any scenario—even in global scenarios that involve major improvements in energy efficiency and major future roles for renewable energy sources. All global energy scenarios are characterised by continuing long-term exports of energy from the Middle East.

Exports from the energy-rich Middle East are projected to remain at current or higher levels long after the peaking of global oil and natural gas production (some 30 to 40 years from now), although the mix of exports is expected to shift over time toward natural gas and its products to reflect the relative magni-

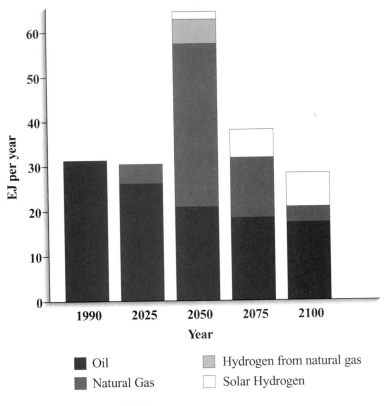

Figure 4.3: Net Exports of Fuels from the Middle East in the Biomass-Intensive, Coal-Intensive and Nuclear-Intensive Variants of the IPCC's LESS Constructions

Oil
Natural Gas
Hydrogen from natural gas
Solar Hydrogen

Source: (IPCC, 1996a)

tudes of remaining oil and gas resources.

Such a continuing major role for Middle East energy is envisioned even in the LESS Constructions, which describe alternative technological paths for global energy that lead by 2100 to a two-thirds reduction of annual global CO_2 emissions from fossil fuel burning.

The continuing importance of Middle East exports in the LESS Constructions is illustrated in Figure 4.3; while in 2050 oil exports from the Middle East are one third less than in 1990, total exports are more than twice the 1990 level, largely because of the projected major expansion of natural gas exports.

A continuing major role for Middle East exports is consistent with achieving deep reductions in CO_2 emissions over the course of the next century. (In fact, burning all estimated remaining conventional oil and natural gas resources and no other fossil fuels would lead to stabilising the atmosphere at near the present CO_2 concentration.)

The growing shift in sustainable development scenarios to inherently clean fuels for transportation (synthetic middle distillates in the near term and hydrogen or hydrogen-rich energy carriers such as methanol in the longer term) also will lead to increased income-generating opportunities for energy-exporting countries. For many decades to come these energy carriers will be derived mainly from natural gas. Making these energy carriers from natural gas will enable natural gas-exporting countries to obtain more added value than could be derived from simply selling natural gas.

4.2.8.3 Nuclear proliferation

Since nuclear power revival is not necessary for sustainable development in a world where emphasis is given to the efficient use of energy and innovation in energy supply technologies, society has the option of choosing not to revive the nuclear fission energy industry, thereby avoiding the nuclear pro-

128

liferation risks inherent in high levels of development of nuclear power.

4.3 Conclusion

It may be concluded that energy systems can be pursued that are not only compatible with, but also are crucial levers for achieving social, economic, environmental and security goals, as expressed in Agenda 21. As a result, energy can be an important instrument for sustainable development. Such energy systems would be based on a much more efficient use of energy, an increased use of renewable energy sources, and a new generation of technologies that make it possible to use both biomass energy and fossil fuels at high efficiency with low adverse impacts on the local, regional and global environments. At present, overall trends are not in this direction and attention must now be turned to an analysis of impediments to sustainable energy futures that are supportive of sustainable development.

5 Making it Happen: Energy for Sustainable Development

5.1 Introduction

Present human activities are unsustainable, and current energy demand and supply patterns are contributing to this problem. Based on an analysis of the important linkages between energy, social, environmental, economic and security issues, it was concluded in Chapter 2 that the world's present energy systems and trends are not compatible with reaching the social and environmental goals and objectives emanating from UNCED and other United Nations global conferences of the 1990s, nor those of the environment-related conventions. Major changes in the energy service delivery system are required to meet these objectives.

It will not be easy to bring about a fundamental reorientation from strategies that focus only on conventional supply expansion to those that emphasise energy services through a combination of energy end-use efficiency improvements, increased use of renewable sources of energy, and a new generation of fossil-fuel-using technologies. Discussions about energy demand still focus on how to increase supplies of energy rather than on the more important question of how to obtain the required energy services. Shifting the existing supply paradigm to a focus on energy services will require fundamental readjustments of public polices to promote and adopt sustainable energy options.

Fortunately, a number of feasible technology options (described in Chapter 3) are available or could become available in the near term to meet energy service demands in a sustainable manner. Considerable benefits in social, environmental, economic and security terms would arise from moving towards a sustainable energy future, as discussed in Chapter 4. Thus, new energy systems that are compatible with sustainable development goals are conceivable, feasible and beneficial.

Energy systems have changed dramatically during the course of history—from the use of wood as the dominant fuel in the early 1800's, to coal in the early 1900's, to the current predominance of oil and natural gas.

These changes, which took place over several decades, were driven by resource availability, technology developments, and prices.

Today, in contrast to the prevailing assumption in the 1970's, shortages of oil and natural gas are not imminent. In fact, the ratios of reserves to production have been growing steadily. In addition, the world has vast coal resources. So, a transition to a new sustainable energy system will not be driven by either limitations of reserves or resource scarcity, for a long time to come (see Section 4.1.3).

Another significant change is the importance of the present environmental situation, locally, regionally, and globally, and the recognition of opportunities to address social concerns through actions related to energy. Concerns in these areas create a new and different set of drivers for change in the energy sector.

Moreover, shifting patterns of demand are creating new opportunities. Historically, most energy technology development has taken place in the industrialised countries, where economic growth has been strong, and rapidly growing markets provided a good context for innovation in energy-intensive processes. Today these conditions have changed radically. The energy-intensive industries are facing stagnation or experiencing slow growth in the markets of industrialised countries, while growth in the demand for energy and material-intensive products in many developing countries is rapid. Growth in the industrialised countries is now primarily in service and knowledge-intensive industries that use little materials or energy. The shift in growth patterns provides new opportunities for developing countries to become leaders of innovation for the development of new energy-efficient and clean production and end-use technologies.

The first step in designing energy systems consistent with the goal of sustainable development is recognition that the measures to advance sustainable development will have to beshaped in the context of current global trends that are operating through, or in conjunction with, strong constraints on traditional actors. This is the topic of the next section.

5.2 The Larger Context: Current Global Trends

Major trends in the overall political and economic environment in which the new global energy system will evolve include globalisation, the information revolution, marketisation, the changing role of governments, governments' fiscal austerity, and popular participation in public sector decision-making.

Globalisation: As markets become globalised, trade barriers between countries are becoming increasingly difficult to erect or maintain. Out-sourcing, the procurement of inputs (materials and services) from distant and foreign sources, is becoming common practice. New technology is diffusing globally, at rates faster than ever before.

Information revolution: World-wide access to information is rapidly improving through the use of modern information technology, including the Internet. Thus, there are new pathways for providing bases for information and dissemination of new technology and know-how. This expansion will facilitate increased awareness of sustainable energy options and deployment of new systems.

Marketisation: Since the end of the Cold War and the collapse of planned economies in central and eastern Europe, significant changes have occurred and continue to occur in the structures of many economies. The questions of what, how, and how much to produce, which in some countries had been a preoccupation of central authorities and bureaucracies, are now being decided by market mechanisms. The allocation of manpower, materials, and financial resources as well as the selection of products and production technologies increasingly is a function of market conditions. The process of marketisation is not restricted to the borders of countries; it is extending beyond national frontiers to regions and the whole world.

Changing role of government: Government functions are increasingly moving towards rule-making and monitoring the application and observance of the rules. Thus, the role of governments is changing drastically towards becoming the caretaker of the rules and regulations that ensure that markets can work efficiently. Governments also have crucial responsibilities that cannot be left to the market—to provide leadership in ensuring that people living in poverty and women have access to modern energy services; to work for the empowerment of communities and regions and strengthen their self-reliance; and to protect the environment.

Governments' fiscal austerity: In most countries, governments currently have budget deficit problems. As a result, only limited government finance is available for infrastructure investments. This affects the role of governments as investors in energy and in research and development, and as Official Development Assistance (ODA) donors. Public fiscal constraints also indicate that measures to implement new energy systems must not create fiscal burdens on public treasuries. Fortunately, as will be discussed below, technological advancement and the development of new policy instruments are resulting in the availability of innovative measures that are not costly to governments.

Popular participation in public sector decision-making: Perhaps the most encouraging development facilitating the emergence of sustainable energy systems is the democratisation that is sweeping the world. Growing awareness and concern about development and environmental issues is beginning to affect elections and consumption patterns. Throughout the world local groups and networks are becoming more involved in the decision-making processes and are having impacts on the formulation of public policies. The challenge of ensuring sustainability is being taken up by public interest groups instead of being left to governments and their bureaucracies alone. Womens' groups, with their natural propensity for concern for the next generation, are getting involved in ensuring that sustainable development stays on the agenda.

5.3 Policy Considerations for Sustainable Energy Strategies

New public policies are needed to promote energy strategies compatible with the sustainable development objectives set forth in the major United Nations conferences and conventions, in light of current global trends and constraints—energy policies that emphasise energy services, promote efficient markets, promote universal access to modern energy services, include external social costs in energy market decisions, acccelerate the development and market penetration of sustainable energy technologies, promote indigenous capacity building, and encourage broad participation of stakeholders in energy decision-making:

Emphasise energy services: People want the services that energy provides, not fuel or electricity. Energy policies should be framed so as not to promote the expansion of energy supplies or consumption levels but instead encourage the provision of energy services in the most cost-effective ways that are compatible with sustainable development objectives. Emphasis on energy services in energy policy-making would facilitate the realisation of energy futures characterised by relatively low levels of energy demand. In such futures sustainability goals are more easily met than in high energy demand futures (see Chapter 4).

Promote efficient markets: The ongoing trends toward privatisation and increased competition can be helpful in meeting sustainable development objectives. Privatisation is bringing needed additional resources to the energy sector that increasingly fiscally constrained governments can no longer provide. Price reforms and the increasing roles of market forces and competition are leading to much greater efficiency in the allocation of resources. Reformed markets will also increase countries' technological choices by freeing them of the need to meet energy needs with the "technology/financing package deals" that have taken place in many developing countries in recent years. Governments have many roles to play in bringing about more efficient energy markets.

Governments can establish and maintain a level playing field among alternative supply and end-use technologies in providing energy services. Reforms needed to accomplish this include elimination of permanent subsidies to particular energy technologies, the pricing of energy to reflect its full cost, measures that improve the flow of information to market decision-makers, and measures that improve the access to capital for technology investments that are discriminated against in current capital markets (e.g. investments in energy end-use efficiency improvement and distributed power generation). Governments can also be helpful in accelerating the development of domestic capital markets (e.g. via establishing pension

funds, insurance funds). And governments can create a policy environment that will build private investor confidence, facilitate the formation of joint ventures, promote equity participation by foreign interests, and promote competition among providers of energy services. The needed policy environment would include, inter alia, clear ownership rules, litigation procedures, protection of intellectual property rights, and the introduction of transparent accounting and auditing. Such conditions have been or are being created in many countries.

Despite the importance of efficient markets, many of the goals of sustainable development cannot be met simply by making markets more efficient.

Promote universal access to modern energy services: While the growing emphasis on market mechanisms in the energy sector will lead to more efficient allocation of resources, market forces alone will not address concerns about equity. Governments have a responsibility to shape the rules that will guide market forces in ways that will promote universal access to modern energy services, giving emphasis to those consumers, e.g., in rural households and low-income households, whom free markets are likely to exclude or serve inadequately.

Include external social costs in energy market decisions: Free markets do not take into account adverse local, regional, and global environmental and safety impacts of energy production and use. Under a sustainable development strategy governments would internalise such "externalities" through imposition of taxes, fees, and/or regulations. Such public policies would encourage the market to choose technologies that are inherently clean and safe.

Accelerate the development and market penetration of sustainable energy technologies: Private firms generally tend to under-invest in research and development, because they cannot avoid the appropriation by free riders of some of the economic benefits of such investments. This traditionally has been the main justification for public-sector support for research and development; under a sustainable development paradigm, government support for research and development would emphasise technologies that are compatible with sustainability objectives. In light of the seriousness of the multiple challenges facing the energy system (see Chapter 2), and the wealth of near-term opportunities for alleviating these problems with new technologies (see Chapter 3), this research and development support should be increased substantially above current levels. Moreover, the significant public benefits that would arise from the successful commercialisation of energy technologies that are compatible with sustainability objectives justifies public sector support, not only for research and development, but also for accelerating the commercialisation of such technologies that are commercially ready. There are many opportunities for cooperation between industrialised and developing countries in these energy innovation-related activities and for developing countries to leapfrog to a development path that is sustainable.

Promote indigenous capacity building: Developing countries cannot leapfrog to a sustainable path for energy without a strong indigenous capacity to create, design, market, build, and manage the needed energy technologies. Developing countries also need a strong indigenous capacity for technology assessment to better inform the energy planning process about opportunities for meeting sustainability objectives with alternative technologies. Capacity-building can be accomplished in various ways, but international joint ventures and other international industrial partnerships can make important contributions to capacity building that warrant particular emphasis in light of ongoing trends towards globalisation and marketisation, particularly if the developing country participants in such collaborations have strong basic skills (STAP/GEF, 1996).

Encourage broad participation of stakeholders in energy decision-making: Evolution of the energy system in ways to make it compatible with sustainable development objectives would be greatly facilitated if there were broad consensus among stakeholders about the needed changes in the energy system. New mechanisms are needed to promote consensus building among industrial, environmental, and consumer stakeholders (both those without and with adequate purchasing power) and to facilitate inputs of these different stakeholders to energy decision-making.

5.4 Improving the Overall Economic Framework

In a market-based economy, the development of new energy systems is strongly influenced by the overall economic framework—the characteristics of capital markets and energy markets and the market treatment of new energy technologies. Current conditions are such that improvements in the overall economic framework must be made if sustainable energy systems are to be put in place. Specifically needed are reforms aimed at ensuring that: *i)* overall capital supplies are adequate to meet expected demands for capital, particularly in developing countries; *ii)* capital resources are allocated in ways that do not discriminate against investments in energy efficiency and small-scale energy production; *iii)* permanent subsidies that distort energy markets are reduced or eliminated; *iv)* environmental costs are internalized in energy markets; and *v)* there are adequate incentives for both research and development on and commercialization of new energy technologies supportive of sustainable development goals.

5.4.1 Accessing Capital for Sustainable Development

Investments in the energy sector are projected to increase significantly. Over the mid-1990s, investments in energy supply worldwide were being made at a rate of about US$400 billion per year (in 1990 dollars). A study carried out jointly by the World Energy Council and the International Institute for Advanced Systems Analysis (WEC/IIASA, 1995) estimated that by 2020 capital requirements will be up to US$750 billion dollars per year (with half of it for electricity). It will be difficult to provide the needed capital from traditional sources, particularly in developing countries.

Traditionally, a major source of capital for infrastructure building has been retained earnings from revenues. However, many electric utilities in developing countries have little or no retained earnings for such purposes because tariffs are low as a result of consumer subsidies (see Section 5.4.3). Moreover, these consumer subsidies have led to poor credit ratings for such utilities, making it difficult for them to raise capital in commercial capital markets. Historically, governments have provided much of the needed capital for utility investments, but increasingly governments are unable to do this because of fiscal constraints (see Section 5.2).

Fiscal constraints are also limiting the availability of financial assistance from ODA sources. For example, in 1994, net total ODA financing amounted to US$67 billion, compared with US$74 billion in 1986, based on 1993 constant dollars (OECD/DAC, 1996). ODA resources also are now being allocated to Central and Eastern European countries. Thus, the ODA pie is becoming smaller, and there are new claimants to the shrinking pie. Multilateral banks and bilateral donors invested approximately US$8 billion per year during the 1980s in the energy sector, mostly for electricity, but that level has not been sustained in the 1990s (WEC/IIASA, 1995).

Sustainable development strategies generally would require less total energy investment (see Section 4.2.6.1) and thus would be easier to finance. However, capital market reforms will be needed even to meet even these reduced capital requirements. A major potential new source of capital for energy-sector investments in developing countries is foreign private capital.

Flows of international private capital to developing countries have increased from US$42 billion in 1990 to US$170 billion in 1995. In 1995, foreign direct investment (FDI) in developing countries reached US$100 billion. However, in order to attract some of this capital to energy investments, prospective private investors must be convinced that the financial risks are acceptable, and the projected returns on investment must be comparable to or larger than for those available on alternative investment opportunities. Clear rules on ownership and a system based on enforced laws and regulations are important elements of a policy that would attract more private capital to energy sector investments. Moreover, in order to attract some of this capital to investments in energy technologies for sustainable development, in particular, investors must be convinced that there will be significant markets for these technologies, with policies in place that promote their deployment (see, for example, Sections 5.4.2 to 5.4.5 and Appendix C).

Nevertheless, foreign private capital is not an overall panacea. First, FDI is distributed very unevenly. The top 10 host developing countries received 76% of FDI in 1993-95, and China alone received approximately 40%.

In stark contrast, all of Africa received only 5% (United Nations, 1996). FDI therefore is not a substitute for ODA in all cases. Furthermore, total needs for capital investment in the energy sectors of developing countries are probably in excess of what can be provided by foreign private capital. Economic reforms, such as proper pricing of energy (see Section 5.4.3) that would make retained earnings a significant source of capital for energy investments and the development of strong domestic capital markets are also important (STAP/GEF, 1996).

5.4.2 Financing Sustainable Energy Technologies via Innovative Credit and Purchase Arrangements

Even if the challenges of providing the volumes of capital needed to support sustainable energy strategies can be overcome, innovative approaches are needed to allocate efficiently these capital resources to energy producers and consumers. The problem has both supply side and demand side aspects.

On the supply side, existing capital markets are generally organised to provide large quantities of capital for energy projects at the scales of conventional energy technologies (e.g., large central-station power plants, oil refineries, or coal mines). But, many of the most promising technologies for meeting sustainable development goals require investments for small-scale energy production systems or for improvements in energy efficiency. Existing capital markets discriminate against investments at such small scales (WEC/IIASA, 1995).

On the demand side, many sustainable energy technologies are cost-effective from the perspective of lifecycle costs evaluated with a discount rate equal to the market rate of interest, but are more capital-intensive than conventional energy technologies. The capital intensity of such technologies poses the problem that many consumers evaluate alternatives primarily on the basis of first costs rather than lifecycle costs. For example, when an energy-efficient device is more expensive than the less efficient alternative, which is often the case, consumers tend to ignore the fact that the life-cycle cost of the energy services obtained are lower with the energy-efficient device. Instead, they tend to choose the less efficient device because it involves a lower initial investment. Sensitivity to first cost, a reluctance to sacrifice present consumption in favour of investment in capital-intensive equipment in order to derive long-term benefits and cost recovery, is a world-wide phenomena. This situation leads to economically inefficient and environmentally sub-optimal investments.

The ability to postpone present consumption for the sake of future benefits derived from a project determines one's discount rate, which in turn determines the present value of all outlays made at various times during the life of the project. The higher the discount rate, the more the emphasis on front-end investments and the less the value one assigns to future benefits. The implicit discount rate used in investment decisions varies dramatically. Studies of consumers of energy-using equipment indicate that as the income of a consumer decreases, the consumer discount rate increases substantially, to levels far higher than the market rate of interest. Consumers with scarce economic resources tend to use these resources for satisfying present needs rather than for future benefits. Thus, low-income people end up spending more in the long run for the same energy service because they are not able to receive the economic benefits from lifecycle cost-based technology choices (Reddy, 1990).

It is essential that policies are implemented to develop a legal and regulatory framework that will provide access to capital markets for investments in various small-scale sustainable energy technologies.

Innovative financing mechanisms for first cost-sensitive investors could be designed to convert the capital cost into an operating cost, so that payments would be aligned with the stream of benefits received. "Microfinancing" (i.e., financial intermediation at the local level) is an effective mechanism for institutions to use in providing households and small businesses access to capital via loans for small-scale investments under flexible, and often non-traditional, lending conditions, so as to expand the market for sustainable energy systems. If a loan is for a more energy-efficient piece of equipment that produces a stream of monetary savings greater than the stream of loan payments, the borrower will realise lower costs. Sometimes an added benefit will be a higher level of energy services obtained from the more efficient equipment, leading to more energy services provided with less energy consumption (see Box 3.1).

To illustrate the importance of such loans, consider, as an example, microfinancing for photovoltaic (PV) systems for lighting and other household activities in rural areas that don't have access to electric utility grids. A World Bank study has shown that in many instances PV systems, though capital-intensive, are less costly on a lifecycle cost basis than current technologies for providing lighting in many developing countries, when the same levels of services are compared. For example, a 100 Watt PV system providing each day 12 hours of area lighting, 14 hours of task lighting, plus 0.15 kWh of electricity for other loads in rural Indonesia would have a total levelised cost over a 25-year period of approximately US$14 per month—about 1/3 less than the currently favoured technology, consisting of 2 kerosene wick lamps, 2 kerosene mantle lamps, and 2 automotive batteries for providing the same level of services. This assessment assumes a 12% discount rate, present PV technology, but a mature, two-step distribution system (i.e., manufacturer-to-dealer and dealer-to-customer) with manufacturer and dealer sales of 5,000 and 200 systems per year, respectively (Cabraal et al., 1996). If financing were available to the consumer via a 5-year loan at 12% interest and a 30% downpayment, the monthly loan repayment rate during this period would be less than 10% more than what the consumer currently pays for lighting with the conventional technology; over the remaining 20 years of the lifecycle, the cost would be zero.

An institutional alternative to microfinancing to deal with the capital allocation problem for small-scale investments is to aggregate many small investments under the umbrella of an energy service company (ESCO). For example, investments in energy end-use efficiency might be financed not by energy suppliers or consumers but rather by third-party ESCOs, which already operate in some countries. In return for providing the capital for the equipment investment, the ESCO collects an agreed-upon fraction of energy savings that arise from the investment.

Although many smaller-scale users are willing to pay market prices for sustainable energy technologies, there remains a critical need to set up financing mechanisms that are suited to the small scales of the capital-intensive equipment they seek to purchase. Once appropriate financing mechanisms are set up to support such energy alternatives, users will be capable of paying the full costs of their purchases.

5.4.3 Reducing Subsidies to Conventional Energy

Subsidies create a non-level playing field among various energy options. One estimate is that in the early 1990s, government subsidies for conventional energy were on the order of US$350-US$400 billion but, by the mid-1990s, these subsidies decreased to US$250-US$300 billion per year (de Moor and Calamai, 1997). Two widely used forms of subsidy are: i) direct subsidies that alter market prices; and ii) indirect subsidies through fiscal and other rules that affect investment decisions.

Subsidies to conventional energy constitute a significant impediment to sustainable energy futures. They make it more difficult for new, sustainable energy technologies to enter the market, while simultaneously reducing the economic efficiency and creating fiscal burdens for government. Reducing permanent subsidies would improve market competitiveness for new technologies whilst yielding the added benefits of improving market efficiency and of considerably decreasing the burden on public spending. However, subsidies provide significant benefits to their recipients, thus creating resistance to their reduction or elimination.

Subsidies are given both on the production and consumption sides. By far, most of the subsidies are given to the fossil fuel and nuclear industries. Production-side subsidies are common in OECD countries. They typically have been utilised to further governments' plans to accelerate the expansion of the energy sector, through support to oil and natural gas exploration, research and development, and market introduction of, for example, nuclear power. Many of these subsidies have remained in place long after the technologies have matured and captured significant market shares. These subsidies can come in the form of direct payments, the creation of more favourable economic conditions, or as mechanisms to reduce risk.

Energy consumers are subsidised in countries where energy prices are below world market prices. Such subsidies are common in the Central and Eastern European states, and in some developing countries. One set of estimates is that in the early 1990s, these subsidies exceeded US$150 billion per year in the former Soviet Union, and were approximately US$50 billion per year in developing countries, (Larsen and Shah, 1995, Koplow, 1993). These amounts are comparable to total official development assistance from all sources, when debt repayment is taken into account. Another estimate is that the financial burden of underpricing electricity in developing countries is on the order of US$90 billion per year (World Bank, 1994). Although these subsidies have been reduced during the last few years (e.g., China has almost eliminated coal subsidies and Russia has significantly reduced the subsides by increasing energy prices) they are still common.

Direct energy subsidies are often provided in the context of helping people who are living in poverty. Not only do low-income households normally spend a higher fraction of their disposable income on energy than do other groups, but also they often pay more for the same level of energy service. They pay more in part because their fuel/equipment systems generally are less efficient than those which wealthier households are able to access and afford, and also because low-income households typically purchase fuel in smaller amounts.

Moreover, energy price subsidies are often an ineffective and inefficient way of helping those living in poverty, who typically receive only a small fraction of the total subsidy given. People living in poverty in rural and urban areas have limited access to electricity, and they cannot benefit from household tariff subsidies meant to guarantee basic needs. Similarly, in the case of kerosene use in Tanzania, subsidies were found to benefit only wealthier (primarily middle-income) households who were able to purchase and use the fuel, while the lowest-income households benefitted little, if at all (Hosier and Kipondya, 1993).

Further, the reduction or elimination of subsidies leading to price increases will be more acceptable if subsidy removal is accompanied by measures to improve end-use efficiency. Where some form of subsidy is believed to be necessary, one way to bring about reform in the electricity sector is to adopt lifeline rates that offer low electricity tariffs up to levels of consumption needed to support basic human needs (e.g., up to 50 kWh per month) and tariffs that reflect marginal costs at higher levels of consumption. Subsidising tariffs at higher consumption levels would benefit richer people more and take away the incentive to improve energy efficiency. Changes in subsidies will always affect the conditions and reactions of the beneficiaries, and changes will be easier to implement if they are part of packages aimed at improving overall energy service delivery and phased in over time.

5.4.4 Internalising Environmental Costs in Energy Markets

Energy prices are also distorted when they fail to include external costs such as environmental costs associated with energy production and use. Environmental costs include the human health impacts of air pollution, land degradation, acidification of soils and waters, and climate change. When market prices do not fully take into account the external costs, the advantages of cleaner energy options are not reflected adequately in the marketplace. With policies designed so that energy prices reflect the true and full costs of energy, sustainable energy options will be much more viable.

Externalities can be internalised by taxes on emissions (IEA, 1993), by fines for damages, or through regulations designed to limit emissions and damages. A great deal of global experience has been accumulated in recent decades with many approaches. Internalising externalities is not straightforward, however. There is no consensus concerning the economic values to assign to environmental damages, or even on the methodologies for estimating such damages. Not only do different analysts and stakeholders tend to assign different values to the same damages, but many values are inherently difficult to quantify in monetary terms. The difficulties in framing appropriate policies for controlling externalities are compounded by the fact that policy changes have to take into account the impacts of new policies on a variety of stakeholders that might be adversely effected by the new policies (e.g. the impacts of higher energy prices from taxa-

tion on low-income consumers and impacts on the competitiveness of industries that are regulated or taxed).

There are two notable trends in formulating policies to deal with externalities. One is to emphasise the role of markets in finding the least costly approaches to achieving a particular objective, once that objective has been decided upon in the political process. For pollutants that have regional or global impacts, governments might choose, for example, to set a ceiling for, or a cap on, total emissions per year. It is then economically efficient to allow market forces to work out the least-cost solution to achieve the emissions objective. Tradable permits have been successfully used for controlling SO_2 emissions in the United States (Stone, 1993). Moreover, strong arguments have been made in favor of the use of tradable CO_2 emission permits in controlling CO_2 emissions at the global level (Epstein and Gupta, 1990). In early 1997 a group of more than 2000 economists, including six Nobel Laureates, called upon the nations of the world to cooperate in addressing the challenge of climate change by using market-based instruments such as the levying of carbon taxes or the auctioning of CO_2 emissions permits that can be traded internationally, using the revenues generated from such policies to reduce government budget deficits or to lower existing taxes. They argued that such policies could be effective in slowing climate change without harming living standards and could in fact improve economic productivity in the long run (Redefining Progress, 1997).

Another recent trend has involved the use of regulations or alternative incentives to force major, rather than incremental, technological change in the pursuit of sustainable development objectives. One notable example is a regulation in the state of California requiring that, by 2003, 10% of new cars sold in the state be characterised by zero air pollution emissions—a regulation that is helping to speed up the development of electric drive vehicles (see Section 3.2.5.4). A non-regulatory example of forcing major technological change is the Partnership for a New Generation of Vehicles, a collaboration between the United States government and United States automakers to develop, in a period of a decade, production-ready prototypes of automobiles that would be three times as fuel-efficient as today's cars, while meeting all air pollution and safety standards and costing no more than conventional cars.

Policies that could speed up the rate of introduction of inherently clean and safe energy technologies should have considerable appeal in developing countries, where environmental problems are often severe both because population densities are high (e.g., 13,000; 50,000; and 95,000 per km^2 in Mexico City, Lagos, and Hong Kong, respectively, compared to 4,000 and 6,000 per km^2 in London and New York), and because rapid growth in demand can quickly erode incremental improvements on conventional energy technologies to reduce pollutant emissions. To the extent such policies can be successful, they would lead to major environmental improvements while providing ancillary benefits. Whereas making incremental environmental improvements in existing technologies typically leads to increased costs for the energy services provided, a major technological innovation typically improves multiple attributes of a product or process simultaneously, often including cost reductions once the new technology becomes well established in the market. The prospect of gaining multiple benefits reduces the importance of gaining precision in the valuation of externalities. Moreover, successful introduction of inherently clean and safe technologies would also reduce the need for large regulatory bureaucracies that would otherwise be engaged in continually tightening regulations that mandate incremental improvements.

The rapid growth in the demand for energy services in developing countries provides a favourable theatre for such innovations. Moreover, if developing countries are successful in bringing about the needed economic reforms in the energy sector (so that decisions regarding energy technology can be decoupled from the securing of financing for energy investments) they would have a great deal of market power in encouraging the introduction of inherently clean and safe technologies through regulations or purchases by state-owned enterprises or utilities. Under such conditions, energy vendors from the industrialised world would be eager to compete in these developing country markets via various kinds of industrial collaborations, including international joint ventures, because these markets account for most energy demand growth world-wide.

To the extent that the introduction of new inherently clean technologies in developing countries leads initially to higher costs for the energy services provided, ways should be found for industrialised and developing countries to work together to share the financial risks of "buying down" the costs of new technologies in exchange for the future shared benefits that would rise from successfully commercialised products.

5.4.5 Developing New Technology

New energy technologies are critical to the realisation of energy futures that are compatible with sustainable development goals, such as those described in Chapter 4. New initiatives relating to both energy research and development and new technology commercialisation are needed to bring about the wide use of such technologies in world energy markets.

5.4.5.1 Reinvigorating research and development

Although there is a consensus among economists that over the long-run, innovation is the single most important source of long-term economic growth and that returns on investment in research and development are several times as high as the returns on other forms of investment, private firms generally tend to under-invest in research and development (Cohen and Noll, 1991). Compounding this long-term historical problem is the fact that both private sector and public sector investments in energy research and development have been declining in recent years (Williams, 1995). This decline is pervasive: it has been taking place in the United States and in much of Europe, in the public and private sectors, and in both the electric utility and the fossil fuel industries.

Overall, government support for energy research and development in International Energy Agency member countries fell by 1/3 in absolute terms and by half as a percentage of GDP in the decade ending in 1992 (see Table 5.1), although there are signs that this downward trend may be ending in some countries. Moreover, in the private sector, there has been declining emphasis on long-term research and development; as a percentage of total research and development, long-

139

Table 5.1: Total reported IEA government R&D budgets (columns 1-7); US$ billion at 1994 prices and exchange rates) and GDP (column 8; US$ trillion at 1993 prices).

Year	1 Fossil Energy	2 Nuclear Fission	3 Nuclear Fusion	4 Energy Conservation	5 Renewable Energy	6 Other	7 Total	8 GDP	9 % of GDP
1983	1.70	6.38	1.43	0.79	1.05	1.08	12.40	10.68	0.12
1984	1.60	6.12	1.44	0.70	1.02	0.99	11.88	11.20	0.11
1985	1.51	6.26	1.42	0.70	0.85	1.04	11.77	11.58	0.10
1986	1.51	5.72	1.31	0.59	0.66	0.94	10.74	11.90	0.09
1987	1.37	4.36	1.23	0.65	0.62	1.04	9.27	12.29	0.08
1988	1.46	3.64	1.13	0.53	0.62	1.19	8.58	12.82	0.07
1989	1.30	4.42	1.07	0.45	0.57	1.33	9.13	13.23	0.07
1990	1.75	4.48	1.09	0.55	0.61	1.15	9.62	13.52	0.07
1991	1.52	4.45	0.99	0.59	0.64	1.39	9.57	13.58	0.07
1992	1.07	3.90	0.96	0.56	0.70	1.28	8.48	13.82	0.06
1993	1.07	3.81	1.05	0.65	0.71	1.38	8.66		
1994	0.98	3.74	1.05	0.94	0.70	1.30	8.72		

Sources: Government energy R&D expenditure data are from IEA (1995); GDP data are from OECD (1994).
IEA, 1995: Energy Policies of IEA Countries: 1994 Review. OECD, Paris France
OECD, 1994: National Accounts: Main Aggregates. Vol. I, 1960-1992. OECD, Paris, France.

term research and development in the major international oil companies declined from 28% in 1982 to 11% in 1992 (Williams, 1995). These declines have been due to several factors—low fossil energy prices, the increasing fiscal constraints on governments, and the ongoing restructuring of the electric power industry. Electric utility restructuring in the United States has led to sharp drops in utility investments in research and development both as a cost-cutting measure to help utilities keep tariffs low so as to minimise the loss of customers to independent power producers and because of the free rider problem created by the emergence of the independent power producer who can benefit from research and development carried out by utilities.

Not only has overall energy research and development spending been declining, but also only modest fractions of research and development spending have been committed to the energy technologies highlighted in this report as being especially important to the realisation of sustainable development objectives—renewable energy and efficient energy-using technologies. Government-supported research and development has generally focused on nuclear technologies (see Table 5.1). On average for International Energy Agency member countries in the period 1983-1994, 48% of government research and development expenditures were committed to nuclear fission and 12% to nuclear fusion. Only 7.5% and 6.5%, respectively, were com-

mitted to renewable energy and energy conservation. Unless efficiency and renewable energy receive large increases, a sustainable energy future will be difficult to realise.

Fortunately, many promising technologies for meeting sustainable development objectives, such as fuel cells and most renewable energy technologies, require relatively modest research and development investments. For example, the World Energy Council has estimated that the research and development expenditures needed worldwide over the next 20 years to advance a range of solar energy technologies is of the order of US$8 billion (WEC, 1994). For comparison, in the United States public-sector support for nuclear fission research and development from 1950-1993 was US$56 billion in constant 1992 dollars (Williams and Terzian, 1993). Such modest costs for solar energy research and development are a reflection largely of the small scale and modularity of these technologies and the fact that they are generally clean and safe (Williams, 1995). After the research phase, the high costs of "scaling up" in the development process can be avoided with small-scale technologies. For technologies that are also characterised by high degrees of inherent safety and cleanliness, research and development resource requirements for improving safety and environmental performance are also small. Enormous research and development resources are sometimes committed to finding effective ways to dispose of harmful residuals of energy systems that are not inherently safe or clean. For example, the United States Department of Energy has spent US$1.7 billion on scientific and technical studies simply to determine the geological suitability of Nevada's Yucca Mountain as a disposal site for radioactive wastes from civilian nuclear power (Whipple, 1996). For comparison, total United States federal government support for photovoltaic research and development, 1972-1994, was US$1.8 billion in constant 1992 dollars (Williams and Terzian, 1993).

Because the research and development costs per technology tend to be relatively modest for many of the technologies that are desirable from a sustainable development perspective, emphasis on such technologies makes it possible to pursue a diversified research and development portfolio, even in times of fiscal austerity. Not all research and development will lead to successful commercial products. But the prospect of some failures should not be used to justify avoiding promising but risky research and development investments. Rather it should lead to the crafting of a diversified research and development portfolio.

In revitalising energy research and development, a major challenge to be addressed is to find new ways to minimise the financial risks of free riders being able to appropriate research and development benefits. Because of increasingly competitive conditions in the energy sector (with highly competitive conditions already dominating the United States energy sector and competitive conditions increasing in many other parts of the world as well), a greater pooling of the risks of supporting energy research and development is needed (Andrews, 1994). In the electric power sector, for example, this means finding ways to make independent power producers as well as utilities responsible for research and development. For "pre-competitive" research, the fostering of collaborations among industrial firms (both potential producers and potential users of future technologies), government laboratories, and universities would be an effective way to deal with the appropriability problem, as well as to minimise duplicated effort, and to promote

effective transfer of technological knowledge to eventual commercial producers. Collaborations in pre-competitive research among competing firms in an industry would make it possible to realise economies of scope or scale in research and development and would be beneficial in expanding the technological base of the industry; each firm in the consortium can then use that technology to develop its own proprietary products (Cohen and Noll, 1994).

The appropriability problem is getting more complicated as a result of the globalisation of economic activity. Because new scientific knowledge flows ever more easily across national borders, it is increasingly difficult for countries to appropriate the economic benefits of investments by their governments in research and development (Andrews, 1995). Accordingly, international research and development collaborations should be encouraged.

New mechanisms are also needed for funding research and development that simultaneously: *i)* reduce the difficulties the private firm finds in appropriating the benefits of its research and development investments; *ii)* reduce the difficulties governments have in financing research and development in periods when fiscal austerity is demanded by the public; *iii)* reduce the growing problem that a country has in appropriating the benefits of its government's investments in research and development; and *iv)* provide support that is sufficiently stable to sustain a viable research and development capacity.

One possibility would be a tax on externalities earmarked for use in supporting research on and the development, demonstration, and commercialisation of new energy technologies.[1] Such a funding mechanism would offer good prospects for being powerfully effective in transforming the energy system, even with relatively modest tax rates. For example, a carbon tax of US$1 per tonne levied on fossil fuel use in OECD countries at the 1990 emissions level would generate annual revenues of US$4.3 billion. This level of revenues is equivalent to half of total energy research and development spending by IEA member countries in 1994 (see Table 5.1); two years of revenues from such a tax

---

[1]   Many economists do not favor earmarked taxes. However, it has been argued that earmarked taxes are desirable in some instances as a mechanism for introducing more taxpayer choice into the process of allocating tax revenues (Buchanan, 1963)

would be adequate to provide the research and development support needed world-wide over the next 20 years to advance a range of solar energy technologies, as estimated by the World Energy Council (WEC, 1994). While such revenues committed to research and development on sustainable energy technology development could make enormous contributions to the realisation of sustainability goals, the cost to consumers would be modest. For example, in the United States such a tax would increase the average price of energy by less than 0.3% and would amount to lessthan US$6 per capita per year.

5.4.5.2 Launching new technologies in the market

Research and development programmes are necessary, but not sufficient, to launch new technologies in the marketplace. Commercial demonstration projects and programmes to stimulate markets for new technologies are also needed. Even after successful demonstration, new technology is typically more expensive initially than the established alternatives, creating a barrier to their increased deployment. This barrier can be overcome through experience and continued incremental technological improvements to bring down the costs.

For many technologies production costs can be expected to decline with the cumulative volume of production, as a result of "learning by doing." A wide range of small-scale, modular energy technologies including most renewable energy technologies and fuel cells are good candidates for cost-cutting via learning by doing (Williams and Terzian, 1993; WEC, 1994). For many of these technologies the cumulative cost of "buying down" the cost of new technologies via progress along learning curves can often be low relative to learning costs for large-scale technologies (see Figure 3.8). The World Energy Council has estimated that to be competitive with conventional options, various solar energy technologies may need, in addition to support for research and development, subsidies of the order of US$7-US$12 billion to support initial deployment until manufacturing economies of scale are achieved to compete with conventional options (WEC, 1994). For the United States, the total investment required over the next 5-10 years to commercialise four different

fuel cell technologies for stationary applications has been estimated to be US$2 billion (Penner et al., 1995).

The economic argument for government support for launching new technologies in the market with temporary subsidies is that sustainable energy technologies provide services in the form of reduced pollution, improved safety, and other attributes that are public rather than private benefits. This argument cannot be applied to energy technologies generally. But even in the case of sustainable energy technologies, the economic argument for government financial support for launching new technologies in the market is weaker than for energy research and development. If a new sustainable energy technology is technically proven and has good prospects for being a commercial success in volume production, private-sector entrepreneurs should be willing to absorb the costs of buying down a new technology if there is a clear large market opportunity for the technology. If such entrepreneurs are available, the government's role might be to focus on helping define and create the market for these technologies via regulatory or other means rather than provide direct financial support. Direct financial support might be needed for technologies that face severe institutional or infrastructure hurdles as well as the challenge of cost buy-down (e.g., various new technologies for electric power generation in distributed rather than central station configurations (Section 3.3.2) or hydrogen fuel cell vehicles (Section 3.2.5.4)). To the extent that direct financial support is provided, subsidies should be designed to decline over time and phased out over a specified period and so as not to hinder technological progress. Governments are experimenting with various approaches for launching new technologies in the market, as illustrated by examples discussed in Appendix C.

5.5 Prospects for Energy Technology Market Leadership in the Developing World
5.5.1 Technology Innovation and Growth

The most favourable theatres for innovation are large, rapidly growing markets. Historically, these conditions have characterised both the energy supply industries and the energy-intensive consuming sectors of the industrialised world, where most energy technology innovation has taken place. The situation is now very different because growth in industrialised countries is slow for both energy production and energy-intensive economic activities. Instead, rapid growth is confined largely to services and knowledge-intensive activities, which tend to require very little materials and energy. The energy-intensive industries are facing either stagnation or only very slow growth in industrialised country markets (see, for example, Figure 3.3). To the extent that innovation is still taking place in the energy producing and consuming sectors of the industrialised countries, it is being driven largely by environmental concerns.

Currently growth is rapid and is expected to continue to be rapid for decades to come for both energy-producing and energy-intensive activities in developing countries, and environmental concerns are likely to be even more intense in developing countries than they have been in industrialised countries. Consequently, the conditions for innovation relating to energy are likely to be far better in developing countries than in industrialised countries. The developing countries now have the opportunity to promote innovative energy technologies that would be helpful in meeting their sustainable development objectives.

5.5.2 Technological Leapfrogging

Developing countries not only have the opportunity to employ the most technologically advanced energy systems available on the world market to meet their energy demands, but also they can consider deploying new, emerging technologies and systems which are not yet in wide use. Pursuing this option would be contrary to the widely held view that the process of commercialising advanced technologies is an inappropriate activity for developing countries. It is often said that developing countries cannot afford the risk-taking of innovation when there are so many pressing development needs to attend to. In addition, some developing countries have had bad experience with efforts to transfer advanced energy technology from industrialised countries. Moreover, the development assistance community has also not been very supportive of innovations in the energy sector. Yet there are many reasons to question this conventional wisdom.

First, many of the industrial technolo-gies now being commercialised in the industrialised countries are capital-intensive and labour-saving—characteristics that are not well-suited to industrial activity in most developing countries, where labour is cheap and capital scarce. Second, the comparative advantages in natural resources are often quite different for many developing countries. Third, human needs are quite different in developing and industrialised countries because of climatological differences, and because the satisfaction of basic needs and infrastructure-building must be given prominent focus in the economic planning of developing countries.

The adoption of advanced technologies is often referred to as "technological leapfrogging" (as in the children's game), whereby developing countries leap over the industrialised countries. In general, because of the importance of technological innovation for development and, in particular, of the multiple benefits inherent in many advanced energy conversion and utilisation technologies, energy planning for developing countries should include technological leapfrogging, where appropriate.

Industries of critical importance for developing countries and thus good candidates for technological leapfrogging are the basic materials processing industries such as iron and steel and cement making—energy-intensive industries that are stagnating in the industrialised countries but are growing rapidly in the many developing countries that are engaged in infrastructure-building. While in many developing countries these industries are much less efficient and more polluting than their counterparts in OECD countries, there has been significant technological leapfrogging experience with these industries in some countries.

Consider first iron- and steel-making. The world's first plants for producing iron by direct reduction (without smelting) were built in Mexico. This technology used in conjunction with electric arc furnaces (EAFs) for steel-making is especially well-suited to many developing countries because favourable economics can be realised at scales of 100,000 tonnes of annual capacity or less, compared to capacities of 2.5 to 3.5 million tonnes per year needed for conventional blast furnaces plus oxygen-blown converters. Moreover, while most of the world's iron-making is based on the use of coke, coal-poor but biomass-rich Brazil has developed a modern charcoal-based process based on the efficient use of eucalyptus grown on plantations; this iron is processed into a high-quality steel that is competitive in world markets.

Smelt reduction is an emerging technology that might dramatically improve iron making, the first and most energy-intensive step in the production of primary steel (Worrell, 1995). Smelt reduction plants are designed to use coal and ores directly in integrated plants, thereby reducing capital costs, pollutant emissions, and the energy intensity of iron-making; and operating costs are reduced because ordinary steam coal can be used instead of the more costly metallurgical coal (see Figure 3.6). The first smelt reduction process to be proven commercially is the COREX process, at a 300,000 tonnes per year plant in South Africa. Although this small scale COREX plant is no more energy-efficient than a modern blast furnace, future developments for this technology are expected to lead to substantial gains in energy efficiency (Worrell, 1995). Hanbo Steel in South Korea is constructing a large new steel-making plant at Asan Bay that will integrate many advanced technologies. This plant will have two COREX C-2000 units, the flue gases of which will be used in a Midrex direct reduction unit to produce 800,000 tonnes/year of sponge iron (used as high grade input in EAF steel-making). The Asan Bay complex is a very compact integrated steel plant with substantially reduced capital costs, energy consumption and environmental impact.

In Taiwan, where annual cement production increased from 3.3 Mtonnes in 1966 to 21.5 Mtonnes in 1992, the cement industry has applied modern technology throughout its expansion. Cement is produced in two steps. First raw materials are burned to produce clinker. The clinker is then mixed with additives. The clinker making is the most energy-intensive production step. Two-thirds of clinker capacity in Taiwan is equipped with pre-calciners (a modern technology), a larger share than in most OECD countries. One of the most energy-efficient clinker plants in the world can be found in Taiwan—the 4800 tonnes per day clinker plant in Hualien (Asia Cement Corporation). The energy efficiency of this plant is second in the world only to that for a plant recently constructed in the United States (Worrell et al., 1995).

While the risks inherent in the innovative process cannot be avoided, they can be managed to acceptable levels in relation to the potential benefits. Risks can be shared in various ways—for example, if innovative projects were pursued as joint ventures between industrialised and developing country companies, or if the international, multilateral and bilateral development assistance organisations were to assume some of the risks of innovation. These development assistance organisations should continue to help build the capacity needed to support a dynamic innovative process in developing countries.

An important example of a development assistance organisation supporting a technological leapfrogging energy project and related capacity-building is the Brazilian project that will demonstrate electricity generation from biomass using thermochemical gasification of woody biomass in combination with a gas turbine/steam turbine combined cycle power plant (Elliott and Booth, 1993) (see Section 3.3.2.6). This project is supported by the Global Environment Facility.

5.5.3 Seizing Market Leadership for Energy Technologies

Developing countries have the opportunity to become market leaders for various state-of-the-art and emerging sustainable energy technologies. In developing countries, large rapidly-growing markets plus lower wage rates at all levels of technical, scientific and engineering skills make both manufacturing and product development attractive options for technology owners (e.g., via international commercial and research and development joint ventures, which could serve global markets). At the time that new technologies are introduced in developing countries, some components could be produced locally. The locally manufactured product content would be expected to increase over time. Local manufacture implies not only local job creation opportunities but also often potentially lower costs than for the same technologies imported from the industrialised world, leading to large domestic markets and opportunities for export growth. The growing emphasis on free trade by governments around the world will facilitate the exploitation of such opportunities.

Therefore, a significant window of opportunity currently exists. Over time, as the global economy becomes more integrated and as developing country economies grow, the wage-rate differential between developing and industrial labour markets is likely to diminish, a situation which could make it more difficult for developing countries to achieve technological leadership in manufacturing and product development (STAP/GEF, 1996).

Seizing opportunities for market leadership will be a challenging task. Three prerequisites for successful outcomes are: *i)* the establishment of an appropriate legal, regulatory, and policy framework; *ii)* the rational pricing of energy; and *iii)* the creation of strong domestic capital markets. Industrial activities consistent with sustainable development objectives could be catalyzed by governments creating and maintaining legal, regulatory, and policy frameworks that: *i)* include elements addressing social and environmental concerns so that the technologies introduced are consistent with sustainable development objectives, and *ii)* are fair to all parties. Rational pricing of energy would go a long way towards overcoming financial weakness in the sector. It would not only attract investment but also it would simultaneously help build a strong, competitive market for technology imports, giving developing countries considerable market power to shape the course of technological change. This technological market power would be enhanced with the creation of strong domestic capital markets via the development of insurance and pension funds, to take advantage of the savings rates that already exist in many developing countries and thereby reduce the need for capital imports.

5.6 The Time for Sustainable Energy Has Come

Concerted efforts are needed at national and international levels involving governments, multilateral institutions, private sector investors, civil society and the energy industries to promote a sustainable energy path and to use energy as an effective instrument for sustainable human development. A number of encouraging developments along these line are underway.

Growing awareness about development and environment issues throughout the world is beginning to have impacts on consumption patterns and political decisions. This increasing awareness is demonstrated by the emergence of local and regional groups that are committed to environmental and clean energy issues. In addition, many countries have adopted policies and programmes that clearly work towards a more sustainable energy future, as illustrated by the examples presented in Appendix C.

A number of international developments in this area are also encouraging. For example, the Framework Convention on Climate Change (FCCC) has entered into force and has been ratified by 164 countries (June 1996). The Global Environment Facility (GEF), as the financial mechanism for the FCCC, devotes a significant fraction of its resources to renewable energy and energy efficiency to reduce greenhouse gas emissions. Multilateral organisations including the United Nations Development Programme, the regional development banks and the World Bank are increasing their sustainable energy efforts. A report of the Secretary-General to the Commission on Sustainable Development (CSD) has detailed the special role of energy in meeting the challenges of sustainable development, reviewed the energy activities of the United Nations system, and recommended areas for future activities by the United Nations system (United Nations, 1997). The countries in the Americas have initiated a process of Hemispheric Energy Co-operation, which has strong mandates to advance efficiency, the use of renewable sources of energy, and rural electrification (Santa Cruz Declaration, 1996). Many developing counties, including China, India, and Brazil, as well as several industrialised countries, have launched sustainable energy programmes. Recently, more than one hundred nations, including ten represented by Heads of State and ten represented by Heads of Government, and another forty by energy or environment ministers, participated in the World Solar Summit in Zimbabwe and expressed their commitment to solar energy.

Internationally, no one organisation is responsible for energy. Within the United Nations system there are numerous agencies that support diverse activities in both conventional and renewable energy. The World Energy Council, representing world energy industries, has called on various occasions for new partnerships between government, the private sector and consumers to facilitate the changes required to move the world to a path of sustainable development (WEC/IIASA, 1995). Many other non-governmental organisations, primarily motivated by environmental and social concerns, have advanced similar propositions.

The ability to move towards a sustainable energy future depends on building coalitions around common development, economic, technological and energy service interests that are part of a sustainable approach to energy. No new international institutions need be established. Rather, a framework through which sustainable energy strategies are promoted and interested parties convened, could be developed to address common interests. A mechanism that encourages better dialogue among governments, the private sector, and non-governmental organisations on the mobilisation of investment funds, technology transfer, management, and training is needed.

In contrast to the past, most future investments in energy systems are likely to be in developing countries. It is of considerable economic and environmental interest to developing countries that new technological opportunities become available to them. If they were to have these opportunities, they would be able to leapfrog to the new generation of cleaner energy technologies, without having to retrace the unsustainable path that the industrialised countries have followed.

This sets the stage for development co-operation. It can contribute to implementing sustainable energy futures and thereby work towards poverty reduction, job creation, the advancement of women and protection of the environment. Key elements in this regard will be human capacity building, the formulation of legal and institutional frameworks supportive of these developments, the demonstration of key new technologies, and national action programmes for sustainable energy.

The international community has dealt with aspects of social, economic and sustainable development through UNCED and the United Nations global conferences of the 1990s. They have identified targets and goals and formulated international agreements, platforms of action, declarations and resolutions adopting these commitments. Energy issues must be squarely dealt with if these commitments are to be fulfilled, and the leadership must come from governments. Within an appropriate framework, energy companies, both privately and publicly owned, investors and civil society can all contribute and support each other to meet the goals of sustainable development. A public sector-led reorientation to promote and adopt sustainable energy is essential to meet the commitments of the global conferences.

Energy can become an instrument of sustainable development. While accomplishing this will not be easily achieved in light of the major changes needed, a continuation of present trends cannot be sustained.

Appendix C: Removing Impediments—Some Examples

The following are examples from around the world of policies that have been enacted or are under consideration for overcoming the barriers to the wide-spread use of sustainable energy technologies.

C.1 Measures to Create Early Markets for New Technology

C.1.1 Renewable energy development in India[1]

Many countries have experience with renewable energy, but few have taken their efforts beyond the pilot stage. A notable exception is India.

Since 1993, the Indian Renewable Energy Development Authority (IREDA), a government- established public bank, has been implementing a US$430 million programme to develop India's renewable energy resources. Supported by US$255 million in multilateral and bilateral loans and grants, the programme provides soft loans to developers of renewable energy projects for up to 75% of project costs.

To date, the majority of loans have gone to wind power development, resulting in the installation of 800 megawatts (MW) of wind power in India, up from 200 MW in early 1995. In addition, the installed bagasse power and solar electric power capacities in India have reached 44 MW and 1 MW, respectively.

IREDA has recently expanded the programmes for solar, biomass, and small hydro power, with the result that projects using these technologies will begin to be installed at a rapid pace. IREDA's mid-range estimate is that 16,000 MW of renewable electric capacity will be on line by 2015 (8% of total generating capacity).

Among the projects under negotiation is a 50 MW solar photovoltaic power plant—the world's largest—in the western state of Rajasthan, sponsored by Amoco-Enron Corporation with support from the Rajasthan State Electricity Board.

C.1.2 The Public Utilities Regulatory Policy Act (PURPA) in the United States

The Public Utilities Regulatory Policy Act (PURPA) of 1978 specified that all utilities in the United States must buy electricity generated by qualifying independent power producers (IPPs), defined as qualifying cogenerators [combined heat and power (CHP) producers] and producers of electricity from small-scale renewable energy sources.

This legislation has encouraged entrepreneurs to establish electricity generating capacity independently of the regulated utilities and has obligated utilities to buy electricity generated by qualified IPPs for their grids at price levels equal to their avoided costs (the costs the utilities could avoid by not having to produce the electricity themselves).

This law proved influential in establishing cogeneration and renewable electricity generation capacity because it secured access to the market and assured fair, predictable prices. Much of the 9,000 MW_e of biomass-fuelled power generation installed in the United States during the 1980s came about because of the incentives provided under this law (Williams and Larson, 1993). Similarly, the development of solar thermal electric and wind energy in California was supported by PURPA, as well through tax incentives provided by the Federal Government and the State of California (de Laquil et al., 1993). Many small hydropower sites, and geothermal sites, have also been developed as a result of the PURPA legislation.

Experience with PURPA has shown that a combination of specific regulatory and legal measures concerning power production can produce favourable results. Among the important measures are:

- *Provisions for long-term power purchase contracts*: Long-term contracts provide for a sufficient amount of time to allow for predictable payment streams. Being able to secure long-term purchase price contracts for electric power was critical for independent power producers to obtain financing and manage their risk, greatly facilitating the establishment of an IPP-based

---

[1]   This subsection is based on (Tata/IREDA and IREDA, 1996).

power industry; and

- *Development of standardised contracts:*
Suggested by the regulatory authorities, standardised contracts provide guidelines for terms and conditions of capacity and energy sales to utilities. Standard contracts have significantly reduced the transaction costs involved with arriving at a negotiated contract that could be financed.

Experience has shown that the IPP industry that evolved under PURPA was able to produce electricity at a lower cost than electric utilities. The avoided cost provisions of PURPA directed the flow of all the net economic benefits generated by qualifying facilities to the IPPs, without penalising consumers with higher electricity prices. This flow of benefits was key to establishing the IPPs in the market as viable alternatives to the regulated electric utilities.

Currently in the United States, the power industry is evolving beyond PURPA-type arrangements towards fully competitive markets for power generation. Under competition the economic benefits of reduced costs offered by IPPs are shared between the IPPs and consumers (in the form of reduced electricity tariffs). However, these reduced tariffs would not be possible had the PURPA legislation not first created a viable IPP-based power-generating industry via the avoided cost provision.

C.1.3 Brazil's Ethanol Programme

Pressed by the rising cost of oil imports that threatened its balance of payments in the 1970s, and seeking a way to stabilise sugarcane production in the context of wide variations in international sugar prices, the Brazilian Government launched in 1976 programmes to encourage the production of ethanol from sugarcane and the adaptation of Brazilian automotive engines to work either on "neat ethanol" (96% ethanol, 4% water) or "gasohol" (78% gasoline, 22 per cent ethanol). The ethanol programme rapidly reached a yearly production of about 200,000 barrels per day of ethanol, replacing one half of the gasoline that would have otherwise been used in automobiles in Brazil (Goldemberg et al., 1993).

Environmental benefits have resulted from this programme since because alcohol use in automotive internal combustion engines leads to reduced CO emissions (see

Section 3.3.5.4). Additionally, as sugar cane is a renewable energy source, the use of cane-derived ethanol as an alternative to gasoline has lead to a major net lifecycle reduction in lifecycle CO_2 emissions. Approximately 15% of Brazil's total CO_2 emissions from fossil fuel use are avoided by the use of ethanol as a replacement for gasoline.

The ethanol programme was almost entirely based on locally manufactured equipment, helping to establish a strong agro-industrial base, and generating a significant number of jobs, both for skilled and unskilled workers. In addition, the programme has led to technological developments, both in agriculture production as well as sugarcane processing leading to lower ethanol cost and the possibility of a large surplus conservation of biomass-based (bagasse and agricultural residues) electricity.

While substantial cost reductions are being made for sugar cane-derived ethanol (Goldemberg et al., 1993), cane-derived ethanol is not yet competitive with gasoline used in internal combustion engine vehicles at the present low world oil price. However, there are good prospects that cane-derived ethanol could become competitive at the present low world oil price if, as a by-product of making alcohol from cane juice, electricity was cogenerated from cane residues using the BIG/GT technology (Williams and Larson, 1993) that will be demonstrated in Brazil by the turn of the century (see Section 3.3.2.6).

C.1.4 The Renewables Non-Fossil Fuel Obligation (NFFO) in the United Kingdom

One way governments can help create markets for renewable sources of energy is to stipulate that utilities incorporate a minimum amount of renewable energy capacity into their portfolios, even if utilities have other, less expensive alternative means of providing power.

The United Kingdom adopted the renewables Non-Fossil Fuel Obligation as part of the 1989 Electricity Act, which privatised the electric power sector. It evolved from the need to find a means of supporting nuclear power, after it was realised that nuclear power could not survive privatisation without a subsidy. The British government was required to obtain permission from the European Commission to levy a tax on electricity in order to subsidise nuclear power. The government asked permission instead for a levy on fossil-based electricity to support non-fossil-based electricity, in a Non-Fossil Fuel Obligation (NFFO)—a request that was granted by the Commission. The NFFO came to be understood to includeboth renewable and nuclear energy (Mitchell, 1995).

The renewables NFFO is a mechanism for moving market-ready renewable energy technologies into the marketplace, and for increasing the number of independent power producers. Despite its origin, the renewables NFFO has turned out to be a great boost for renewables. The major outcome of the renewables NFFO has been the establishment of a renewable energy industry in the United Kingdom. The goal of the policy is to bring into operation, by the year 2000, a baseload equivalent of 1,500 MW$_e$ of renewable electric supplies. Several orders of projects have been developed under the renewables NFFO: the first, in 1990, provided 75 contracts for 152 MW of electric capacity; the second, in 1991, 122 contracts and 472 MW, and the third, in 1994, 141 contracts and 627 MW. By early 1997, some 428 MW of renewables capacity from NFFO-1, NFFO-2, and NFFO-3 was already operational. For the fourth and largest renewables order, NFFO-4, 195 projects with a total capacity of 843 MW were approved early in 1997 (DTI, 1997). The fifth order, NFFO-5, will take place in 1998.

The renewables NFFO requires that producers have a minimum of their supply capacity in renewable energy-based generation, and regional electricity companies are required to purchase a certain amount of renewable electricity (Mitchell, 1995). Because a premium price is paid for the renewable electricity, the incremental price is reimbursed to the regional electricity companies by the Non-Fossil Purchasing Agency. The public electric suppliers pay these generators a premium price for renewable electricity, and the difference between the premium price and the market electricity price is paid for by a tax on fossil fuels consumed by the utilities. The extra cost for the renewables NFFO is paid for by the ratepayers, but the effect has been small (an increase of 0.1 to 0.5% in electricity price since 1990).

Over the last several years, the renewables NFFO has made cost convergence between renewables and conventional energy

an explicit goal, as explained by the Minister of Energy in July 1993 (Mitchell, 1995): "...the purpose of the NFFO Orders is to create an initial market so that in the not too distant future the most promising renewables can compete without financial support. This requires a steady convergence under successive Orders between the price paid under the NFFO and the market price. This will only be achieved if there is competition in the allocation of NFFO contracts."

Indeed there have been substantial price reductions—from an average price of 7.2 pence/kWh for NFFO-2 to 4.35 and 3.46 pence/kWh for NFFO-3 and NFFO-4, respectively (Mitchell, 1995; DTI, 1997).

Lessons learned include the desirability of co-ordinating better market penetration programmes such as the renewables NFFO with research and development programmes, and the importance of finding ways to adjust the requirements or expectations of key actors (e.g., bankers, investors, regulators, utilities, and sometimes governments) to the characteristics of renewables (e.g., often small-scale, capital-intensive, decentralised, and/or intermittent), which can be dealt with effectively, but require approaches and procedures different from those for conventional energy technologies (see Section 3.2.3).

C.1.5 A Renewables Portfolio Standard

A variation on the renewables NFFO being explored in many states and also at the federal level in the United States is a "Renewables Portfolio Standard" (RPS). The RPS is intended to maximise the use of market forces in establishing renewable energy industries in the context of a restructured and competitive electric industry in which retail electricity consumers are free to choose their electricity suppliers and grid owners are required to serve as common carriers for all suppliers (Rader and Norgaard, 1996)—a structure towards which the electric industry is evolving in the United States. Under the RPS, each retail supplier of electricity must provide a minimum percentage (specified by the State or the federal government) of renewable energy in its portfolio of electricity supplies. Individual obligations would be tradable through a system of renewable energy credits (RECs), which is intended to add flexibility in meeting the standard.

One REC is the equivalent of 1 kWh of

electricity generated from a renewable source. Retailers could choose from either owning their own renewable energy facilities to obtain RECs, purchasing them from other suppliers of renewable electricity, or purchasing them from a broker.

The administrative requirements of government are less under a RPS than under a NFFO, because the market, rather than an administrative process, would choose winning technologies and suppliers. A major role of the government would be to decide on the number of RECs required in relation to the total electricity sales by each retailer, based on renewable energy resources in the region, policy objectives, and potential costs. Separate requirements might be made for alternative classes of renewables (e.g. wind and photovoltaic sources) to account for different levels of progress in cost reduction. The number of RECs required might start at a low level, and increase over time as renewable energy capacity increased. Government would also certify the production of RECs and monitor compliance (Wiser et al., 1996).

In December 1996, both the states of Maine and Arizona adopted RPS mandates as part of their electricity utility structuring plans. The Arizona RPS mandate requires that at least 0.5% of electricity sold competitively in Arizona for the four-year period beginning in 1999 must come from photovoltaic or solar thermal-electric sources—a requirement that could increase to 1% beginning in 2002. Regulatory staff expect that this will lead to 75-200 MW of photovoltaic capacity in Arizona before 2003; for comparison, total world-wide PV sales amounted to 91 MW in 1996 (Curry, 1997). At the federal level, all the bills being considered in the United States Congress dealing with a restructured electric utility industry in early 1997 have RPS mandate provisions.

C.2 A Measure that Would Raise Funds for Purposes Relevant to Sustainable Energy (e.g. Research and Development): a System Benefits Charge in California

In Section 5.4.5.1 an earmarked carbon tax was discussed as a novel mechanism for funding research and development on energy technologies that would be compatible with sustainable development objectives. It was shown that a US$1 per tonne carbon tax, which would have a very small impact on energy prices, could provide large resources for supporting such R&D.

A similar instrument has recently been adopted in the State of California in the United States as a mechanism for dealing with the problem that the ongoing process of restructuring of the electric utility industry in favour of increased competition has decimated energy research and development activities by the electric utilities in the State. In August 1996, California enacted legislation designed to raise funds to correct this problem. This legislation imposes a surcharge, or System Benefits Charge, on all electricity sold at the retail level in the State (by both utilities and independent power producers) to raise funds to be used for energy research and development and other activities of vital public interest that the free market will not support (Wiser et al., 1996). As in the case of the proposed carbon tax, a surcharge that would have a very small impact on consumer electricity prices would be able to support a substantial R&D programme focussed on sustainable energy technologies.

C.3 Measures to Advance More Efficient Use of Energy

C.3.1 Market transformation through technology procurement by NUTEK in Sweden

Governments might use their convening power to create a demand for new technologies and in doing so have a large impact. For example, in the late 1980s, the Swedish government agency responsible for energy, NUTEK, created a technology procurement programme to facilitate a market transformation to products with higher energy efficiency (Nilsson, 1996). In the programme, the government acts as a catalyst by convening consumers to define the need, thereby encouraging the equipment producers to meet the need by improving equipment performance and efficiency. The cost to the government is very small, and the programme has a record of more than a dozen successful projects.

To illustrate the approach, consider household refrigerator-freezers. About half of the market for such appliances in Sweden is accounted for by a few public and private companies owning apartments. NUTEK convened a group of buyers, who agreed to issue a request for proposals for more energy-efficient, freon-free refrigerator-freezers. The winning model was freon-free, and its electricity requirements were one-third less than for the most energy-efficient model on the market, and two-thirds less than the market average.

This approach has also proven effective for lighting, windows, heat pumps, clothes washers and dryers, and even electric vehicles, where significant market transformations have been observed, and energy use has been reduced by 20% to 50%, compared to the best products on the market. In addition, the energy-efficient products often have other advantages such as being higher quality and having reduced noise (Nilsson, 1996).

The NUTEK technology procurement programme has proven to be an efficient mechanism for bringing new technologies into the market. However, other institutional improvements, such as labelling, performance standards, product campaigns, and professional training, are needed in order for the new products to penetrate and saturate the market, thus leading to a sustained impact. These changes need to be made in ways that appreciate the realities of operating businesses in a competitive environment.

C.3.2 The PROCEL electricity conservation programme in Brazil

In 1985, the PROCEL programme was launched in Brazil to promote the rational use of electricity. It is estimated that, as a result of PROCEL, 250 MW of generating capacity (1150 GWh per year of electricity)has been saved over the past decade—corresponding to savings of at least US$400 million in foregone investments in generation, transmission and distribution. Expenditures in this programme were US$15 million in 1995, and approximately US$100 million since the programme started (i.e., only one quarter of the savings arising from not having to build the extra new electricity supplies).

The primary activities in PROCEL have been energy audits, appliance labelling, and public lighting projects. Estimated savings from energy audits have ranged from 65 to 100 GWh per year, and the appliance labelling effort has realised an estimated annual savings of 390 GWh—one-third of all the savings realised under PROCEL. The success of the labelling programme is attributed to collaboration between government, industry and research laboratories, in spurring

appliance manufacturers to improve the efficiency of their products and to retire inefficient models from the market. Public lighting, which accounts for roughly 3% of electricity consumption in Brazil, was significantly overhauled under PROCEL by replacing incandescent bulbs with mercury vapour lamps and efficient, high-pressure sodium lamps.

Presently PROCEL is actively engaged in a series of other activities which are expected to reduce by 1,600 MW the generating capacity of the system. Main activities include programmes to install compact fluorescent lighting, plans to limit the demand of 2 million electric showers and air conditioners, and increase the use of high efficiency motors.

C.3.3 The Building Measurement and Verification Protocol (BMVP) for measurement and evaluation of energy efficiency improvements

A significant obstacle to contracting energy efficiency improvements has been the uncertainty about how to measure and evaluate the performance of the measures that have been implemented and methods to ensure consistency of the results. However, in a new approach to these problems, a North American energy efficiency protocol has been developed to develop standards on how to implement, measure, and verify efficiency savings. This was done through a public-private partnership involving American, Canadian, and Mexican industry and energy organisations and a range of finance firms. Published in early 1996, the Building Measurement and Verification Protocol (BMVP) has been widely adopted in the United States, Canada, and Mexico (USDOE, 1996).

The Protocol establishes standard approaches to project implementation and emphasises real-time measurement of actual savings. The Protocol is being translated into French, Spanish, Russian, Portuguese, and Hungarian. A growing range of governments, businesses and NGOs are joining the Protocol development process to refine and extend its application. By adopting the Protocol as a requirement for retrofit of existing buildings and design of new buildings, governments can sharply cut the cost of energy bills and provide for better quality work environments. For example, the adoption of the

Protocol by the United States Federal Government and by a growing number of American states is already resulting in the development of better quality, lower cost investments in energy efficiency improvement. The World Bank has structured US$350 million in new financing for large-scale, energy-efficiency improvement projects that involve this Protocol. The Protocol is being applied in commercial buildings and schools to introduce designs that are 30% more energy-efficient than the norm, with little or no increase in first costs. For fast growing countries that are experiencing a 'building boom', application of the Protocol offers an important tool for cutting costs and limiting growth in energy use, as well as a reduction in the generation of pollutants.

C.3.4 Energy-efficient lighting in Mexico[3]

Faced with an annual electricity growth rate of 6%, and an estimated 10-year power system expansion cost of US$43 billion, Mexico's national electric utility, Commission Federal de Electricidad (CFE) chose in 1992 to begin exploring energy-efficient technologies such as compact fluorescent lamps (CFLs).

Distribution of CFLs through utility-sponsored demand-side management (DSM) programmes is a cost-effective alternative to building new power plants. A CFL provides the same lighting as an incandescent lamp, however uses as little as 25% as much energy, and lasts 10 to 13 times as long.

In 1995 CFE began implementing an energy-efficient lighting project in the cities of Monterrey and Guadalajara. Known as Illumex, the project involves sales of CFLs to customers through CFE's district offices, where most customers go to pay their bills. Customers have the option of purchasing the lamps with cash, or paying for them over time through their electric bills. With an estimated 1.8 million lamps installed, Illumex is the largest project in the history of the lighting industry.

In the course of its 10,000-hour life, each CFL will accrue net savings of several tens of dollars, and allow the utility to defer over one hundred dollars of investment in generation, transmission, and distribution/ expansion costs. Over their lifetimes, these 1.8 million lamps will save CFE US$180 million, leading to lower utility rates and cleaner air. Annual fuel savings will be equivalent to 265,000 barrels of oil per year, reducing CO_2 emissions by 27,500 tonnes C per year, SO_2 emissions by 1,500 tons per year, and NO_x emissions by 175 tons per year.

C.3.5 Appliance and equipment efficiency standards in the United States[4]

In the United States, energy efficiency standards for appliances and other equipment have been used effectively by both state governments and the federal government to reduce energy use and consumer energy bills. Appliance and equipment efficiency standards set minimum efficiency requirements for newly manufactured appliances and other energy-consuming products. The standards prohibit the production, import, or sale of products less efficient than the minimum requirements. Appliance standards were first adopted by California and a number of other states in the 1970s and early 1980s, and laid the groundwork for adoption of federal standards.

In the National Appliance Energy Conservation Act (NAECA) of 1987, the federal government mandated standards for such products as refrigerators, water heaters, furnaces and boilers, central air conditioners and heat pumps, room air conditioners, clothes washers, dryers, dishwashers, ovens, and lighting ballasts. NAECA requires a periodic update on all standards, with the timing of new standards differing among products.

Nation-wide, standards already in force will reduce total U.S. energy use in 2015 by a projected 2.7%, and standards now under development will raise the savings to 4.3% of projected U.S. energy use. As a result, by 2015, these standards will reduce U.S. electric-generating-plant needs by approximately 75,000 MW and will result in net consumer benefits of approximately US$140 billion (in 1993 dollars).

In addition to saving energy, appliance- and equipment-efficiency standards can increase local employment and reduce pollution emissions. Due to these multiple benefits, it is important for governments and electric utili-

---

[3]   Source: (IRT/IIEC).

[4]   Source: (Nadel, 1996).

ties to include the savings potential of standards in their energy use forecasts and plans.

C.3.6 ASEAN commercial building codes[5]

Economic expansion in Indonesia, Malaysia, the Philippines, Thailand, Singapore, and Brunei has been accompanied by rapid growth in energy use, particularly in commercial buildings. Electricity use by commercial buildings has increased in these six countries from 4.3 billion kilowatt-hours (kWh) in 1970 to 23 billion kWh in 1987, at a rate of more than 10% per year over this period. To address the losses due to energy-inefficient buildings, the ASEAN organisation, starting in 1982, began working with its member governments to establish energy-efficiency building codes.

By 1992, all the member governments, with the exception of Brunei, had adopted building energy codes. The codes focus on improving the efficiency of building shells (exterior building envelopes), cooling equipment, and lighting systems. Each country has adopted a slightly different set of codes based on local climatic conditions and the judgements of local energy planners. The codes are mandatory in Singapore and the Philippines and are expected to be mandatory in Thailand in the near future. In Indonesia and Malaysia, the codes are voluntary, providing a guideline that building designers are encouraged to use. Long-term energy savings of 20% can be realised from full adoption of the codes.

Since the codes were established through a multilateral organisation, ASEAN, regionally-consistent standards have been developed. Furthermore, participating countries together have gained a wealth of experience in the process of designing building energy codes. The region has instituted a system whereby architects and engineers make it a custom to design energy-efficient buildings.

C.4 Institutional Mechanisms to Encourage Investment in Sustainable Energy Technologies

C.4.1 Rural credit and purchase mechanism: the Sudimara story for Indonesia

The high initial cost of renewable energy systems requires financing mechanisms to make them affordable to consumers. PT Sudimara Energi Surya, based in Indonesia, has been successful in selling solar home systems in rural Indonesia using innovative credit arrangements and services (de Lange, 1996).

Between 1993 and 1995, Sudimara sold over 7800 solar panels for home systems to rural customers, through a network of local service centres that are responsible for sales, service, and credits. The average monthly payments with solar systems is less than the monthly costs of conventional energy systems. Additionally, with these systems, consumers obtained increased levels of energy services. Thus far, there has been a 100% collection rate on the loans (i.e., there have been no defaults on loan payments by the customers).

By combining all of the operational and financial functions at a local level, it is possible to open up new markets and also serve the needs of the rural communities, as shown by this example. Sales and distribution are maximised by building a good relationship with the customers and providing service that is both inexpensive and easy to access. In addition, this type of programme has helped to build capacity and expertise in the country by manufacturing and assembling system components in Indonesia. Once the appropriate mechanisms are set up to provide alternatives to the local community, experience has shown that there are significant numbers of consumers who are willing to pay the full cost to purchase these sustainable energy systems.

C.4.2 Curitiba: towards sustainable urban development

Curitiba is the capital of the state of Parana, in southern Brazil, currently with a population of 2.3 million in its metropolitan area. The city had been growing at the rate of 10% a year in expanding concentric circles from the city centre. In the early 1970's, city authorities began to implement the urban design structure that counteracted unplanned urban sprawl and emphasized linear growth along five pre-determined structural axes. Land use legislation was enacted to guide this growth, allowing for higher housing densities in streets served by public transport. These arrangements also allowed the city to spread out while developing public transport that kept shops, work places and

---

homes readily accessible to one another. Curitiba's road network and public transport system are probably the most influential elements accounting for the present shape of the city. Total priority was given to public transport throughout the entire city and to pedestrians downtown.

Each structural axis was designed as a "trinary road system": the central road has two restricted lanes in the middle for express buses flanked by two local roads. There are high capacity one-way streets into and out of the central city one block on either side of this central road. In the areas adjacent to each axis, land use legislation has encouraged high density occupation, together with services and commerce.

The city augmented these spatial changes with a bus-based public transportation system designed for convenience and speed. The five sets of express bus lanes along the structural axes are complemented by interdistrict and feeder buses that have expanded as the city has grown. There are large bus terminals at the end of the five express busways where people can transfer to interdistrict, feeder or intercity buses. Medium-sized terminals are located every two kilometers along the express routes, and a single fare allows passengers to transfer from the express routes to interdistrict and local buses. In high demand routes, tubular, subway-style boarding stations speed boarding times through pre-payment and level boarding. This system replicates some of the advantages of a subway system at the surface, costing approximately 200 times less than a conventional subway. Articulated and bi-articulated buses (for 270 passengers) double and triple, respectively, the capacity of the express busways. The whole system has been implemented in partnership with private bus companies that buy buses and operate the system, following guidance established by the city.

Curitiba has over 500,000 private cars (more per capita that any Brazilian city except Brasilia). Remarkably, 75% of all commuters (more than 1.3 million passengers per day) take the bus. This has resulted in fuel consumption rates that are 25% lower than comparable Brazilian cities and has contributed to the city having one of the lowest rates

of ambient air pollution in the country. Finally, the average Curitiba resident spends only about 10% of his or her income on transport, which is a relatively low percentage in Brazil.

C.4.3 The rural electricity development concession in Argentina[6]

Over the last several years, the government of Argentina has put into place a number of structural economic reforms. One of the most significant of these is the privatisation of government-owned electric utilities and the restructuring of its electric power sector.

The effort to increase private sector participation in the power sector has fostered the development of an innovative experiment in Northwest Argentina to establish an electricity concession market for 1.4 million currently unserved inhabitants. It is an alternative to the conventional—and costly—approach of extending the existing electricity grid to remote areas. Private purchasers of the concessions will provide electricity to dispersed rural residences and public facilities (e.g., schools, medical centres, drinking water services, etc.) through a range of energy technologies determined by what the concessionaire considers to be is the least costly. Solar photovoltaic panels, small wind mills, hydraulic microturbines, and diesel-driven generators will compete on the basis of the lowest cost of provided energy.

Preliminary analyses show that renewable technologies will often be competitive with diesel generators. Specifically, it is likely that a large share of residences will receive power from household photovoltaic systems.

The winning bids for the concessions will be those that seek the lowest government subsidy per energy hook-up. The total investment for this programme amounts to US$314 million, which will be financed by fees paid by private users (US$142 million), subsidies from already-existent funds managed by provincial states (US$75 million), and national subsidies (US$97 million). The concessions are expected to be approved in 1997, and concessionaires will be expected to provide electric power to "significant" portions of their service population within three years.

---

[6]   Source: (SDE, Argentina, 1996).

C.4.4 A wind energy resource development concession

Because most renewable energy technologies are small and modular, their manufacture can benefit from the economies of producing large numbers of identical units. However, consumers cannot capture the full potential economic benefits of mass production if the market volume per supplier is small and if there are large transaction costs associated with accessing this limited market. The Argentine rural electric development concession is a mechanism that aggregates the market for these small-scale systems, thereby both facilitating the realisation of the economies of mass production and making possible substantial reductions in transaction costs per customer, by granting to a single supplier as a result of acompetitive process, exclusive market development rights in a delineated region over a specified period of time in exchange for the supplier's agreement to meet the terms specified in the concession.

Concessions are likely to play important roles in renewable energy development. Another example illustrating the importance of concessions is the wind energy resource development concession (Brennand, 1996), proposed as an instrument that is especially promising for harnessing large, high-quality wind energy resources that are concentrated in regions that are remote from major electricity markets, as is the case in the United States (Cavallo, 1995) and China (Lew et al., 1995). In order to exploit substantial fractions of these resources, it is necessary to transmit the produced electricity to distant markets via long-distance transmission lines. The long-distances involved dictate that the transmission lines be of high capacity (typically more than 1 GW) and loaded at high capacity factor in order to be cost-effective. These requirements, in turn, require that even larger (multi-GW) wind farms be constructed to serve these lines, often in conjunction with energy storage systems (e.g., compressed air energy storage), to facilitate "baseloading" the transmission lines (Cavallo, 1995; Lew et al., 1996). Such wind farms are far larger than those constructed today; at present a 50 - 100 MW wind farm is considered to be large. The wind energy resource development concession is an instrument that would facilitate the attraction of private-sector capital resources to the development for such projects

The *resource development concession* is a concept that has proved to be very effective in developing resources in the mineral extraction industries (e.g. petroleum, natural gas, metals). This concept, as applied to wind power development might work as follows. In a delineated region of high-quality wind resources, the government would offer concessions to companies for the exploration and development wind energy in the region over a specified period of time. Besides issuing the concessions via some competitive process, the government's roles would be to issue and enforce the rules and regulations that would define and guide concessions (including the payment of royalties and specifications for technology transfer), and to issue and enforce the rules and regulations that would define and guide the relationships among the electricity producers, transmitters, and buyers, including long-term electricity purchase agreements. This approach offers advantages both for the government and for prospective wind energy developers.

The government would gain, at very little risk, greater control over the rate and scale of wind energy development, since all front-end risks are borne by the wind energy developers. Concessions issued via competitive bidding processes could help to reassure the government authority that it was getting a fair deal, and the negotiating process would enable the authority to gain experience of how much the "market" can bear. Moreover, the issuance of concessions for gigawatt-scale wind projects would start to attract a new generation of larger companies organised as international joint ventures and other collaborations that could bring together the needed financial and technical resources for such large wind energy development projects. The institutional establishment of the concession, together with the emergence of this new generation of wind energy developers, would lead to lower costs through the scale economies of wind turbine production and large wind-farm development and make it possible to speed up the timetable on which wind energy would be able to make substantial contributions to overall electricity supplies.

For prospective wind energy developers,

the concession offers the opportunity to participate in far larger wind energy projects than has heretofore been possible. The concession would also attract a wider range of potential developers than has been typical for wind energy development. Furthermore, the concession, with its detailed rules and regulations, would add a great deal of transparency to the negotiating process relative to present-day private power market development negotiations in many developing countries. This transparency would encourage competition and reduce the financial risks for would-be developers.

References

Chapter 1

Beijing Declaration and The Platform for Action, 1995 United Nations Conference on Women and Development. United Nations, New York, 1996.

HABITAT Agenda, 1996: Chapter IV Global Plan of Action: Strategies for Implementation, United Nations Development Programme (UNDP), New York.

Report of the Global Conference on the Sustainable Development of Small Island Developing States, Bridgetown, Barbados, 25 April-6 May 1994, United Nations.

Report of the International Conference on Population and Development, Cairo 5-13 September 1994. United Nations, New York, 1995.

Report of the World Summit for Social Development, Copenhagen 6-12 March 1995, United Nations, 1996.

United Nations Convention to Combat Desertification in those Countries Experiencing Serious Drought and/or Desertification, Particularly in Africa. United Nations, New York, 1994.

UNCED, 1993: Report of the United Nations Conference on Environment and Development, Rio de Janeiro, 3-14 June 1992, Vol. I, Resolutions Adopted by the Conference, Agenda 21, Document A/Conf. 151/26/Rev.1.United Nations, New York.

UNFCCC, 1992: United Nations Framework Convention on Climate Change. United Nations, New York.

Chapter 2

ACDA (Arms Control and Disarmament Agency), 1997: *Signatories and Parties to the Treaty on the Non-Proliferation of Nuclear Weapons*. Washington, DC, January.

Agarwal, B., 1986: Cold Hearths and Barren Slopes: The Woodfuel Crisis in the Third World. 2ed Books, London, p.24.

ASTRA, 1982: Rural Energy Consumption Patterns—A Field Study. *Biomass*, **2** (4), September.

Baldwin, S., 1984: New directions in wood stove development. *VITA News*, January.

Batliwala, S., 1982: Rural Energy Scarcity and Undernutrition. *Economic and Political Weekly*, **XVII** (9), February 27.

Batliwala, S., 1987: Women's Access to Food. *The Indian Journal of Social Work*,. **XLVIII** (3), October, 255-271.

Batliwala, S., 1984: Rural Energy Situation: Consequences for Women's Health. *Socialist Health Review*, **1** (2), September, pp.75.

Batliwala, S., and Reddy, A.K., 1996: Energy for Women & Women for Energy: Engendering Energy and Empowering Women, Brainstorming Meeting of ENERGIA: Women and Energy Network, University of Twente, Enschede, The Netherlands, June 4-5, 1996.

Beijing Declaration and The Platform for Action, 1995 United Nations Conference on Women and Development. United Nations, New York, 1996.

Berkhout, F., A. Diakov, H. Feiveson, H. Hunt, E. Lyman, M. Miller, and F. von Hippel, 1993: Disposition of separated plutonium. *Science and Global Security*, **3**, 161-213.

BEST, 1988: Biomass Energy Services and Technology; The Use of Wood Fuels in Rural Industries in Asia and Pacific Region. Regional Wood Energy Development Programme in Asia. Food and Agriculture Organisation (FAO), Bangkok.

Bos, E., My T. Vu, E. Massiah, R.A. Bulatao, 1994: World Population Projection, 1994-1995 Edition—Estimates and Projections with Related Demographic Statistics. The World Bank. Johns Hopkins University Press.

Cecelski, E., 1990: Energy and Women—Forward Looking Strategies in ESMAP (Energy Sector Management Assistance Programme). Household Energy Unit, ESMAP, The World Bank.

Cecelski, E., 1992: Women, Energy and Environment: New Directions for Policy Research, Working Paper, GSD-2, International Federation of Institutes of Advanced Study.

Cecelski, E., 1995: From Rio to Beijing: Engendering the Energy Debate. *Energy Policy*, **23** (6), July.

Chen, B.H. et al, 1990: *World Health Statistics Quarterly*, **43** (3), 127-138.

CISAC (Committee on International Security and Arms Control of the National Academy of Sciences), 1994: *Management and Disposition of Excess Weapons Plutonium.* National Academy Press, Washington, DC.

Coale, A.J., 1973: The Demographic Transition Reconsidered, International Population Conference, Liege.

Coale, A.J., 1983: Recent Trends in Fertility in Less Developed Countries. *Science*, (221), 26 August, 828-832.

Dasgupta, P.S., 1993: *Scientific American*, February, 26-31.

EIA (Energy Information Administration), 1994: *International Energy Annual 1992.* DOE/EIA-0219(92). United States Department of Energy, U S Government Printing Office, January.

Ellegard, A. and H. Egneus, 1993: Urban Energy: exposure to biomass fuel pollution in Lusaka. *Energy Policy*, **21** (5), 01 May, 615-621.

FAO (Food and Agriculture Organisation), 1992: Protect and Produce: putting the pieces together. FAO, Rome.

FAO (Food and Agriculture Organisation), 1990: Land Evaluation for Development. FAO, Rome.

FAO (Food and Agriculture Organisation), 1991: Soils Bulletin # 64: A study of the reasons for success or failure of soil conservation projects.

FAO (Food and Agriculture Organisation), 1993: Guidelines for Land use Planning. FAO, Rome.

FAO (Food and Agriculture Organisation), 1995: World Agriculture: Towards 2010. An FAO Study. N. Alexandratos (ed.). John Wiley, Chicester, UK.

FAO (Food and Agriculture Organisation), 1997: Irrigation and Water Resources Potential in Africa. FAO, Rome.

FAO (Food and Agriculture Organisation) World Soil Resources Reports: #60 Revised legend, Soil Map of the World. FAO/UNESCO, ISRIC, 1990.

FAO (Food and Agriculture Organisation) World Soil Resources Reports: #71 Agroecological land resources for agricultural development planning, 1994.

FAO (Food and Agriculture Organisation) World Soil Resources Reports: #80 Soil survey perspectives andstrategies for the 21st century, 1995.

FAO (Food and Agriculture Organisation), 1979: Fighting World Hunger. FAO, Rome.

FAO (Food and Agriculture Organisation), 1995: Food, Agriculture and Food Security: The Global Dimension. FAO, WFS 96/TECH/1, March.

Feiveson, H.A., 1978: Proliferation-resistant nuclear fuel cycles. *Annual Review of Energy*, **3**, 357-394.

Flavin, C. and Lenssen, N., 1994: Power Surge. New York: W.W. Norton & Company.

Foell, W., M. Amann, G. Carmichael, M.J. Chadwick, J.-P. Hettelingh, L. Hordijk, and Zhao, Dianwu (eds.), 1995: RAINS-ASIA: An Assessment Model for Air Pollution in Asia. Final Report Submitted to the Bank by the Project Team. Resource Management Associates, Wisconsin, USA.

Goldemberg, J., T.B. Johansson, A.K.N. Reddy, and R.H. Williams, 1985: Basic Needs and Much More with One Kilowatt per Capita. *Ambio*, **14** (4-5), 190-200.

Goldemberg, J., T.B. Johansson, A.K.N. Reddy, and R.H. Williams, 1988: Energy for a Sustainable World. Wiley-Eastern Limited, New Delhi, 55-60.

Gordon, J., 1986: Biomass Energy Devices for Income Generation at the Household or Community Level. ITDG, London.

HABITAT Agenda, 1996: Chapter IV Global Plan of Action: Strategies for Implementation. United Nations Development Programme (UNDP), New York.

Haile, F., 1991: Women Fuelwood Carriers in Addis Ababa and the Peri-Urban Forest. International Labour Organisation (ILO), Geneva.

Hall, D.O, H.E. Mynick, and R.H. Williams, 1991a: Cooling the greenhouse with biomass energy. *Nature*, **353** (11-12), September.

Hall, D.O, H.E. Mynick, and R.H. Williams, 1991b: Alternative roles for biomass in coping with greenhouse warming,. *Science and Global Security,* **2 (1-39)**.

HDR, 1995: Human Development Report 1995. United Nations Development Programme (UNDP), New York. Oxford University Press.

HDR, 1996: Human Development Report 1996. United Nations Development Programme (UNDP), New York. Oxford University Press.

Holdren, J.P., 1990: Energy in transition. *Scientific American*, **263** (3), 156-163.

Hosier, R.H. and Dowd, J., 1987: Household fuel choice in Zimbabwe: An empirical test of the Energy Ladder Hypothesis. *Resources and Energy*, **13** (9), 347-361.

Hube, J.H., 1982: Food Science and Nutrition: The Gulf between the Rich and the Poor. *Science*, (216) June 18, 1291-1294.

Hyman, L.S., and D.C. O'Niell, 1995: Financing energy expansion: 1990-2020. *World Energy Council Journal*, December, pp. 7-12.

IDRC (International Development Research Centre), 1980: Nutritional Status of the Rural Population of the Sahel: Report of a Working Group; Paris, France, 28-29 April, 1980/Sponsored by the International Union of Nutritional Scientists et al., Ottawa.

IPCC (Intergovernmental Panel on Climate Change), 1990: *Climate Change: The IPCC Scientific Assessment.* [Houghton, J.T., G.J. Jenkins, and J.J. Ephraums (eds.)]. Cambridge University Press, Cambridge and New York.

IPCC (Intergovernmental Panel on Climate Change), 1992: *Climate Change 1992: The Supplementary Report to the IPCC Scientific Assessment. Report of Working Group I.* [Houghton, J.T., B.A. Callander, and S.K. Varney, (eds.)]. Cambridge University Press, Cambridge.

IPCC (Intergovernmental Panel on Climate Change), 1994: *Radiative Forcing of Climate Change and an Evaluation of the IPCC Emission Scenarios.* [Houghton, J.T, L.G Meira Filho, J. Bruce, Hoesung Lee, B.A. Callander, E. Haites, N. Harris, and K. Maskell, K (eds.)]. Reports of Working Groups I and III of the IPCC, forming part of the IPCC Special Report to the first session of the Conference of Parties to the UN Framework Convention on Climate Change Cambridge University Press, Cambridge.

IPCC (Intergovernmental Panel on Climate Change), 1996a: *Climate Change 1995: The Science of Climate Change. Contribution of Working Group I to the Second Assessment Report of the Intergovernmental Panel on Climate Change.* [Houghton, J.T., L.G. Meiro Filho, B.A. Callander, N. Harris, A. Kattenberg, and K. Maskell K (eds.)]. Cambridge University Press, Cambridge and New York.

IPCC (Intergovernmental Panel on Climate Change), 1996b: *Impacts, Adaptations and Mitigation of Climate Change: Scientific-Technical Analyses. Contribution of Working Group II to the Second Assessment Report of the Intergovernmental Panel on Climate Change.* [Watson, R.T., M.C. Zinyowera, and R.H. Moss, (eds.)]. Cambridge University Press, Cambridge and New York.

IPCC (Intergovernmental Panel on Climate Change), 1996c: Summary for Policymakers: Scientific-Technical Analyses of Impacts, Adaptations, and Mitigations of Climate Change. In: *Impacts, Adaptations and Mitigation of Climate Change: Scientific-Technical Analyses. Contribution of Working Group II to the Second Assessment Report of the Intergovernmental Panel on Climate Change.* [Watson, R.T., M.C. Zinyowera, and R.H. Moss, (eds.)]. Cambridge University Press, Cambridge and New York, p.15.

Jackson, C., 1992: Doing What Comes Naturally? Women and Environment in Development. *World Development*, **21** (12) 1947-1963.

Kumar, S.K. and D. Hotchkiss, 1988: Consequences of Deforestation for Women's Time Allocation, Agricultural Production and Nutrition in Hill Areas of Nepal. International Food Policy Research Institute, Washington DC.

Kuylenstierna, J.C.I, H. Cambridge, S. Cinderby and M.J. Chadwick, 1995: Terrestrial ecosystem sensitivity to acidic deposition in developing countries. *Water, Air and Soil Pollution*, **85**, 2319-24.

Leach, G., 1992: The energy transition. *Energy Policy*, **20** (2), 01 February, 116-123.

Leach,G., 1995: *Global Land and Food in the 21ˢᵗ Century: Trends and Issues for Sustainability.* Polestar Series Report No. 5, Stockholm Environment Institute, Stockholm, Sweden.

Lilienthal, D.E., C.I. Barnard, J.R. Oppenheimer, C.A. Thomas, and H.A. Winne, 1946: *A Report on the International Control of Atomic Energy.* A report prepared for the Secretary of State's Committee on Atomic Energy. U.S. Government Printing Office, Washington, DC, 16 March.

Maidique, M.A. and B.J. Zirger, 1988: The New Product Learning Cycle In : *Strategic Management of Technology and Innovation* [Burgleman R.A. and Maidique M.A] Irwin.

Masters, C., Attanasi E., and Root, D., 1994: World Petroleum Assessment and Analysis, Proceedings of the 14th World Petroleum Congress, Stavanger, Norway. John Wiley and Sons Ltd.

Monthly Energy Review 1995: Energy Information Administration. *Monthly Energy Review*, June, 130-136.

Moreira, J.R, and Poole, A.D., 1993: Hydropower and its constraints. In: *Renewable Energy-Sources for Fuel and Electricity.* [Johansson, T.B., Kelly, H., Reddy, A.K.N., and Williams, R.H. (eds.)]. Island Press, Washington DC, 73-119.

Mumford, J.L. et al, 1990: Lung cancer and indoor air pollution in Xuan Wei, China; possibly due to smoky vs. Smokeless coal use indoors, 9 January, 1987. *Science*, 235, 217-220.

Nilsson H.E., 1995: Market Transformation: An Essential Condition for Sustainability. Energy for Sustainable Development, **1** (6) 20-30.

Posch, M., de Smet, P.A.M., Hettelingh, J-P., and Downing, R.J. (eds.), 1995: Calculation and Mapping of Critical Thresholds in Europe. Co-ordination Centre for Effects. RIVM, Bilthoven, The Netherlands.

Ravallion, M. and Chen, S., 1996: The World Bank, Working Paper No.1, The Poverty, Environment and Growth Working Paper Series, Washington, DC, April.

Reddy, A.K.N., and B.S. Reddy, 1994: Substitution of energy carriers for cooking in Bangalore. *Energy*, **19** (5), 01 May, 561-571.

Report of the Global Conference on the Sustainable Development of Small Island Developing States, Bridgetown, Barbados, 25 April-6 May 1994, United Nations, New York.

Report on the International Conference on Population and Development, Cairo 5-13 September 1994. United Nations, New York, 1995.

Report of the World Summit for Social Development, Copenhagen 6-12 March 1995, United Nations, New York, 1996.

Ravallion, M. and Chen, S., 1996: Working Paper No.1, The Poverty, Environment and Growth Working Paper Series, The World Bank, Washington, DC, April.

Robinson, John B. 1991. The Proof of the Pudding—Making Energy Efficiency Work. *Energy Policy*, September, 631-45.

Rodhe, H., J. Langner, L. Gallardo and E. Kjellstrom, 1995: Global scale transport of acidifying pollutants. *Water, Air and Soil Pollution*, **85**, 37-50.

RWEDP, 1996: FAO/RWEDP Report of the Sub-Regional Training Course on Women in Wood-EnergyDevelopment, Bangkok.

Scrimshaw, N.S. and Taylor, L., 1980: Food. *Scientific American*, **243** (3), 74-84.

Sen, Amartya, 1994: Population: Delusion and Reality. *The New York Review of Books*, **XLI** (15), 22 September, pp.1-8.

Sims, J., 1994: Women, Health & Environment: An Anthology. World Health Organisation, Geneva.

Skutsch, M., 1996: *Forthcoming*

Smith, K.R., 1990: Health Effects in Developing Countries In : *Bioenergy and the Environment*, [Pasztor, Janos and Kristoferson (eds.)] Westview, Boulder, Colorado, USA.

Smith, K.R., 1987: Biofuels, Air Pollution and Health—A Global Review. Plenum Press, New York.

Smith, K.R., 1993: Fuel combustion : Air pollution exposures and health in developing countries. *Annual Review of Energy and Environment*, (18), 529-566.

Spitzner, M., 1993: Approaches to Reducing Road Traffic Volumes. Contribution to the First Season of the Wuppertal International Advisory Council, Wuppertal Institute for Climate, Environment and Energy, Wuppertal, North Rhine-Westphalia, Germany, 14-15 June.

Swisher J.N., 1996: Regulatory and Mixed Policy Options for Reducing Energy Use and Carbon Emissions. The Netherlands: Kluwer Academic Publishers. *Forthcoming.*

Pakistan, 1991: Pakistan Integrated Household Survey, Final Results, 1991. Federal Bureau of Statistics, Pakistan, March 1992.

Tinker, I., 1990: The real rural energy crisis: women's time In: *Human Energy*, [Deasi, A.V. (ed.)] Wiley, New Delhi.

United Nations, 1995: *Report of the Secretary-General on the Status of the Implementation of the Plan for the Ongoing Monitoring and Verification of Iraq's Compliance with Relevant Parts of Section C of Security Council Resolution 687 (1991)*. United Nations Document S/1995/284, April 10.

United Nations Convention to Combat Desertification in those Countries Experiencing Serious Drought and/or Desertification, Particularly in Africa. United Nations, New York, 1994.

UNCED, 1993: Report of the United Nations Conference on Environment and Development, Rio de Janeiro, 3-14 June 1992, Vol.1, Resolutions Adopted by the Conference, Agenda 21, Document A/Conf. 151/26/Rev.1. United Nations, New York.

UNDP/WMO (United Nations Development Programme/World Meteorological Organisation), 1995: Climate Change 1995: Impacts, Adaptations and Mitigations of Climate Change: Scientific-Technical Analyses; Edited by Watson, R.T., Zinyowera, M.C., Moss, R.H.; Cambridge University Press, 15.

UNEP/WHO (United Nations Environment Programme/World Health Organisation), 1992: In Expanding Environmental Perspectives—Lessons of the Past, Prospects for the Future. Department of Environmental and Energy Systems Studies. Lund University Press.

UNFCCC, 1992: United Nations Framework Convention on Climate Change. United Nations, New York.

UNIFEM (United Nations Development Fund for Women), 1987: Oil Extraction: Food Technology Source Book. (UNIFEM), New York.

UNIFEM (United Nations Development Fund for Women), 1988: Cereal Processing—Food Technology Source Book. (UNIFEM), New York.

UNIFEM (United Nations Development Fund for Women), 1994: Report of the Expert Group Meeting on Women, Science and Technology: New Visions for the 21st Century, UNIFEM, New York.

Urasa, I., 1990: Women and Rural Transport: An Assessment of their Role in Sub-Saharan Africa. International Labour Office (ILO), Geneva.

van Horen, C., A. Eberhard, H. Trollip, and S. Thorne, 1993: *Energy Policy*, 623-639.

Vietnam LSMS, 1992-93: Vietnam Living Standards Measurements Survey, 1992-93. Basic Information, Poverty and Human Resources Division, World Bank, December 1994.

Wakeman, W., 1995: Gender Issues Sourcebook for Water and Sanitation Projects. United Nations Development Programme/World Bank Water and Sanitation Program/PROWESS, The World Bank, Washington, DC.

WEC (World Energy Council), 1993: *Energy for Tomorrow's World.* Kogan Page, St. Martin's Press, New York, 277

WEC (World Energy Council), 1994: New Renewable Energy Resources—A Guide to the Future. Kogan Page, London, UK.

WEC (World Energy Council), 1995: Financing Energy Development: The Challenges and Requirements of Developing Countries. Report prepared by the Tata Energy Research Institute for the World EnergyCouncil.

WEC/IIASA (World Energy Council/International Institute for Advanced Systems Analysis), 1995: Global Energy Perspectives to 2050 and Beyond. London and Laxenburg, Austria, 84.

WHO (World Health Organisation), 1997: Health and Environment for Sustainable Development. WHO, Geneva.

Williams, R.H., and H.A. Feiveson, 1990: Diversion-resistance criteria for future nuclear power. *Energy Policy*, **18** (6), 543-549.

World Bank, 1994: World Development Report 1994. The World Bank, Washington DC. 121-122.

World Bank, 1996: Rural Energy and Development: Improving Energy Supplies for Two Billion People. The World Bank, September.

World's Women, 1995: Trends and Statistics. United Nations, New York. pp. 48 and pp. 53.

WRI (World Resources Institute), 1992: World Resources 1992-1993, Oxford University Press, New York.

Chapter 3

Acker, D.R. and D.M. Kammen, 1990: The quiet (energy) revolution: analyzing the dissemination of photovoltaic power systems in Kenya. *Energy Policy*, **24**(1), 81-111.

Ahuja, D.R., 1990: Research needs for improving biofuel burning cookstove technologies. *Natural Resources Forum*, May, 125-134.

Alexander, A.G., 1985: *The Energy Cane Alternative*. Sugar Series, Vol. 6, Elsevier, Amsterdam, The Netherlands.

ASE, ACEEE, NRDC, UCS (Alliance to Save Energy, American Council for an Energy Efficient Economy, Natural Resources Defense Council, Union of Concerned Scientists), 1992: *America's Energy Choices—Investing in a Strong Economy*. Union of Concerned Scientists, Cambridge, Massachusetts, USA.

Ayres, R.U., 1989: *Energy Inefficiency in the US Economy: a New Case for Conservation*. Report IIASA-RR-89-12, International Institute for Advanced Systems Analysis, Laxenburg, Austria.

Ayres, R.U., and U.E. Simonis (eds.), 1994: *Industrial Metabolism: Restructuring for Sustainable Development*. United Nations University Press, Tokyo, Japan.

Bakker, W., 1996: Advances in solid-oxide fuel cells. *EPRI Journal*, **21** (5), 42-45.

Baldwin, S. et al., 1985: Improved woodburning cookstoves: signs of success. *Ambio*, **14** (4-5), 280-287.

Baldwin, S.F., 1986: *Biomass Stoves: Engineering Design, Development, and Dissemination*. Volunteers in Technical Assistance, Rosslyn, VA, and Center for Energy and Environmental Studies, Princeton University, Princeton, New Jersey, USA.

Barnes, D.F., K. Openshaw, K.R. Smith, and R. van der Plas, 1994: *What Makes People Cook With Improved Biomass Stoves?* World Bank Technical Paper #242, Energy Series, World Bank, Washington, DC.

Bernardini, O., and R. Galli, 1993: Dematerialization: long-term trends in the intensity of use of materials and energy. *Futures*, May, 431-448.

Birk, M. and D. Bleviss, eds., 1991: *Driving New Directions: Transportation Experiences and Options in Developing Countries*. International Institute for Energy Conservation, Washington, DC.

Birk, M. and C. Zegras, 1993: *Moving Toward Integrated Transport Planning: Energy, Environment, and Mobility in Four Asian Cities*. International Institute for Energy Conservation, Washington, DC.

Blok, K., R.H. Williams, R.E. Katofsky, and C.A. Hendriks, 1997: Hydrogen production from natural gas, sequestration of recovered CO_2 in depleted gas wells and enhanced natural gas recovery. *Energy*, **22** (2-3), 161-168.

Borroni-Bird, C., 1996: Is there a fuel cell in the automobile's future? Paper presented at the Intertech Conference on Commercializing Fuel Cell Vehicles, Chicago, Ill., 17-19 September 1996.

Bowers, W., 1992: Agricultural field equipment. In: *Energy in Farm Production*. [Fluck, R.C., ed.]. *Energy in World Agriculture, Vol. 6*. Elsevier Science Publishers, Amsterdam, The Netherlands, 117-129.

Brohard, G.J. (Pacific Gas and Electric Company), 1992: ACT² pilot project: results to date from the pilot demonstration building. *Proceedings of the ACEEE 1992 Sum-*

mer Study on Energy Efficiency in Buildings. Panel 1. Commercial Technologies: Design and Operation. American Council for an Energy-Efficient Economy, Washington, DC, 1.27-1.38.

Bystroem, S., and L. Loennstedt, 1995: Waste paper usage and fiber flow in Western Europe. *Resources, Conservation and Recycling,* **15,** 111-122.

Cabraal, A., M. Cosgrove-Davies, and L. Schaeffer, 1996: *Best Practices for Photovoltaic Household Electrification Programmes—Lessons from Experiences in Selected Countries,* World Bank Technical Paper No. 324, Asia Technical Department Series, World Bank, Washington, DC.

Calvert, J.G., J.B. Heywood, R.F. Sawyer, and J.H. Seinfeld, 1993: Achieving acceptable air quality: some reflections on controlling vehicle emissions. *Science,* **261,** 37-45.

Cavallo, A., 1995: High capacity factor wind energy systems. *Journal of Solar Engineering,* **117,** 137-143.

Christiansen, K., B.B. Nielsen, P. Doelman, and F. Schelleman, 1995: Cleaner technologies in Europe. *Journal of Cleaner Production,* **3,** 67-70.

Colombo, U. and U. Farinelli, 1994: *The Hybrid Car as a Strategic Option in Europe.* Paper presented at the Dedicated Conference on Supercars (Advanced Ultralight Hybrids), Aachen, Germany, 31 October-4 November.

Comptroller and Auditor General of India, 1994: *Report of the Year Ended March 1993.* Hyderabad, India.

Corman, J.C., 1996: H gas turbine combined cycle technology and development. ASME paper 96-GT-11, presented at the International Gas Turbine and Aeroengine Congress and Exhibition, Birmingham, UK, 10-13 July 1996.

Cowan, W.D., 1990: Conflicts of Interest, Technical and Social Rationality: Photovoltaic Applications in a Divided Society. In: Energy and the Environment into the 1990s—*1st World Renewable Energy Congress.* Pergamon Press, Oxford, 331-336.

Cowley, P. 1996: Photovoltaic building integration in Japan. *Sun World,* March.

Crouch, M., 1989: *Expansion of Benefits: Fuel Efficient Cookstoves in the Sahel, The VITA Experience.* Volunteers in Technical Assistance, Rosslyn, VA, July.

CTOFM (Committee on Tropospheric Ozone Formation and Measurement, National Research Council), 1991: *Rethinking the Ozone Problem in Local and Regional Air Pollution.* National Academy of Sciences, Washington, DC.

Curry, R., 1996a: Amoco/Enron to build $7 million, 4 MW PV system in Hawaii during 1997. *Photovoltaic Insider's Report,* **XV** (2) 1.

Curry, R., 1996b: Four groups chosen by CSTRR to negotiate for 270 MW of power systems. *Photovoltaic Insider's Report,* **XV** (3), 1.

Curry, R., 1997: Sparked by U.S. sales, worldwide PV module shipments high record 90.6 MW. *Photovoltaic Insider's Report,* **XV** (3), 1.

Decicco, J., and M. Ross, 1994: Improving automotive efficiency. *Scientific American,* **6** (6), 52-57.

De Laquil, P., D. Kearney, M. Geyer, and R. Diver, 1993: Solar-thermal electric technology. In: *Renewable Energy: Sources for Fuels and Electricity.* Johansson, T.B., H. Kelly, A.K.N. Reddy, and R.H. Williams (eds.), Island Press, Washington, DC, 213-296.

DeLuchi, M., 1991: *Emissions of Greenhouse Gases from the Use of Transportation Fuels and Electricity; Volume 1: Main Text.* Report prepared for the Argonne National Laboratory, ANL/ESD/TM-22.

De Neufville, R., S.R. Connors, F.R. Field III, D. Marks, D.R. Sadoway, and R.D. Tabors, 1996: The electric car unplugged. *Technology Review,* **99** (1), 30-36, January.

DEPE (Department of Environmental Protection and Energy), Ministry of Agriculture, People's Republic of China, 1992: *Biogas and Sustainable Agriculture: The National Experience.* Exchange Meeting on Comprehensive Utilization of Biogas, Yichang City, Hubei Province, Bremen Overseas Research and Development Association, Bremen, Germany, 10-15 October.

DMEE (Danish Ministry of Environment and Energy), 1996: *Agenda 21: The Danish Government's Action Plan for Energy 1996.* Copenhagen.

Dunnison, D.S., and J. Wilson: 1994: PEM fuel cells: a commercial reality. In: *A Collection of Technical Papers: Part 3, 29th Intersociety Energy Conversion Engineering Conference.* Monterey, California, USA, 7-11 August, 1260-1263.

Dutt, G.S., and N.H. Ravindranath, 1993: Bioenergy: direct applications in cooking. In: *Renewable Energy: Sources for Fuels and Electricity.* Johansson, T.B., H. Kelly, A.K.N. Reddy, and R.H. Williams (eds.), Island Press, Washington, DC, 653-697.

Eberling, L.E. (Pacific Gas and Electric Company), 1992: ACT² project: residential maximum energy efficiency. *Proceedings of the ACEEE 1992 Summer Study on Energy Efficiency in Buildings. Panel 2. Residential Technologies: Design and Operation.* American Council for an Energy-Efficient Economy, Washington, DC, 2.45-2.52.

Eberling, L.E., and R.C. Bourne (Pacific Gas and Electric Company), 1994: ACT² project: maximizing residential new construction energy efficiency. *Proceedings of the ACEEE 1994 Summer Study on Energy Efficiency in Buildings. Panel 3. Technology Research, Development and Evaluation.* American Council for an Energy-Efficient Economy, Washington, DC, 3.57-3.66.

EIA (Energy Information Administration), 1994: *International Energy Annual 1992.* DOE/EIA-0219(92). US Department of Energy, US Government Printing Office, Washington, DC, January.

EIA (Energy Information Administration), 1995: *International Energy Outlook 1995.* DOE/EIA-0484(95). US Department of Energy, US Government Printing Office, Washington, DC.

EIA (Energy Information Administration), 1997: *Monthly Energy Review.* DOE/EIA-0035(97/01). US Department of Energy, US Government Printing Office, Washington, DC, January.

Eketorp, S., 1987: Energy considerations of classical and new iron- and steel-making technology. *Energy,* **12** (10/11), 1153-1168.

Elliott, P., and R. Booth, 1993: *Brazil Biomass Power Demonstration Project.* Special Project Brief, Shell International Petroleum Company, London.

Elliott, R.N, 1994: *Carbon Reduction Potential from Recycling in Primary Materials Manufacturing.* American Council for an Energy Efficient Economy, Washington, DC.

EPRI (Electric Power Research Institute), 1995: 2-MW direct carbonate fuel cell demonstration. *Technical Brief, Gas and New Coal Generation Business Unit.* TB-105733, Electric Power Research Institute, Palo Alto, California, USA, October.

Farmer, R. (ed.), 1989: *Gas Turbine World 1988-89 Handbook.* Pequot Publishing, Inc., Fairfield, Connecticut, USA.

Farmer, R., (ed.), 1995: *Gas Turbine World 1995 Handbook.* Pequot Publishing, Inc., Fairfield, Connecticut, USA.

Fisher, J., 1974: *Energy Crises in Perspective.* John Wiley and Sons, New York.

Fitzgerald, K.B., D. Barnes, and G. McGranahan, 1990: *Interfuel Substitution and Changes in the Way Households Use Energy: The Case of Cooking and Lighting Behavior in Urban Java.* Industry and Energy Department, World Bank, Washington, DC, 13 June.

Fleisch, T., McCarthy, C. and Basu A.; and Udovich, C. (Amoco Corporation); Charbonneau, P. and Slodowske, W. (Navistar International Transportation Corporation); Mikkelsen, S-E (Haldor Topsoe A/S); and McCandless, J. (AVL Powertrain Engineering, Inc.), 1995: A new clean diesel technology: demonstration of ULEV emissions on a Navistar diesel engine fueled with dimethyl ether. Paper 950061, SAE Technical Paper Series, presented at the SAE International Congress and Exposition, Detroit, Michigan, USA, 27 February-2 March.

Floor, W., and R. van der Plas, 1991: *Kerosene stoves: their performance, use, and constraints.* Draft report prepared for the World Bank and United Nations Development Programme, Energy Sector Management Assistance Program, Washington, DC, 7 March.

Ford, K.W., G.I. Rochlin, and R.H. Socolow, eds., 1975: *Efficient Use of Energy. Part I: a Physics Perspective.* AIP Conference Proceedings No. 25, American Institute of Physics, New York, 1-151.

Frosch, R.A., 1994: Industrial ecology: minimizing the impact of industrial waste. *Physics Today,* **47** (11), 63-68.

Geller, H.S., 1988: *Residential Equipment Efficiency: a State of the Art Review.* Contractor report prepared by the American Council for an Energy Efficient Economy for the Office of Technology Assessment, US Congress, Washington, DC, May.

Goldemberg, J., T.B. Johansson, A.K.N. Reddy, and R.H. Williams, 1985: Basic needs and much more with one kilowatt per capita. *Ambio,* **14** (4-5), 190-200.

Goldemberg, J., T.B. Johansson, A.K.N. Reddy, and R.H. Williams, 1988: *Energy for a Sustainable World,* Wiley-Eastern, New Delhi.

Goldemberg, J., L.C. Monaco, and I.C. Macedo, 1993: The Brazilian fuel-alcohol program. In: *Renewable Energy: Sources for Fuels and Electricity.* Johansson, T.B., H. Kelly, A.K.N. Reddy, and R.H. Williams (eds.), Island Press, Washington, DC, 841-863.

Greenpeace Germany, 1991: *Weniger Muell, Mehr Wald. Konzepte zum Einsparen und Recyclen von Papier*. Greenpeace Deutschland, Hamburg, Germany.

Grubb, M.J. and N.I. Meyer, 1993: Wind energy: resources, systems and regional strategies. In: *Renewable Energy: Sources for Fuels and Electricity.* Johansson, T.B., H. Kelly, A.K.N. Reddy, and R.H. Williams (eds.), Island Press, Washington, DC, 157-212.

Gyftopoulos, E.P., L.J. Lazaridis, and T.F. Widmer, 1974: *Potential Fuel Effectiveness in Industry*. A report of the Energy Policy Project of the Ford Foundation, Ballinger, Cambridge, MA.

Heidarian, J. and G. Wu, 1994: *Power Sector Statistics for Developing Countries (1987-1991)*.Industry and Energy Department, World Bank, Washington, DC.

Helsel, Z.R., 1992: Energy and alternatives for fertilizer and pesticide use. In: *Energy in Farm Production*. Fluck, R.C., ed.. *Energy in World Agriculture, Vol. 6*. Elsevier Science Publishers, Amsterdam, The Netherlands.

Hendriks, C.A., 1994: *Carbon Dioxide Removal from Coal-Fired Power Plants*. Ph.D. Thesis, Department of Science, Technology, and Society, Utrecht University, Utrecht, The Netherlands.

Hendriks, C.A., W.C. Turkenburg, and K. Blok, 1993: Promising options to remove carbon dioxide from large power plants. In: *Proceedings of the International Symposium on CO_2 Fixation and Efficient Utilization of Energy*. Tokyo Institute of Technology, Tokyo, Japan.

Hoff, T.E., H.J. Wenger, and B.F. Farmer, 1995: Distributed generation. An alternative to electric utility investments in system capacity. *Energy Policy,* **24** (2), 137-148.

Holloway, S. (British Geological Survey), ed., 1996: *The Underground Storage of Carbon Dioxide*. Report prepared for the Joule II Programme (DG XII) of the Commission of the European Communities, Contract No. JOU2 CT92-0031, Brussels, February.

Horst, E., 1996: Building integrated PV in The Netherlands. *Sun World*, March.

IEA (International Energy Agency), 1994: *Biofuels*. IEA/OECD (Organization for Economic Cooperation and Development), Paris.

IEA (International Energy Agency), 1996: CO_2 Capture and Storage in the Natuna NG Project. *Greenhouse Issues,* **22,** 1.

IIED (International Institute for Environment and Development), 1995: *The Sustainable Paper Cycle* (Phase 1 Review Report, 2nd Draft). World Business Council for Sustainable Development/International Institute for Environment and Development, London.

IISA (International Iron and Steel Institute), 1992: *Steel Statistical Yearbook 1992*. Brussels, Belgium.

IPCC (Intergovernmental Panel on Climate Change), 1992: *Climate Change 1992: The Supplementary Report to the IPCC Scientific Assessment. Report of Working Group I.* Houghton, J.T., B.A. Callander, and S.K. Varney, (eds.), Cambridge University Press, Cambridge, UK.

IPCC (Intergovernmental Panel on Climate Change), 1996a: Chapter 20: Industry, and Chapter 22: Mitigation Options for Human Settlements. In: *Climate Change 1995. Impacts, Adaptations and Mitigation of Climate Change: Scientific-Technical Analysis. Contribution of Working Group II to the Second Assessment Report of the Intergovernmental Panel on Climate Change.* Watson, R.T., M.C. Zinyowera, and R.H. Moss, (eds.), Cambridge University Press, Cambridge and New York, 649-678 ; 713-744.

IPCC (Intergovernmental Panel on Climate Change), 1996b: Chapter 19: Energy Supply Mitigation Options. In: *Impacts, Adaptations and Mitigation of Climate Change: Scien-*

tific-Technical Analyses. Contribution of Working Group II to the Second Assessment Report of the Intergovernmental Panel on Climate Change. Watson, R.T., M.C. Zinyowera, and R.H. Moss, (eds.), Cambridge University Press, Cambridge and New York, 585-647.

IPCC (Intergovernmental Panel on Climate Change), 1996c: Part I—Introduction Materials B: Energy Primer. In: *Impacts, Adaptations and Mitigation of Climate Change: Scientific-Technical Analyses. Contribution of Working Group II to the Second Assessment Report of the Intergovernmental Panel on Climate Change.* Watson, R.T., M.C. Zinyowera, and R.H. Moss, (eds.), Cambridge University Press, Cambridge and New York, 77.

Jensen, J., and B. Sørensen, 1984: *Fundamentals of Energy Storage.* John Wiley and Sons, New York.

Johansson, T.B., H. Kelly, A.K.N. Reddy, and R.H. Williams, 1993: Renewable fuels and electricity for a growing world economy: defining and achieving the potential. In: *Renewable Energy: Sources for Fuel and Electricity.* Johansson, T.B., H. Kelly, A.K.N. Reddy, and R.H. Williams (eds.), Island Press, Washington, DC, 1-72

Jones, D.W., 1988: Some simple economics of improved cookstove programs in developing countries. *Resources and Energy*, **10**, 247-264.

Jones, H.M., 1989: *Energy Efficient Stoves in East Africa: An Assessment of the Kenya Ceramic Jiko (Stove) Program.* Oak Ridge National Laboratory, report No. 89-01, 31 January.

Kaarstad, O., 1992: Emission-free fossil energy from Norway. *Energy Conversion. Management,* **33** (5-8), 781-786.

Kammen, D.M, and W.F. Lankford, 1990: Cooking in the sunshine. *Nature* **348**, 385-386, 29 November.

Kammen, D.M., 1995: Cookstoves for the developing world. *Scientific American*, **273** (1), 72-75, July.

Karekezi, S., 1992: The development of stoves and their effectiveness. *Renewable Energy Technology and Environment, Vol. 1.* Pergamon Press, 46.

Karekezi, S., 1994: Disseminating renewable energy technologies in sub-Saharan Africa. *Annual Review of Energy and Environment*, **19**, 387-421.

Karekezi, S. and R. Karottki, 1989: *A Contribution to the Draft Paper on the Role of New and Renewable Sources of Energy from the Perspective of the Environmental Problems Associated with Current Patterns of Energy Use and Consumption.* Foundation for Woodstove Dissemination/Danish Centre for Renewable Energy, Nairobi, Kenya.

Kartha, S., E.D. Larson, J.M. Ogden, and R.H. Williams, 1994: Biomass-integrated gasifier/ fuel cell electric power generation and cogeneration. Prepared for Fuel Cell Seminar 1994: Demonstrating the Benefits, San Diego, California, 28 November- 1 December.

Kartha, S., T.G. Kreutz, and R.H. Williams, 1997: *Rural Electrification via Small-Scale Biomass Gasifier/Solid Oxide Fuel Cell/Gas Turbine Power Plants*, Center for Energy and Environmental Studies, Princeton University, March.

Kassler, P., 1994: *Energy for Development.* Shell Selected Paper, Shell International Petroleum Company, London, England, November.

Katihabwa, J., 1993: *Economic and Environmental Implications of the Diffusion of RETs in Burundi.* African Energy Policy Network, Nairobi, Kenya.

Kelly, H., and CJ. Weinberg, 1993: Utility strategies for using renewables. In: *Renewable Energy: Sources for Fuel and Electricity.* Johansson, T.B., H. Kelly, A.K.N. Reddy, and R.H. Williams (eds.). Island Press, Washington, DC, 925-1000.

Ketoff, A.N., and O.R. Masera, 1990: Household electricity demand in Latin America. *Proceedings of the ACEEE 1990 Summer Study on Energy Efficiency in Buildings, Panel 9: Residential Data, Design, and Technologies.* American Council for an Energy-Efficient Economy, Washington, DC, 9.143-9.156.

Kircher, R., S. Birkle, C. Noelscher, and H. Voigt, 1994: *PEM fuel cells for traction: system technology aspects and potential benefits.* Paper presented at Symposium on Fuel Cells for Traction Applications Royal Swedish Academy of Engineering Sciences, Stockholm, Sweden, 8 February.

Kreutz, T., M. Steinbugler, and J. Ogden, 1996: *Onboard Fuel Reformers for Fuel Cell Vehicles: Equilibrium, Kinetic and System Modeling.* Poster paper presented at the 1996

Fuel Cell Seminar, Orlando, Florida, 17-20 November.

Lamarre, L., 1994: Activity in IGCC worldwide. *EPRI Journal,* **9** (5), 6-15.

Larson, E.D., E. Worrell, and J.S. Chen, 1996a: *Clean Fuels from Municipal Solid Waste for Transportation in New York City and Other Major Metropolitan Areas.* PU/CEES Report No. 293, Center for Energy and Environmental Studies, Princeton University, Princeton, NJ.

Larson, E.D., E. Worrell, and J.S. Chen, 1996b: Clean fuels from municipal solid waste for fuel cell buses in metropolitan areas. *Resources, Conservation, and Recycling,* **17**, 273-298.

Lew, D.J., R.H. Williams, S. Xie, and S. Zhang, 1996: *Industrial-Scale Wind Power for China.* Report prepared for the Working Group on Energy Strategies and Technologies of the China Council for International Cooperation on Environment and Development, Beijing, China, August.

Leydon, K., and H. Glocker, 1992: *Energy in Europe: A View to the Future* (chapter 2). Analysis and Forecasting Unit of the Directorate General for Energy, European Commission, Brussels, Belgium.

Little, A.D., 1995: *Fuel Cells for Building Cogeneration Applications—Cost/Performance Requirements and Markets.* Final Report prepared for the Building Equipment Division, Office of Building Technology, U.S. Department of Energy, NTIS, Springfield, Virginia, USA.

Lysen, E.H., C.D. Ouwens, M.J.G. van Onna, K. Blok, P.A. Okken, and J. Goudriaan, 1992: *The Feasibility of Biomass Production for The Netherlands Energy Economy.* The Netherlands Agency for Energy and the Environment (NOVEM), Apeldoorn, The Netherlands.

MacKenzie, J. and M. Walsh, 1990: *Driving Forces: Motor Vehicle Trends and their Implications for Global Warming, Energy Strategies, and Transportation Planning.* World Resources Institute, Washington, DC.

Marchetti, C., 1989: How to solve the CO_2 problem without tears. *International Journal of Hydrogen Energy,* **14**, 493-506.

Mark, J., J.M. Ohi, and D.V. Hudson, 1994: Fuel savings and emissions reductions from light duty fuel-cell vehicles. In: *A Collection of Technical Papers: Part 3, 29th Intersociety Energy Conversion Engineering Conference.* Monterey, California, USA, 7-11 August, 1425-1429.

Masters, C.D., E.D. Attanasi, and D.H. Root, 1994: World petroleum assessment and analysis. *Proceedings of the 14th World Petroleum Congress.* Stavanger, Norway.

Mitchell, W.L., J.H.J. Thijssen, J.M. Bentley, and N.J. Marek, 1995: Development of a catalytic partial oxidation ethanol reformer for fuel cell applications. *Proceedings of the 1995 SAE Alternative Fuels Conference.* SAE Technical Paper Series 952761, 209-217.

Moreira, J.R., and A.D. Poole, 1993: Hydropower and its constraints. In: *Renewable Energy: Sources for Fuel and Electricity.* Johansson, T.B., H. Kelly, A.K.N. Reddy, and R.H. Williams (eds.), Island Press, Washington, DC, 73-119.

Mukunda, H., Dasappa, S., Srinivasa, U. 1993. Open-top wood gasifiers. In: *Renewable Energy—Sources for Fuel and Electricity.*Johansson, T.B., H. Kelly, A.K.N. Reddy, and R.H. Williams (eds.). Island Press, Washington, DC, 699-728.

Mukunda, H., S. Dasappa, P. Paul, N. Rajan., and U. Srinivasa, 1994: Gasifiers and combustors for biomass. *Energy for Sustainable Development,* **1**(3), 27-38.

MVMA (Motor Vehicles Manufacturers Association of the United States), 1982: *MVMA Motor Vehicle Facts and Figures '82.* Detroit, Michigan, USA.

MVMA (Motor Vehicles Manufacturers Association of the United States), 1992: *MVMA Motor Vehicle Facts and Figures '92.* Detroit, Michigan, USA.

Nørgard, J.S., 1989: Low electricity appliances options for the future. In: *Electricity: Efficient End Use and New Generation Technologies, and their Planning Implications.* Johansson, T.B, B. Bodlund, and R.H. Williams (eds.), Lund University Press, Lund, Sweden, 125-172.

Ogden, J.M., E.D. Larson, and M.A. DeLuchi, 1994: *A Technical and Economic Assessment of Renewable Transportation Fuels and Technologies.* Report prepared for the Office of Technology Assessment, US Congress, Washington, DC, 27 May.

OTA (Office of Technology Assessment, US Congress), 1991: *Energy in Developing Coun-*

tries. US Government Printing Office, Washington, DC.

OTA (Office of Technology Assessment, US Congress), 1992a: *Green Products by Design: Choices for a Cleaner Environment.* OTA-E-516, US Government Printing Office, Washington, DC, October.

OTA (Office of Technology Assessment, US Congress), 1992b: *Fueling Development: Energy Technologies for Developing Countries.* OTA-E-516, US Government Printing Office, Washington, DC, April.

OTA (Office of Technology Assessment), 1995: *Renewing our Energy Future.* OTA-ETI-614, US Government Printing Office, Washington, DC.

Peters, R., F. Kijek, R. Maya, and M. Wacwani, 1992: *Study on NRSE Pricing in the SADC Region.* Southern African Development Community, Luanda, Angola.

Pimental, D., and C.W. Hall, 1984: *Food and Energy Resources.* Academic Press, Orlando, Florida, USA.

Pinon, R., 1983: About solar cookers. *Passive Solar Journal,* **2** (2), 133-146.

Prasad, K.K., 1982: *Cooking Energy.* Paper presented at Workshop on End-Use Focused Global Energy Strategies, Princeton University, Princeton, New Jersey, USA, 21-29 April.

Prasad, K.K., E. Sangen, and P. Visser, 1985: Woodburning cookstoves. In: *Advances in Heat Transfer.* Hartnett, J.P., and T.F. Irvine, Jr. (eds.). Academic Press, New York.

Prater, K., 1994: Polymer electrolyte fuel cells: a review of recent developments. *Journal of Power Sources,* **51**, 129-144.

PSI (Pilkington Solar International), 1996: *Status Report on Solar Thermal Power Plants.* Report sponsored by the German Federal Ministry for Science, Research, and Technology, January.

Rabinovitch, J., 1995: A sustainable urban transportation system. *Energy for Sustainable Development,* **II** (2), July, 11-18.

Rajabapaiah, P., S. Jayakumar, and A.K.N. Reddy, 1993: Biogas electricity—the Pura Village case study. In: *Renewable Energy: Sources for Fuels and Electricity.* Johansson, T.B., H. Kelly, A.K.N. Reddy, and R.H. Williams (eds.), Island Press, Washington, DC, 787-815.

Raju, S.P., 1953; reprinted 1961: *Smokeless Kitchens for the Millions.* Christian Literature Society, Madras, India.

Ravindranath, N., 1993: Biomass gasification: environmentally sound technology for decentralized power generation, a case study for India. *Biomass and Bioenergy,* **4**, 49-60.

Ravindranath, N.H. and D.O. Hall, 1995: *Biomass Energy and Environment: A Developing Country Perspective from India.* Oxford University Press, Oxford, UK.

Reddy, A.K.N., G.D. Sumithra, P. Balachandra, and A. D'Sa, 1991a: A development-focused end-use-oriented electricity scenario for Karnataka, part I. *Economic and Political Weekly,* 6 April, 891-910.

Reddy, A.K.N., G.D. Sumithra, P. Balachandra, and A. D'Sa, 1991b: A development-focused end-use-oriented electricity scenario for Karnataka, part II. *Economic and Political Weekly,* 13 April, 983-1001.

Reddy, A.K.N., 1994: *Electricity Planning: Current Approach and Resulting Problems. Module M2, Course Materials for Workshop for Policy-makers on Electricity Planning and Development,* January 4-5 (Bangalore, India: International Energy Iniative).

Reddy, A.K.N., V. Balu, G.D. Sumithra, A. D'Sa, P. Rajabapaiah, and H.I. Somasekhar, 1994: *Replication of rural energy and water supply utilities (REWSUs): an implementation package and proposal.* Paper presented at Bioresources '94 Biomass Resources: A Means to Sustainable Development, Bangalore, India, 3-7 October.

Ringland, J.T., 1994: *Safety Issues for Hydrogen-Powered Vehicles.* Systems Research Department, Sandia National Laboratory, Livermore, California, SAND94-8226 UC0407.

Rogner, H.H., and F.E.K. Britton, 1991: *Energy, Growth and the Environment: Towards a Framework for an Energy Strategy.* Think-piece submitted to the Directorate General for Energy (DG XVII), Commission of the European Communities, Brussels, Belgium.

Ross, M., 1987: Industrial energy conservation and steel industry of the United States. *Energy,* **12** (10/11), 1135-1152.

Ross, M., and W. Wu, 1995: Fuel economy analysis for a hybrid concept car based on a buffered fuel-engine operating at an optimal point. Reprinted from: *Design Innovations in Electric and Hybrid Electric Vehicles.* Paper presented at the International Congress and Exposition, Detroit, MI, 27 February-2 March 1995, SAE Technical Paper Series 950958, Society of Automotive Engineers, Warrendale, Pennsylvania, USA.

Ross, M., R. Goodwin, R. Watkins, M. Wang, and T. Wentzel, 1995: *Real-World Emissions from Model Year 1993, 2000, and 2010 Passenger Cars.* Report sponsored by The Energy Foundation, Lawrence Berkeley Laboratory, and Oak Ridge National Laboratory, and distributed by the American Council for an Energy-Efficient Economy, Washington, DC.

Ross, M., W. Wu, J. Musser, and F. Walker, F., 1996: A parallel hybrid automobile with less than 0.1 kWh of energy storage. SAE paper 961282, Society of Automotive Engineers, Warrendale, Pennsylvania, USA.

Sachs, H., J. DeCicco, M. Ledbetter, and U. Mengelberg, 1992: Heavy truck fuel economy: a review of technologies and potential for improvement. *Transportation Executive Update,* July/August, 6-13.

Sathaye, J., S. Taylor, and N. Goldman, 1994: Transportation, fuel use and air quality in Asian cities, *Energy,* **19**, 573-586.

SEIA (Solar Energy Industries Association), 1996: *Bulletin on Japanese and German Government Programs to Promote PV Technology.* SEIA, Washington, DC.

SFA Pacific, 1993: Coal gasification guidebook: status, applications, and technologies. Final Report EPRITR-102034 prepared for the Gasification Power Plants Program, Generation and Storage Division, Electric Power Research Institute, Palo Alto, California, USA, December.

Schafer, F., and R. van Basshuysen, 1995: *Reduced Emissions and Fuel Consumption in Automotive Engines.* Springer-Verlag, New York.

Shugar, D., 1990: Photovoltaics in the utility distribution system: the evaluation of system and distributed benefits. Paper presented at the 21st IEEE Photovoltaics Specialty Conference, Las Vegas, Nevada, USA.

Shukla, K.C., J.R. Hurley, and M. Grimanis, 1985: *Development of an Efficient, Low NOx Domestic Gas Range Cooktop, Phase II.* Report No. TE4311-36-85, prepared by Thermo Electron Corp., Waltham, Massachusetts, for the Gas Research Institute, Chicago, Illinois, USA, GRI-85/0080.

Sinton, J.E., and M.D. Levine, 1994: Changing energy intensity in Chinese industry. *Energy Policy,* **19**, 239-255.

Ski Electric Co., 1996: *The Bangkok Metropolitan Electric Bus Development Project.* Inception report prepared for the Pollution Control Department, Ministry of Science, Technology and Environment, Bangkok.

Sloggett, G., 1992: Estimating energy use in world irrigation. In: *Energy in Farm Production.* Fluck, R.C., (ed). *Energy in World Agriculture, Vol. 6.* Elsevier Science Publishers, Amsterdam, The Netherlands, 203-217.

Smith, K.R., 1987: *Biomass Fuels, Air Pollution, and Health: A Global Review.* Plenum Publishing Company, New York.

Smith, K.R., 1989: Dialectics of improved stoves. *Economic and Political Weekly,* 11 March.

Socolow, R., C. Andrews, F. Berkhout, and V. Thomas (eds.), 1994: *Industrial Ecology and Global Change.* Cambridge University Press, Cambridge, UK.

Sørensen, B., 1981: A combined wind and hydro power system. *Energy Policy,* **9** (1), 51-55.

Sørensen, B., 1984: Energy storage. *Annual Review of Energy,* **9**, 1-29.

Sørensen, B., 1987: Current status of energy supply technology and future requirements. *Science and Public Policy,* **14**, 252-256.

Soussan, J., 1987: Fuel transitions within households. Discussion paper No. 35. In: *Transitions Between Traditional and Commercial Energy in the Third World.* Elkan, W., et. al. (eds.). Surrey Energy Economics Center, University of Surrey, Guildford Surrey, UK, January.

Sperling, D., and S. Shaheen (eds.), 1995: *Transportation and Energy: Strategies for a Sustainable Transportation System.* American Council for an Energy Efficient Economy, Washington, DC.

Sperling, D., 1995: *Future Drive. Electric Vehicles and Sustainable Transportation.* Island

Press, Washington, DC.

Sperling, D., 1996: The case for electric vehicles. *Scientific American,* **275** (5), November, 54-59.

Stambler, I., 1996: Progress in IGCC and advanced cycles outlined at EPRI meeting. *Gas Turbine World,* **26** (1), 16-23.

STAP/GEF (Scientific and Technical Advisory Panel to the Global Environment Facility), 1996: *Outlook for Renewable Energy Technologies, Strategic Considerations Relating to the GEF Portfolio and Priorities for Targeted Research.* Report prepared by the Scientific and Technical Advisory Panel of the Global Environment Facility, Nairobi, Kenya, September.

Stoll, H., and Todd, D.M., 1996: Competitive power generation costs for IGCC. Paper presented at the EPRI Gasification Technologies Conference, San Francisco, California, USA, 2-4 October.

Strong, S., 1996: The dawning of solar electric architecture. *Sun World*, March.

Summerfield, I.R., S.H. Goldhorpe (British Coal Corporation), and N. Williams, and A. Sheikh (Bechtel, Ltd), 1993: Costs of CO_2 disposal options. *Energy Conversion and Management,* **34** (9-11), 1105-1112.

Szargut, J., and D.R. Morris, 1987: Cumulative energy consumption and cumulative degree of perfection of chemical processes. *Energy Research*, **11**, 245-261.

Tijm, P.J.A. (Shell International Gas, Ltd., London), J.M. Marriott (Shell International Petroleum Company, Ltd., London), H. Hasenack (Koninklijke Shell Laboratorium, Amsterdam), M.M.G. Senden (Shell Internationale Petroleum Maatschappij B V, The Hague), and Th. van Herwijinen (Shell MDS (Malaysia) Sdn Bhd, Kuala Lumpur), 1995: The markets for Shell middle distillate synthesis products. *Alternate Energy '95.* Vancouver, Canada, 2-4 May.

Turkenburg, W.C., 1992: CO_2 removal: some conclusions. In: *Proceedings of the First International Conference on Carbon Dioxide Removal.* Blok, K., W. Turkenburg, C. Hendriks, and M. Steinberg, (eds.). *Energy Conversion and Management,* **33** (5-8), 819-823.

van der Burgt, M.J., J. Cantle, and V.K. Boutkan, 1992: Carbon dioxide disposal from coal-based IGCCs in depleted gas fields. In: *Proceedings of the First International Conference on Carbon Dioxide Removal.* Blok, K., W. Turkenburg, C. Hendriks, and M. Steinberg, (eds.). *Energy Conversion and Management,* **33** (5-8), 603-610.

van Weenen, J.C., 1995: Towards sustainable product development. *Journal of Cleaner Production,* **3**, 95-100.

Veyo, S.E., and W.L. Lundberg, 1996: Tubular SOFC and SOFC/gas turbine combined cycles-status and prospects. Paper presented at the 1996 Fuel Cell Seminar, Orlando, Florida, USA,17-20 November.

Walker, B. and S. Kishan (Radian International LLC), 1996: *On-Road Evaluation of Electric Tuk-Tuks in Bangkok, Thailand.* Final report prepared for the Ministry of Science, Technology, and Environment (MOSTE), Pollution Control Department, Bangkok, Thailand, 20 September.

Wall, G., 1988: Energy flows in industrial processes. *Energy*, **13**, 197-208.

WEC (World Energy Council), 1993: *Energy for Tomorrow's World.* Kogan Page, St. Martin's Press, New York.

WEC (World Energy Council), 1994: *New Renewable Energy Resources—A Guide to the Future.* Kogan Page, London, UK.

WEC (World Energy Council), 1995a: *Efficient Use of Energy Utilizing High Technology: an Assessment of Energy Use in Industry and Buildings.* London, UK.

WEC (World Energy Council), 1995b: *Global Transport Sector Energy Demand Towards 2020.* London, UK.

WEC/IIASA (World Energy Council/International Institute for Advanced Systems Analysis), 1995: *Global Energy Perspectives to 2050 and Beyond.* London, UK, and Laxenburg, Austria.

Williams, M.C., and C.M. Zeh (technical coordinators), 1995: *Proceedings of the Workshop on Very High Efficiency Fuel Cell/Gas Turbine Power Cycles.* Morgantown Energy Technology Center, Office of Fossil Energy, US Department of Energy, DOE/METC-96/1024, 19 October.

Williams, R.H. 1993: Fuel cells, their fuels, and the U.S. automobile. In: *Proceedings of the First Annual World Car 2001 Conference*, University of California at Riverside, Riverside, California, USA.

Williams, R.H., 1994: Fuel cell vehicles: the clean machine. *Technology Review*, April, 21-30.

Williams, R.H., 1996: *Fuel Decarbonization for Fuel Cell Applications and Sequestration of the Separated CO_2*. PU/CEES Report No. 295, Center for Energy and Environmental Studies, Princeton University, Princeton, New Jersey, USA.

Williams, R.H., 1997: Fuel decarbonization for fuel cell applications and sequestration of the separated CO_2. In: *Ecorestructuring*. Ayres, R.U. et al. (eds.). United Nations University Press, Tokyo, Japan (forthcoming).

Williams, R.H., E.D. Larson, and M.H. Ross, 1987: Materials, affluence, and industrial energy use. *Annual Review of Energy,* **12**, 99-144.

Williams, R.H., and E.D. Larson, 1989: Expanding roles for gas turbines in power generation. In: *Electricity: Efficient End Use and New Generation Technologies, and their Planning Implications.* Johansson, T.B, B. Bodlund, and R.H. Williams (eds.). Lund University Press, Lund, Sweden, 503-554.

Williams, R.H. and E.D. Larson, 1993: Advanced gasification-based biomass power generation. In: *Renewable Energy: Sources for Fuels and Electricity.* Johansson, T.B., H. Kelly, A.K.N. Reddy, and R.H. Williams (eds.), Island Press, Washington, DC, 729-785.

Williams, R.H., and E.D. Larson, 1996: Biomass gasifier gas turbine power generating technology. *Biomass and Bioenergy,* **10** (2-3), 149-166.

Williams, R.H., E.D. Larson, R.E. Katofsky, and J. Chen, 1995a: Methanol and hydrogen from biomass for transportation. *Energy for Sustainable Development,* **1** (5), 18-34.

Williams, R.H., E.D. Larson, R.E. Katofsky, and J. Chen, 1995b: *Methanol and Hydrogen from Biomass for Transportation, with Comparisons to Methanol and Hydrogen from Natural Gas and Coal.* PU/CEES Report No. 292, Center for Energy and Environmental Studies, Princeton University, Princeton, New Jersey, USA, July

World Bank, 1989a: *World Development Report 1989.* Oxford University Press, New York.

World Bank, 1989b: *China: County-Level Rural Energy Assessments: A Joint Study of ESMAP and Chinese Experts.* Activity Completion Report No. 101/89; World Bank/UNDP, May.

Worrell, E., 1995: Advanced technologies and energy efficiency in the iron and steel industry in China. *Energy for Sustainable Development,* **II** (4), November, 27-40.

Worrell, E., R.F.A. Cuelenaere, K. Blok, and W.C. Turkenburg, 1994: Energy consumption of industrial processes in the European Union. *Energy,* **19**, 1113-1129.

Worrell, E., R. Smit, D. Phylipsen, K. Blok, F. van der Vleuten, and J. Jansen, 1995a: International comparison of energy efficiency improvement in the cement industry. *Proceedings of the ACEEE 1995 Summer Study on Energy Efficiency in Industry (Volume II).* American Council for an Energy Efficient Economy, Washington, DC, 123-134.

Worrell, E., A.P.C. Faaij, G.J.M. Phylipsen, and K. Blok, 1995b: An approach for analyzing the potential for material efficiency improvement. *Resources, Conservation, and Recycling,* **13**, 215-232.

Worrell, E., B. Meuleman, and K. Blok, 1995c: Energy savings by efficient application of fertilizers. *Resources, Conservation, and Recycling,* **13**, 233-250.

Worrell, E., M. Levine, L. Price, N. Martin, R. van den Broek, and K. Blok, 1997: *Potentials and Policy Implications of Energy and Material Efficiency Improvement.* A Report of the United Nations, New York.

WRR (Netherlands Scientific Council for Government Policy), 1992: *Grounds for Choice: Four Perspectives for the Rural Areas in the European Community.* Working Document 42. The Hague, The Netherlands.

Wyman, C., R. Bain, N. Hinman, and D. Stevens, 1993: Ethanol and methanol from cellulosic feedstocks. In: *Renewable Energy: Sources for Fuels and Electricity.* Johansson, T.B., H. Kelly, A.K.N. Reddy, and R.H. Williams (eds.), Island Press, Washington, DC, 865-923.

Chapter 4

Blok, K., R.H. Williams, R.E. Katofsky, and C.A. Hendriks, 1997: Hydrogen production from natural gas, sequestration of recovered CO_2 in depleted gas wells and enhanced natural gas recovery. *Energy,* 22 (2-3), 161-168.

British Petroleum, 1996: *BP Statistical Review of World Energy 1996.* British Petroleum Company p.l.c, Britannic House, London.

Chakma, A., 1992: CO_2 Separation and recycling—a route to zero net production of CO_2 in the Alberta energy industry. *Energy Conversion Management.,* 33 (5-8), 795-802.

Clement-Jones, R. and J. R. Mercier, 1995: *Towards a Renewable Energy Strategy for Sub-Saharan Africa: Phase 1: Photovoltaics Applications.* Paper No. 9. Environmentally Sustainable Development Division, Africa Technical Department, World Bank, Washington, DC.

Dessus, B., 1996: *Energie, un défi planétaire.* Belin, Paris, 160 pp.

Edmonds, J., M. Wise, and C. MacCracken, 1994: *Advanced Energy Technologies and Climate Change: An Analysis Using the Global Change Assessment Model (GCAM).* Report prepared for the IPCC Second Assessment Report, Working Group IIa, Energy Supply Mitigation Options, PNL-9798, UC-402, Pacific Northwest Laboratories, Richland, WA.

Fulkerson, W., and T. Anderson, 1996: World's appetite for energy may crave nuclear power. *Forum for Applied Research and Public Policy,* 11 (1), 96-100, Spring.

IPCC (Intergovernmental Panel on Climate Change), 1992: *Climate Change 1992: The Supplementary Report to the IPCC Scientific Assessment. Report of Working Group I.* [Houghton, J.T., B.A. Callander, and S.K. Varney, (eds.)]. Cambridge University Press, Cambridge, UK.

IPCC (Intergovernmental Panel on Climate Change), 1994: *Radiative Forcing of Climate Change and an Evaluation of the IPCC Emission Scenarios.* [Houghton, J.T, L.G. Meira Filho, J. Bruce, Hoesung Lee, B.A. Callander, E. Haites, N. Harris, and K. Maskell, (eds.)]. Reports of Working Groups I and III of the IPCC, forming part of the IPCC Special Report to the first session of the Conference of Parties to the UN Framework Convention on Climate Change Cambridge University Press, Cambridge, UK.

IPCC (Intergovernmental Panel on Climate Change), 1996a: Chapter 19: Energy supply mitigation options. In: *Impacts, Adaptations and Mitigation of Climate Change: Scientific-Technical Analyses. Contribution of Working Group II to the Second Assessment Report of the Intergovernmental Panel on Climate Change.* [Watson, R.T., M.C. Zinyowera, and R.H. Moss, (eds.)]. Cambridge University Press, Cambridge and New York, pp. 585-647.

IPCC (Intergovernmental Panel on Climate Change), 1996b: Summary for policymakers: scientific-technical analyses of impacts, adaptations, and mitigation of climate change. In: *Impacts, Adaptations and Mitigation of Climate Change: Scientific-Technical Analyses. Contribution of Working Group II to the Second Assessment Report of the Intergovernmental Panel on Climate Change.* [Watson, R.T., M.C. Zinyowera, and R.H. Moss, (eds.)]. Cambridge University Press, Cambridge and New York, p. 15.

Johansson, T.B., H. Kelly, A.K.N. Reddy, and R.H. Williams, 1993a: Renewable fuels and electricity for a growing world economy: defining and achieving the potential. In: *Renewable Energy—Sources for Fuel and Electricity.* [Johansson, T.B., H. Kelly, A.K.N. Reddy, and R.H. Williams (eds.)]. Island Press, Washington, DC, USA.

Johansson, T.B., H. Kelly, A.K.N. Reddy, and R.H. Williams (eds.), 1993b: *Renewable Energy - Sources for Fuel and Electricity.* Island Press, Washington, DC, USA.

Johansson, T.B., R.H. Williams, H. Ishitani, J.A. Edmonds, 1996: Options for reducing CO_2 emissions from the energy supply sector. *Energy Policy,* 24 (10/11), 985-1003.

Kassler, P., 1994: *Energy for Development.* Shell Selected Paper, Shell International Petroleum Company, London, England, November, 11 pp.

Larson, E., C. Marrison, and R. Williams, 1997: *CO_2 Mitigation Potential of Biomass Energy Plantations in Developing Regions.* PU/CEES Report, Center for Energy and Environmental Studies, Princeton University, Princeton, NJ.

Marrison, C.I. and E.D. Larson, 1996: A preliminary analysis of the biomass energy production potential in Africa in 2025 considering projected land needs for food production. *Biomass and Bioenergy,* 10 (5/6), 337-351.

Masters, C.D., E.D. Attanasi, W.D. Dietzman, R.F. Meyer, R.W. Mitchell, and D.H. Root, 1987: World resources of crude oil, natural gas, natural bitumen, and shale oil. *Proceedings of the 12th World Petroleum Congress.* Houston, Texas.

Masters, C.D., E.D. Attanasi, and D.H. Root, 1994: World petroleum assessment and analysis. *Proceedings of the 14th World Petroleum Congress*. Stavanger, Norway.

Riedacker, A. and B. Dessus, 1991: Increasing productivity of agricultural land and forest plantations to slow down the increase of the greenhouse effect. In: *Intensification Agricole et Reboisement dans la Lutte contre le Renforcement de l'Effet de Serre*. [Grassi, G., A. Collina, and H. Zibetta (eds.)]. Proceedings of the 6th European Conference on Biomass for Energy, Industry, and Environment. Elsevier Applied Science, London, England, pp. 228–232.

Shell International Petroleum Company, 1995: *The Evolution of the World's Energy System 1860-2060*. Shell Centre, London, December.

Stoll, H., and Todd, D.M., 1996: *Competitive Power Generation Costs for IGCC*. Paper presented at the EPRI Gasification Technologies Conference, San Francisco, CA, 2-4 October.

Sunquist, E.T., and G.A. Miller, 1981: Oil shales and carbon dioxide. *Science*, **208**, 740-741.

WCED (World Commission on Environment and Development), 1987: *Our Common Future*. Oxford University Press, Oxford/New York, 400 pp.

WEC (World Energy Council),1993: *Energy for Tomorrow's World*. Kogan Page, St. Martin's Press, New York.

WEC (World Energy Council), 1994: *New Renewable Energy Resources—A Guide to the Future*. Kogan Page, London, UK.

WEC/IIASA (World Energy Council/International Institute for Advanced Systems Analysis), 1995: *Global Energy Perspectives to 2050 and Beyond*. London, UK, and Laxenburg, Austria.

Williams, R.H., 1995a: *Variants of a Low CO_2-Emitting Energy Supply System (LESS) for the World*. Report prepared for the IPCC Second Assessment Report, Working Group IIa, Energy Supply Mitigation Options, PNL-10851, Pacific Northwest Laboratories, Richland, WA.

Williams, R.H., 1995b: *Making R&D an effective and efficient instrument for meeting long-term energy policy goals*. Paper presented at Energy Futures to 2020, Directorate General for Energy (DG XVII), European Union, Brussels, 19 June.

Williams, R.H., 1996: *Fuel Decarbonization for Fuel Cell Applications and Sequestration of the Separated CO_2*. PU/CEES Report No. 295, Center for Energy and Environmental Studies, Princeton University, Princeton, NJ.

Williams, R.H. and E.D. Larson, 1993: Advanced gasification-based biomass power generation. In: *Renewable Energy: Sources for Fuels and Electricity*. [Johansson, T.B., H. Kelly, A.K.N. Reddy, and R.H. Williams (eds.)]. Island Press, Washington, DC, pp. 729–785.

Worrell, E., M. Levine, L. Price, N. Martin, R. van den Broek, and K. Blok, 1997: *Potentials and Policy Implications of Energy and Material Efficiency Improvement*. A Report to the United Nations Division of Sustainable Development, NY.

WRI (World Resources Institute), 1994: *World Resources 1994—95: People and the Environment*. Oxford University Press, New York.

Chapter 5

Andrews, C., 1994: *Evaluating risk management strategies in resource planning*. Paper presented at the IEEE/PES Summer Meeting, San Francisco, CA, 24-28 July.

Andrews, C., 1995: Scaling up. *Technology and Society,* **14**(2), Summer.

ASEAN Building Codes: Rumsey, P., and Flanigan, P., 1995: Asian Energy Efficiency Success Stories; Global Energy Efficiency Initiative and the International Institute for Energy Conservation. Washington, DC; September.

Brennand, T., 1996: *Concessions for Windfarms: a New Approach to Wind Energy Development. Report prepared for the Working Group on Energy Strategies and Technologies of the China Council for International Cooperation on Environment and Development,* Beijing, China, August.

Buchanan, J.M., 1963: The economics of earmarked taxes. *Journal of Political Economy,* **LXXI**(5).

Cabraal, A., M. Cosgrove-Davies and L. Schaeffer, 1996: *Best Practices for Photovoltaic Household Electrification Programmes—Lessons from Experiences in Selected Countries; World Bank Technical Paper*. World Bank, Washington, DC.

Cavallo, A., 1995: High capacity factor wind energy systems. *Journal of Solar Engineer-*

ing, **117**, 137-43.

Cohen, L.R., and R.G. Noll,1991: The Technology Pork Barrel. Brookings Institution, Washington, DC.

Cohen, L.R., and R.G. Noll,1994: Privatising public research. *Scientific American,* **271** (11), September, 72-77.

Curry, R., 1997: Effects of Arizona's new utility solar power mandate could be felt soon. *Photovoltaic Insider's Report,* **XVI**(2), 2 February.

de Lange, R., 1996: Sudimara Marketing Strategy, In: *Seminar Proceedings, Decentralized Electrification Issues,* Marrakech, 13-17 November, 1995, 353-65 (available from Ademe, Paris).

de Laquil III, P., D. Kearney, M. Geyer, R. Diver, 1993: Solar-Thermal Electric Technology. In: *Renewable Energy-Sources for Fuels and Electricity* [Johansson,T.B., H. Kelly, A.K.N. Reddy, and R.H. Williams (eds.)]. Island Press, Washington, DC.

de Moor, A. and Calamai, P., 1997: Subsidising Unsustainable Development—Depleting the Earth with Public Funds, February.

DTI (Department of Trade and Industry), 1997: Richard Page Turns Up the Heat for Renewables. Press Notice, London, 6 February.

Elliott, P., and R. Booth, 1993: Brazil Biomass Power Demonstration Project. Special Project Brief, Shell International Petroleum Company, London.

Epstein, J.M and R. Gupta, 1990: Controlling the Greenhouse Effect: Five Global Regimes Compared. Brookings Occasional Papers. The Brookings Institution, Washington, DC.

Epstein, J.M, C. Flavin, and N. Lenssen, 1994: Power Surge. New York: W.W. Norton & Company.

Goldemberg, J., L.C. Monaco, and I.C. Macedo, 1993: The Brazilian fuel-alcohol program. In: *Renewable Energy: Sources for Fuels and Electricity.* [Johansson, T.B., H. Kelly, A.K.N. Reddy, and R.H. Williams (eds.)]. Island Press, Washington, DC, 841-63.

Hosier, R. H. and W. Kipondya, 1993: Urban household energy use in Tanzania: Prices, Substitutes, and Poverty. *Energy Policy,* **21**(3), May, 454-73.

IEA (International Energy Agency), 1993: Taxing Energy: Why and How. Organisation for Economic Cooperation and Development (OECD)/IEA, Paris.

IEA (international Energy Agency), 1995: Energy Policies of IEA Countries: 1994 Review. OECD/IEA, Paris.

IREDA: Singh, V., 1996: India looks into private investors to sustain renewable energy growth. *Clean Energy Finance.* Arlington, VA; Winrock International and Energy Ventures International; **1**(3), Third Quarter.

IRT Environment, Aspen, CO; The International Institute for Energy Conservation, Washington, DC; and Commission Federal de Electricidad, Mexico.

IRT/IIEC: IRT Environment, Aspen, CO, and the International Institute for Energy Conservation, Washington, DC., based on information from Wong, R., Nanyang Technological Institute, Singapore; Kannan, K.S., Institute Satter Iskanidar, Malaysia, Khun Promote Iamsiri, Dept. of Energy Development and Promotion, Thailand; and Jesus Annunciacion, Department of Energy, Philippines.

Koplow, D.N.,1993: Federal Energy Subsidies: Energy, Environment and Fiscal Impact. The Alliance toSave Energy, Washington, DC.

Larsen, B., and A. Shah, 1995: Energy prices and taxation options for combating the greenhouse effect. In: *Proceedings of the Workshop on Climate Change: Policy Instruments and their Implications,* Working Group III of the Intergovernmental Panel on Climate Change (IPCC), Tsukuba, Japan, 17-20 January.

Lew, D.J., R.H. Williams, S. Xie, and S. Zhang, 1996: Industrial-Scale Wind Power for China. Report prepared for the Working Group on Energy Strategies and Technologies of the China Council for International Cooperation on Environment and Development, Beijing, China, August.

Maidique, M.A. and B.J. Zirger, 1988: The New Product Learning Cycle. In: *Strategic Management of Technology and Innovation.* [Burgleman, R.A. and Maidique, M.A.] Irwin.

Mitchell, C.,1995: The renewables NFFO: *A Review. Energy Policy,* **23**, 1077-91.

Nadel, S., 1996: The Future of Standards. American Council for an Energy Efficient Economy (ACEEE), Washington DC, October.

Nilsson, H. (NUTEK, Sweden), 1996: Looking inside the box of market transformation. Proceedings of the 1996 ACEEE Summer Study on Energy Efficiency in Buildings (Pacific Grove, CA, 26-30 August), Vol. 5. pp. 5.181-5.189. American Council for an Energy-Efficient Economy (ACEEE), Washington, DC.

OECD (Organisation for Economic Cooperation and Development), 1994: National Income Accounts : Main Aggregates, Vol. 1, 1960-1992. OECD, Paris.

OECD/DAC (Organisation for Economic Cooperation and Development/ Development Assistance Committee), 1996: Development Cooperation, 1995 Report. OECD, Paris, Table 1.

Penner, S.S., A.J. Appleby, B.S. Baker, J.L. Bates, L.B. Buss, W.J. Dollard, P.J. Farris, E.A. Gillis, J.A. Gunsher, A. Khandkar, M. Krumpelt, J.B. O'Sullivan, G. Runte, R.F. Savinell, J.R. Selman, D.A. Shores, and P. Tarman, 1995a: Commercialisation of fuel cells. *Energy The International Journal*, **20** (5), 331-470.

Penner, S.S., A.J. Appleby, B.S. Baker, J.L. Bates, L.B. Buss, W.J. Dollard, P.J. Farris, E.A. Gillis, J.A. Gunsher, A. Khandkar, M. Krumpelt, J.B. O'Sullivan, G. Runte, R.F. Savinell, J.R. Selman, D.A. Shores, and P. Tarman, 1995b: Commercialisation of fuel cells. *Progress in Energy and Combustion Science*, **21** (2), 145-151.

Rader, N.A., and R.A. Norgaard, 1996: Efficiency and sustainability in restructured electricity markets: the renewables portfolio standard. *The Electricity Journal*, **9** (6), 37-49, July.

Redefining Progress, 1997: Economists' Statement on Climate Change. San Francisco, CA, USA.

Reddy, B.S., 1990: The Energy Sector of the Metropolis of Bangalore. Ph.D. Thesis Submission, Indian Institute of Science, Bangalore.

Santa Cruz Declaration, 1996: Hemisphere Meeting of Ministers of Energy, Santa Cruz de la Sierra, Bolivia, July 30th-August 2nd, 1996.

Robinson, J. B., 1991. The Proof of the Pudding—Making Energy Efficiency Work. *Energy Policy*, September, 631-45.

SDE, Argentina: Susecretaria de Energia, Republic of Argentina; Personal Communication, Spencer, Richard; World Bank, September, 1996.

Schaeffer, L., 1996: World Bank Technical Paper No. 324, Asia Technical Department Series. World Bank, Washington, DC.

STAP/GEF (Scientific and Technical Advisory Panel/Global Environment Facility), 1996: International Industrial Collaboration for Accelerated Adoption of Environmentally Sound Energy Technologies in Developing Countries. Report prepared by the Scientific and Technical Advisory Panel of the Global Environment Facility, Nairobi, Kenya, September, 1996.

Stone, C.D., 1993: Chapter VI: The economist's prescriptions: taxes and tradable permits. In: *The Gnat is Older than Man: Global Environment and Human Agenda*. Princeton University Press, Princeton, NJ, USA.

Tata/IREDA: The Tata Energy Research Institute and the Indian Renewable Energy Development Authority.

UNDP/UNISE: The UNDP Initiative on Sustainable Energy. United Nations Development Programme (UNDP), New York, June 1996.

United Nations, 1996: World Investment Report. United Nations, New York.

United Nations, 1997: Report to the Secretary-General : Inventory of Ongoing Energy-Related Programmes and Activities of Entities within the United Nations System, on Co-ordination of Such Activities and on Arrangements Needed to Foster the Linkage between Energy and Sustainable Development within the System. Economic and Social Council of the United Nations, New York, 15 January.

USDOE (United States Department of Energy), 1996: North American Energy Measurement and Verification Protocol (NEMVP). United States Department of Energy, Washington, DC, March.

WEC (World Energy Council), 1994: World Energy Council Report, 1994.

WEC (World Energy Council), 1995: World Energy Council Report; Financing Energy Development: The Challenges and Requirements of Developing Countries.

WEC/IIASA (World Energy Council/International Institute for Advanced Systems Analysis), 1995: Global Energy Perspectives to 2050 and Beyond. London and Laxenburg, Austria, 84.

Whipple, C.G., 1996: Can nuclear waste be stored safely at Yucca Mountain? *Scientific American,* **274**(6), 72-79.

Williams, R.H. and E.D. Larsson, 1993: Advanced Gasification-Based Biomass Power Generation, Renewable Energy-Sources for Fuels and Electricity. [Johansson, T.B., H. Kelly, A.K.N. Reddy, and R.H. Williams (eds.)]. Island Press, Washington, DC.

Williams, R.H., and G. Terzian, 1993: A benefit/cost analysis of accelerated development of photovoltaic technology. *PU/CEES Report No. 281,* Center for Energy and Environmental Studies, Princeton University, Princeton, NJ, USA, 47pp.

Williams, R. H., 1995: Making Research and Development an Effective and Efficient Instrument for Meeting Long-term Energy Policy Goals. Directorate General for Energy (DG XVII), European Union, Brussels, Belgium, 19 June, 1995, 59pp.

Wiser, R, S. Pickle, and C. Goldman, 1996: California Renewable Energy Policy and Implementation Issues—an Overview of Recent Regulatory and Legislative Action. LBL-39247, UC-1321, Energy and Environment Division, Lawrence Berkeley National Laboratory, University of California, Berkeley, CA, September.

World Bank, 1994: World Development Report 1994. World Bank, Washington DC, *121-122.*

World Bank, 1994a: Memorandum on A Proposed Grant From the Global Environment Facility For A High Efficiency Lighting Pilot Project. Report No.12448-ME. World Bank, Washington DC, March 8.

World Energy Council, 1994: New Renewable Energy Resources—A Guide to the Future. Kogan Page, London.

Worrell, E., 1995: Advanced technologies and energy efficiency in the iron and steel industry in China. *Energy for Sustainable Development,* **II** (4), November, 27-40.

Worrell, E., R. Smit, D. Phylipsen, K. Blok, F. van der Vleuten, and J. Jansen, 1995: International comparison of energy efficiency improvement in the cement industry. Proceedings of the ACEEE 1995 Summer Study on Energy Efficiency in Industry (Vol. II). American Council for an Energy Efficient Economy, Washington, DC, 123-34.